C000304157

Touchlines and Deadlines

Touchlines and Deadlines

A Compendium of South African Sports Writing

edited and compiled by

Tom Eaton & Luke Alfred

DOUBLE STOREY
a juta company

First published 2005 by Double Storey Books,
a division of Juta & Co. Ltd,
Mercury Crescent, Wetton, Cape Town

ISBN 1-919930-88-4

Proofread by Wendy Priilaid
Page layout by Claudine Willatt-Bate
Cover design by Andy Jamieson
Printing by Formeset Printers

Contents

COMMENT AND ANALYSIS

RUGBY WORLD CUP 1995

THE WAY IT WAS

HUMOUR

THE BEAUTIFUL GAME

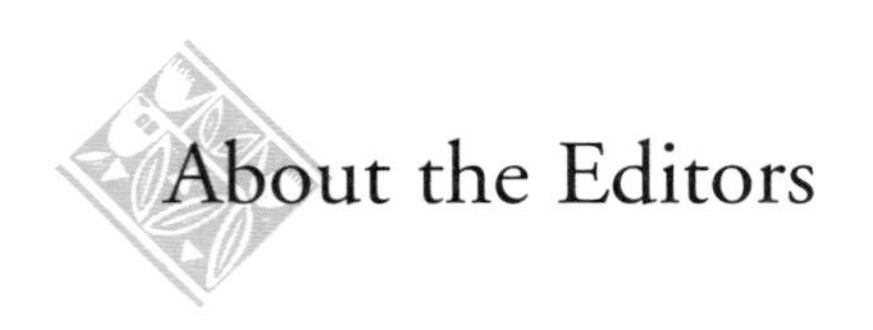

About the Editors

Tom Eaton completed his MA in Creative Writing under the supervision of Nobel Laureate J.M. Coetzee in 2001 at the University of Cape Town, and spent two years as a sports journalist and editor at the 365 Digital group before going freelance. Since then he has written a weekly column in the *Mail & Guardian*, while producing work for, among others, the *Guardian* (UK), *SA Sports Illustrated*, *GQ*, *Femina*, *SL* magazine, and both *Laugh It Off* annuals. He is also the editor of *New Contrast*, South Africa's leading literary journal, and is an adjunct supervisor in UCT's MA in Creative Writing programme. In July 2005 Double Storey Books published a selection of his *Mail & Guardian* articles, entitled *Twelve Rows Back*.

Luke Alfred is an experienced and widely travelled sports journalist, who has worked for the *Mail & Guardian*, *The Star* and the *Sunday Independent*. He is currently news editor for sport at the *Sunday Times* in Johannesburg. Luke is the author of two well-received books on South African cricket, one of which, *Lifting the Covers: The Inside Story of South African Cricket*, is currently being made into a film. He is also a regular contributor to SAfm's Saturday afternoon sports programme with his irreverent take on matters sporting both local and international, 'From Left Field'.

Preface

This book is not definitive. We have not tried to present a comprehensive history or catalogue of the best South African sports writing: to make those highly subjective choices for our reader would have been presumptuous in the extreme; and besides, no South African anthology of any kind featuring only English writing can ever claim to have covered anything but a fairly small proportion of what is out there.

Indeed, our decision to exclude the wealth of Afrikaans sports writing on offer was not born out of any kind of prejudice towards the language or disregard for its magnificently juicy journalism and evocative literature. On the contrary, we recognised that if we opened those particular floodgates, we would be swamped with quality; a happy deluge perhaps, but one that would take years rather than months to navigate.

Less frustrating to us as editors, but considerably more sobering to as us white South Africans, was the gaping hole where black mother-tongue sports writing should have been. The new histories of black sport are flourishing, resurrecting and honouring the dashing young men and women of the townships and the heartland and the inner cities, illuminating the showmen, the bullies, the maestros; the mumbling kid with the thunderbolt left hook and the Brylcremed gent with the lavish cover-drive. It is a mythology in turn brash and poignant, triumphant and despairing; and it must have seemed appallingly dangerous to the old regime. (It was, after all, much easier to sell Apartheid to an electorate who believed it was resisting a godless Communist terrorist Marxist Africanist horde rather than a country of sports fans who wanted to be free not so that they could bayonet whites and nationalise swimming pools, but to have the right to go to a game on a Saturday afternoon, or enjoy a beer with friends listening to the match, or go to sleep in a real bed looking at posters on the wall of Pele and Garfield Sobers and Mohammad Ali, to dream of sweet victories and freshly cut grass.)

Yes, the histories have survived, but their languages haven't. From Mr Drum's curious Hollywood-meets-Hillbrow hep-cat lingo in the 1950s, to the professional writers with their clichés and hyperboles in today's black newspapers and magazines, English has prevailed; and, unfortunately for the genre and for us as editors, it has usually prevailed as a second or third language. However, the briefest skim through fifty years of black sports writing in English reveals that it has been improving exponentially in the last decade, and no doubt many of those who currently inhabit the (still largely white) press boxes of cricket and rugby stadiums, writing their sedate prose for sedate English readers, will soon have to stop their bemused and faintly paternal grinning at the explosive radio commentary in Sesotho or Zulu or isiXhosa going on next door, set aside the second slice of milk tart and start typing like madmen.

The second, and glaringly obvious, reason why this book cannot purport to be a history (even of sports writing in English!) is its flagrant disregard for the past. This was a concern to us: sports fans who care about what they read have an intimate knowledge of and deep fondness for historical sporting literature. Ask them who won a Test series or a Cup Final in 1923, and they will trundle to a vast bookshelf, lovingly poring over their volumes, allowing themselves to be sidetracked into leafing through entirely unconnected tomes, until they find the right page and tell you the final score, the crowd attendance, and what the band played. Others forgo physical libraries entirely, and simply quote chapter and verse from memory. In other words, this is a tough room: presenting them with an anthology in which very little predates 1980 seemed to be asking for trouble.

But there are two good reasons for our relatively modern selections. The first has to do with the Golden Age of Sports Journalism. This was the time, somewhere between 1930 and 1970, when every sports writer penned lyrical and incisive odes to incomparable sporting titans, and readers sat agog and agape at the sheer wonderfulness of it all. Of course this is a big lie, no doubt passed down by pundits who became increasingly impossible to please in their old age, or by honest souls who, as time passed, had simply amplified the mild pleasures of long ago. The reality of sports writing before 1980 is that most of it is dull, plodding and glaringly obvious; in other words, much like most sports writing after 1980. The Golden Age is a myth, and today's readers can be reassured that in some respects they've never had it this good.

But of course not all historical sports writing in South Africa is pedestrian. Over the last 100 years the best writers, when they have emerged, have been very good. So where are they?

The answer to this is that they are where they should be: in old treasured volumes in well looked-after collections. And it is best that they stay there, waiting for the enthusiast or the specialist to hunt them down; because they could easily have been damaged by appearing in this collection.

The better sports writing of pre-1980 white South Africa is the prose of the British Empire somewhere around 1930. It is delicate, refined, slightly dusty, often ponderously rhetorical, and always (to a modern sensibility) maddeningly understated. It has a gentleness and a confidence about it that can never stand up to the brash, opinionated, insecure, showy writing of our modern era; and it would only suffer by crude comparison, like a candle-lit shadow-puppet show compared to a Hollywood blockbuster. In itself it can be quite lovely, and it deserves to keep its delicate dignity intact by not being paraded with the usual (current) suspects.

Even the advertisements around its borders display a reserve and naivety completely alien to the modern world. A large advertisement in *Drum* magazine in 1953 for Aspro tablets, illustrated with a dashing black cricketer and an elegant young woman playing a tennis backhand, claims, 'To be good at sport you must be healthy and strong, so that you can play well all the time – whatever sport you play, football – tennis – golf – baseball, etc. Steady nerves help to keep you in top form. That is why ASPRO is a wonderful aid to those who play sport … Furthermore IT STEADIES THE EYE NERVES which makes all the difference!'

It steadies the eye nerves? Clearly this is a world with different priorities to our own, one in which science and money have not yet been installed as gods, in which steady nerves (harking back to the steady nerves and stout hearts of pre-Industrial heroes) still hold more clout than trim figures, big houses, fast cars and blonde hair. This is everything David Beckham isn't.

It is also a world full of now-extinct words and phrases: a wizard match, a queer little fellow, a bracing cigarette. This was a world in which 'doyens' roamed and wrote: few other words conjure a certain kind of writer in a certain kind of era, writing in a certain kind of room, as certain kinds of native inhabitants discreetly make him certain kinds of alcoholic drinks. South African sports writing had its doyens; it doesn't seem likely that there will be any more. Just as flying-boats gave way to Airbuses and Protectorates gave way to Republics, doyens have passed away in favour of journalists, columnists, correspondents and presenters.

Of course, just because we've never had it so good, it doesn't mean that there isn't room for improvement. Those who write in English in this country tend to use the United Kingdom and Fleet Street as their literary compass, often emulating the tone, idiom and focus of their British counterparts, with all the laboured waffling after watery punchlines that can entail. The danger here is obvious: if you insist on writing British sports journalism, the British will always be better than you.

Worse still, you might never look up and see American sports journalism. For fifty years the United States has been the driving force behind modern literature in English, whether poetry, fiction or non-fiction; its writers more than filling the slippers left vacant by Commonwealth authors when they shuffled off into University syllabi. And the sports writers have been in the vanguard of their advance. Neville Cardus and his fellow doyens have their place, but nobody writes sport like the Americans. We look westward for all our other influences: surely one more cultural loan – this time a few pointers on how to write sizzling, intelligent prose about a game – couldn't hurt?

But perhaps when your view of the game is straight and clear, you don't need to look anywhere else; and certainly those writers assembled in this book have demonstrated a clarity of vision throughout their careers. Some are professional sports journos, grizzled veterans who have wolfed a thousand pre-packed lunches in press boxes around the globe; others are part-timers, dipping in and out of sport with an amateur's lightness of touch. But all are eminently readable, and together they provide us with a wonderful vantage point over this maddening, exulting thing called sport, and in their own way, show us another South Africa, one both new and strange.

And if we have overlooked any of the greatest shadow-puppeteers of past times, please forgive us.

Tom Eaton & Luke Alfred

THE PLAYERS

Sport is bigger than individuals.

Sure. Tell that to fans of Michael Schumacher, David Beckham, Sachin Tendulkar and Ronaldo …

Teams and stadia and managers and coaches are the skeleton of sport, but the players are its heart and soul. To the supporters they are the epicentre of all emotion: the fan loves them, hates them, cheers them, curses them, hangs their picture on the wall on one year and stuffs it into the attic the next. And always there is that peculiar tension between us and them. I could be him, the fan says, if I watched my weight and took my game seriously. They say she's just an ordinary girl-next-door type: I bet if we met at a party we'd be best mates. And yet all the while the fan knows that it's wishful thinking. The sports star is different, separate, and ultimately unattainable. Which is just the way we like it.

– Tom Eaton

Forget the hype, here was a brave young man delivering on the day

Rodney Hartman

Sport is better than the theatre for one very cogent reason: no one writes the plot.

If you missed, for example, the opening act of *Hamlet*, you could still arrive late in your seat assured of no major departures from the script. But if you watched only the closing act of the Olympic marathon, you would have been bewildered to discover that an unheralded extra was currently upstaging road running's equivalents of Sir Laurence Olivier.

Where else can one be so surprised and entertained?

The inherent drama of sport is to confound all predictions. This was nowhere so profound as when a maintenance worker from the Koornfontein Coal Mine ran triumphantly into the Olympic stadium in Atlanta.

Had you ever heard of Koornfontein colliery? Had you ever heard of Josia Thugwane? Has Larry Olivier ever brought you to tears? Well, okay, maybe, but not quite so unexpectedly.

This was the Olympics as it should be; no swank or smirk, no hype or hubris; only a brave young man delivering on the day. Here, amid all the big deals of the track and field, the men and women who easily tell you just how good they are, was a mere amateur by comparison in the true Corinthian tradition.

Here, moreover, was the epitome of Olympic competition … the ultimate test of mind and body; here, indeed, is the most romantic bridge between the ancient and modern Games.

Michael Johnson pronounced on more than one occasion the importance of his sprinting prowess. He claimed, even before the Games had begun, that his was *The Story* of the 1996 Olympics. While there is no denying the man's historic feat in achieving his golden double, there is every reason to ask why the final of the 400 metres or the 200 metres was not staged on the final day.

That slot was reserved for the marathon for the very good reason that, unlike the ephemeral sprints, it is guaranteed to end the Games on the highest note for body and spirit. In what is seen as the most fitting climax to any Olympiad, it invites us to live through all the tactical excellence, the heroics and heartbreak, of the greatest race of all.

As to those who would acclaim the Johnsons and the Lewises as the athletes of the century, there is a gentle reminder today of the man from Czechoslovakia who went to Helsinki in 1952. After his achievements in those Olympics, Emil Zatopek was acclaimed as the greatest runner that ever lived. Having won the gold medals and setting new Olympic records in both the 5 000 and 10 000 metres, he then decided to enter the marathon for the first time. He won that too, in a new Olympic record. The balding Czech had completed the most exceptional feat in athletics ... something that was even beyond the grasp of the best scriptwriters.

That one of our own should now conquer the select field of the Olympic marathon was as outstanding as it was surprising. As opposed to the glamour events of the track, there were no pre-race interviews, no breathless hyperbole, no one strutting around in gold running shoes for the benefit of the kitch addicts. There was just honest to goodness endeavour on the day; and some very shrewd tactics besides.

Unlike Johnson's golden slippers, Thugwane's sunglasses were not there for effect, neither were they there to give some sponsor a cheap thrill. He wore them to hide the most telling features of the long-distance runner, indeed of any sportsman in head-to-head combat. By observing your opponents' eyes you are able to read a lot about his strength and will. Had we been able to see a close up of Thugwane's eyes on that long road towards the stadium, we might have known that his intentions were not going to be disturbed.

His wife knew it all right. Back home in their neat little pale-blue corrugated iron shack, she said, 'Well, look, he's been away so long that I knew he must bring home a gold medal.' No hyperbole, no fuss. With down-home honesty, she acknowledged without any noticeable excitement that her man had done his job. What self-respecting husband would go away for so long, to some big land across the seas, and not return home with tangible evidence of his sweat and toil?

But did the nation know? No, it didn't. There were muted suggestions that Thugwane might finish stronger than his two teammates because the humid conditions would suit him better, but no one could ever imagine that he would beat the likes of Dionicio Ceron or Martin Fiz.

This newspaper last week gave him an honourable mention ('the Witbank mine employee … is being increasingly talked about as our big gun') but it also gave his name as Josiah Thungwane. This was no sin, mind, because several statistical handbooks spell his name this way and, about a month before the Games had even begun, I telephoned the National Olympic Committee and asked them to clarify the spelling. They told me they weren't sure; that it always seemed to be changing.

It was not as if he was a newcomer … but, outside of his immediate circle, he remained a virtual unknown. Even among the cognoscenti of South African road running it is likely that he was not seen as a major force because his personal best time of 2:11:46 this year was well down an all-time list headed by Zithulele Sinqe's 2:08:04.

You have to ask if there is any precedent for an Olympic champion in so high profile an event being so anonymous in his own home country … but then I would remind you that sport is the only stage that can throw up such wonderful surprises.

… [Late into the race] Thugwane changed direction and cut back in order to grab his drinks bottle. Only a very fit and strong marathoner can deliberately break his rhythm at such a late stage of a marathon, and then slip straight back into the lead pack.

Our only fear was that the Kenyan runner would enter the stadium with Josia. The Kenyans are famous for their devastating sprint finishes and even exhausted runners are often able to muster a last desperate sprint at the sight of the finish line. But Josia made his decisive move just before the stadium and made certain that nothing was left to chance. It is interesting to note how fast the three leaders were finishing.

In an era when times in the 2:08–2:09 range are commonplace, a winning time of 2:12 may appear to be a little on the slow side; but the last few kilometres were far from slow. The kilometres, in the second half, were rattling past at a little over three minutes a kilometre. I timed Josia's last 400 m at 73 seconds or so and he was forced to run very wide for half of his last lap. The world former No 1, Martin Fiz of Spain, was almost flying in pursuit of the leading trio and he could make no impression.

Josia Thugwane's triumph was a wonderful, uplifting achievement for both himself and his country but just as important was the credibility he gave to our claim that we have some of the world's best long-distance runners. In the past some people have scoffed at the idea that we can be as good as the Kenyan or Ethiopian distance runners. Perhaps those people had a right to scoff. Marathoners such as Willie Mtolo, Gert Thys, David Tsebe and Xolile Yawa won some of the world's big city marathons. They also did so in superb times, but up until now we had only flattered to deceive. (Of course Mark Plaatjes' win in the 1993 world championship marathon in Stuttgart was a warning of our potential.) Our much-vaunted teams failed in Barcelona, in Stuttgart and in Gothenburg. Those of us who believed in our potential became concerned and a little depressed.

Until the 30 km mark of last Sunday's Olympic marathon that is ... And so we have our second Olympic marathon champion. I for one still have to pinch myself to believe that it is true. I have a feeling, however, that I will be doing a lot more pinching in the future. Josia Thugwane's win is certain to act as an inspiration to our other top marathoners.

(Sunday Independent, 11 August 1996)

From miner to major

Grant Shimmin

There was something serenely symbolic in the fact that each time steepening gradients stretched Josia Thugwane's hamstrings and tendons that little bit further during the Atlanta Olympic marathon, the expression on his face remained virtually unchanged.

Whenever one of his rivals surged to try to spread the field, he did what was necessary to stay in touch with the man up front, but his expression bore no hint of stress or strain as the race wore on.

Clearly, here was a man aware of all the obstacles the course or the field could throw in his path and at peace with his ability to overcome each one. For, if the race had been a metaphor for his life, the sight of each new obstacle in his path would have prompted a slide to pop up in his mind bearing an image of a more difficult one already conquered.

When Thugwane promised friends and family before his departure for the States that he would bring back a medal from the Games, it wasn't an attempt to emulate the noisy, hot-aired hype that precedes heavyweight boxing bouts. A life such as his has been too simple and sincere to have been touched by the concept of arrogant bluster for the sake of effect. He made his promise because he knew he had it in him, and on 4 August he made good on his promise.

There would have been easier times and places for Thugwane to be born than in the early 1970s on the conservative Eastern Transvaal platteland.

His birthplace, Bethal, where he has lived all his 25 years, is part of a triangle with Witbank and Middelburg in which life still consists in the main of farming and coal-mining.

Thugwane's early childhood would have encompassed the explosion of racial hatred that was the Soweto riots; a time when life became extremely difficult for black people all over the country, but particularly in the northern half.

In Extension 5 of Mzinoni, the treeless township outside Bethal where Thugwane now lives with his wife Zodwa and young daughters Zandile and Thandile, the demoralising effect of those times can be seen on drink-ravaged faces.

As the men gathered round to congratulate him after he returned there last week, one sensed in some an element of envy at the one among their number who'd survived the oppression of the apartheid era as a whole man, and grasped the opportunities engendered by the system's dissolution.

Perhaps Thugwane sensed it too, when he said: 'Not everybody is happy that I won the gold medal. Some are jealous.'

Ironically, his hitherto low social standing in South Africa, where he built his own corrugated iron house on a dusty, sloping site, probably worked in his favour in Atlanta. While spoilt brat basketball and tennis stars were deserting the Olympic Village in favour of luxury hotels, the accommodation would have seemed positively palatial to Thugwane and surely helped him to relax ahead of the great occasion.

Just about all of Thugwane's working life has been spent on Koornfontein mine, 30 km from Bethal, where he now performs the humble tasks of a member of the maintenance crew in the hostels and offices.

He first worked at the mine as a cook with a catering company contracted to Koornfontein, and it was there, in 1988, that he got into running on the encouragement of Job Mahlangu and Joseph Skosana.

Ironically, in an area so flat, he developed a love for hills and his victories include last year's Foot of Africa at Bredasdorp.

In 1993, Thugwane made his first big break into the limelight when he won the SA Marathon championship, as well as the Hyper-to-Hyper 42 km race, achievements that were all but forgotten in the euphoria surrounding his amazing Atlanta victory.

But a new hurdle was looming.

Thugwane left his job at the mine before embarking on the ritual of circumcision that his culture demands to signal the passage from boyhood into manhood. In other cultures his running exploits would already have made him a man among men, but he had to go through the ritual. However, there were serious complications and his running career could have ended then.

Perhaps it's no surprise, therefore, that since enduring what stretched into two years of unemployment, before returning to the mine in his new, humbler position, he has been virtually unstoppable on the road.

To Thugwane, the mere fact he was able to preserve his running career must have seemed a blessing and not one he was about to take lightly.

For the past 18 months, Thugwane has been under the wing of the mine's personnel manager, Ray Dibden, who has helped with race entries, physiotherapists and visas: 'It's never been a problem for him to get time off for his running. We let him go to the States two months early to get ready for the Olympics,' said Dibden.

Victories in Bredasdorp, Honolulu, Cape Town and now Atlanta have followed his return to the road, but another obstacle threatened to stop him even attempting the last and hitherto most important step up the ladder.

In early March, after his win at the SA Championships in Cape Town and with Georgia on his mind, Thugwane was hijacked on the road between Bethal and Kriel. The man is a fighter and a thinker. His chin bears the brunt of the first quality, the horizontal scar almost mimicking the shape of the bullet the hijackers used to show they would take no prisoners. They eventually didn't, but only because Thugwane's quick thinking persuaded him to jump from the moving vehicle, effectively abandoning it but staying alive.

His community retrieved the bakkie the same day. Bringing his life back would have presented a sterner challenge.

'I hurt my head, my back and my elbow when I jumped out and I thought the Olympics were over for me,' he said.

The mine's help in getting him to a physio regularly and sheer guts pulled him through.

Ironically, Thugwane's greatest victory may have helped set before him his highest hurdle, the lure of the limelight. Sponsorships, advertising contracts and endorsements are all set to swell his personal bank balance, potentially pulling his eyes off the quest to remain at the top.

But while he now intends to buy a house in Hendrina, 45 km from Bethal, on the strength of his new-found fortune, Thugwane declares boldly that: 'I would love to keep living a simple life.'

A strong, fair managerial hand is what he needs to realise that wish while continuing with his burgeoning career.

Thugwane realises his success may compel him to subject his introvert personality to more of the media glare, but don't expect to see him streaking through the stratosphere, hanging on the tail of a rocket called 'High Flyer'.

He may have earned the right to join Gary Player as one of South Africa's 'little big men', but one senses that Thugwane will be happiest out pounding the roads in training, alone or with friends, or at home with his young family, watching his beloved Kaizer Chiefs on the box.

(SA Sports Illustrated, 2 September 1996)

The flip sides of Penny

Mike Behr

In the beginning (circa 1991, when she was just becoming a household name), Penelope Heyns was, in her own words, 'a complete pain in the arse'. Her life revolved around two things: swimming and God. Today, those things are still the focus of Penny's life, but now she's learnt to add balance to the mix. By all accounts, it's turned her into a less uptight, bright new Penny.

'I gave my life to the Lord in Standard 3,' she explains. (Stick around, this doesn't turn into a sermon.) 'But I only understood the implications in 1991 when I was in Standard 9 at Amanzimtoti High. In retrospect I now see that I went totally overboard. I destroyed all my secular music and played only Christian music; I immersed myself in Christian literature and I did most of my socialising at church youth clubs. After matric, during my first year at the University of Nebraska on a swimming scholarship [she's studying psychology], I'd refuse to go into a house or a party where people were drinking. And I was a real nerd at the Barcelona Olympics in '92 – when I wasn't in the pool I was in my hotel room reading Christian works.'

Growing up in America changed all that. 'One night I thought, bugger it, I want to know what it's like to get drunk. So I joined my roommate and two South African friends for a couple of beers while we watched a football game. It took only three beers and I was *gone*,' she recalls with a mischievous smile. 'Afterwards I felt so guilty I thought I'd go straight to hell – which is ridiculous. It took a while, but I've come to realise that being a good Christian is not about following strict rules. I can go out and have a few drinks and dance and still be a Christian.'

Typically flip in manner, Penny makes it sound as if one night of dorm recreation changed her life, when it was actually a gradual, osmotic process. 'I'll be honest …' she says, using a preface that crops up often in her conversation, leading the listener to wonder just when she *isn't* being entirely frank. 'America changes your views. At first, because I was so naïve, I was shocked by what I encountered over there, especially the promiscuity. But lately I've become a lot more broad-minded.'

Part of Penny's chilling-out process included developing a penchant for partying. The university town of Lincoln (where Penny shares a house with two friends) doesn't offer much in the way of night life. So the students tend to spend a lot of time in bars or throwing house parties. Penny prefers house parties because there she can indulge in her other love – dancing.

I didn't get to witness her skill first hand but, according to those who saw her raise the roof one September night at Rattlesnakes Diner in Rivonia, she is as fluid on the dance floor as she is in the pool. 'Her speciality is a sort of *Dirty Dancing* derivative,' says one of the Absa Bank promotional team who were celebrating the end of a particularly gruelling countrywide post-Olympic Games promotional roadshow. (Absa Trust is one of Penny's main sponsors.) 'Penny's got a wonderful sense of rhythm and looks very sexy. She had a rave and attracted a lot of attention. Many guys came over and asked her to dance.'

Of course, there is more to the new Penny than the party animal. One side can be seen [in camera shots], where she demonstrates the ability not only to flirt comfortably with a new look, but to turn it into a stunning photographic spread. There was no knowing how Penny, an unknown quantity in the studio, would perform in front of the camera. But as in Atlanta (where, to refresh memories, she became the first *ever* South African to clinch double Olympic gold), Penny performed like a seasoned pro.

That's the confident Penny. But she's also a typical Scorpio. (Is it any surprise that she's a fixed water sign?) So flip her over and you could quite easily discover that beneath her calm and very self-controlled exterior hides a vulnerability that often expresses itself in humour (she's forever joking and teasing), and other times in insecurity, especially where looks are concerned. At times there are even hints of an emotional tug-of-war.

Her insecurity first revealed itself en route from Cape Town International Airport to the Cellars Hohenort Country House Hotel in Constantia, the venue for *Fair Lady*'s shoot. It was clear that she was nervous about the assignment. It was only when we reached our destination and the beauty editor briefed Penny on what clothes she would be wearing that she relaxed. 'I was really concerned that you'd put me in dresses,' Penny explained. 'It's not that I have a problem wearing dresses – I quite enjoy them when I do – it's just that my legs are very hairy and I'd like to keep that private. That's one of the main reasons I wear jeans so often.' (The other reason is that Nebraska's cold.)

So why, you may ask, doesn't Penny do what most other women do and shave? Because, she explains, the less a swimmer shaves, the better the effect on race day. Then she shaves everywhere – her arms, back, legs, whatever is not covered by her swimsuit – not only to remove body hair, but the first layer of skin as well.

'The idea is to make yourself more streamlined and more sensitive to the water, because swimming has a lot to do with feel. For me, shaving down is also psychological. It's the final step.

'My coach says that it turns me into a completely different swimmer. It's almost as if I shave away the self-doubt that is with me during "hairy" starts. When I stand on the starting block shaved, there's absolutely *no* doubt in my mind that I'll swim my best time. In Atlanta I felt terrible in the water the day before I shaved down. But afterwards I felt great.' Double-gold great, we now know.

An appealing aspect of Penny Heyns is the way she frankly, sometimes intimately, reveals herself, often without much coaxing. At the start of our interview in Room 43, Penny tauntingly slumped back into an elegant chaise longue, pinned me with eyes still smouldering seductively with photographic shoot make-up, and declared with a chuckle, 'Now analyse me.' On one level it was a joke, but on another it was as if Penny was inviting me to probe. Because, as she contends, Penny Heyns has got nothing to hide.

Jumping at the opportunity, I discover that on the romantic side Penny has a very specific taste in men. 'My perfect man would have to be someone I could respect and trust and someone who would reciprocate. He'd also have to be successful, preferably not as a swimmer though, because that could cause problems. I'd like it if he was a sporty outdoor type. He'd also have to be goal oriented and have similar interests, especially when it comes to travel, because I want to see more of the world. He'd also have to have a sense of humour, be intelligent and deep. Obviously I'd want to be physically attracted to him, but I'd have to be able to talk to him.

'Have I met him yet? Let's just say I've met some men who have shown signs of perfection. No, no, no, don't put that,' she says chuckling. 'It makes me sound very judgmental.'

Penny reveals that she was dating a South African during her first year at Nebraska, but having a long-distance relationship proved too demanding. 'When I came back to Durban in May '94, I knew I only had two weeks to spend with my family – we're very close – and my friends. Understandably my boyfriend wanted to spend time alone with me, but I wasn't – and I'm still not – at that point in my life where I can give that much time to just one person. Maybe it's selfish, but I want to come and go as I please.'

Back in Nebraska is a Scotsman who is keen to get more intimate. The feeling is mutual, says Penny, but once again she's applied the brakes on this budding relationship. 'Even though I am a bit of a control freak, I realise that I won't always have control over precisely when I get romantically involved. And as my mother says, I'd be a fool to let Mr Perfect slip through my fingers. But I'll be honest … right now I don't want commitment in my life because it wouldn't benefit my swimming. I only have four years left to compete with the best. Besides,' and another mischievous grin creeps across her face, 'why make one person happy and so many others unhappy?'

In the meantime, Penny confesses that a relationship on a superficial level is not unthinkable. 'But I'd be clear from the start that it couldn't get serious. And no matter how tempting, I wouldn't jump into bed with him, because I haven't yet made up my mind whether that would conflict with my religious principles. And besides, I think that sex too soon can ruin a relationship. First you have to become best friends. The person I end up marrying will have to be my soul mate, and that doesn't happen easily if you get physical first.'

On the subject of her new-found fame, Penny reveals that it's a many-faceted beast. On the one hand her two gold medals have laid golden eggs. In addition to their ongoing sponsorship, Absa Trust paid her R100 000 for her Olympic victories. Fulfilling a pre-Olympic promise, the government presented her with a cheque for R300 000. Her achievements also spawned a Vodacom sponsorship that is worth a million rand in incentives. In the air, SAA are her official carrier to the tune of R80 000 in free flights.

Penny is aware that her celebrity status can open doors, even when she does not expect it. On several occasions proud restaurateurs have refused to let her pay for her meal, alert airline staff have upgraded her to business class, and recently a club bouncer turned a blind eye when she went to a Durban dance club with her younger brother and some friends. One of the girls was under the age limit, but the magic words, 'She's with Penny Heyns,' did the trick.

There are other times though, claims Penny, when people give her a hard time simply because she's now a big name. 'There have been occasions when I would have been served quicker had I been an anonymous person in the crowd. It's almost as if some people think an Olympic medallist automatically has a big head and therefore has to be brought down a peg or two.'

But the biggest strain about fame is the awareness that people are watching every move with a critical eye. 'I had a big yearning before the Olympics – I think it was a way of handling my nervousness – to go out, have a couple of drinks, dance and go crazy. It worried me, but my coach said I needed it. For so long my life had just been swimming, swimming, swimming. After my races I couldn't wait for the Olympics to end so that I could party, because my other Olympic goal was to enjoy myself socially.

'Then suddenly the desire was gone. I think it was because I realised that people were watching me. One day I was having a beer with a friend at the Olympic Village Pavilion and I overheard someone saying, "Look at Penny, she's drinking!" Even though I wasn't doing anything wrong, I decided then that I wasn't going to give anyone the opportunity to criticise me.'

The spinoff of that little encounter is that the first time Penny let her hair down in South Africa was weeks after her arrival, when Absa organised a private function with people she felt safe with. 'Only then did I drop my guard and enjoy myself.'

What is surprising is that a maverick athlete like Penny Heyns cares a jot what anyone thinks about her. She certainly wasn't bothered by what her university swimming teammates and the coaching staff thought when she declined to get involved in team building exercises, or when she walked out of a two-week training camp in Puerto Rico and stormed back to Nebraska to do things *her* way.

What is also unexpected is Penny's response when I ask her whether she'd like more opportunity to express the side of her that we photographed. 'Because I grew up with two brothers I'm a bit of a tomboy. I'm also very sporty, so I'm not a very fashion-conscious person. At the same time I'm perfectly comfortable with the way I was styled today. It's just that I'm not sure where this look fits into my life. And I'm hesitant to change my image because I'm not sure what people will say if I do. I'm not comfortable enough with myself yet to make those sorts of fashion decisions. Someone's got to do that for me.'

Which is one of the reasons that Penny's agent took her shopping in Atlanta and bought her a Dolce & Gabbana pants suit (Penny calls it a Dolce Gabocci) for a cool $2 195. 'It's very nice, but I think it's crazy to spend that kind of money on one outfit. I've only worn it twice!'

If you hear rumours of Penny's partying, the occasional profanity in her speech, the odd dirty or politically incorrect joke and – horror of all horrors – a recent starkers midnight streak across an Amanzimtoti rugby field with two friends (she says she did it for a dare), don't judge her too harshly. It has nothing to do with the flying Springbok tattoo on her back just below her left shoulder (she did it to shock her critics), which some people laughably suggest is the work of the devil. All Penny has done is replace her holier-than-thou image with a lightness of being.

At an Absa Trust cocktail party held recently in Cape Town in Penny's honour, bronze medalist Marianne Kriel told the audience that wherever she held coaching workshops, children sang the praises of her friend and Olympic teammate. So high was their regard that none could remember who was placed second and third in Penny's races. All except one little boy, who revealed to Marianne that God had come second on both occasions. When asked to explain himself, the boy told her that Penny Heyns had said on the television news that God had been behind her the whole way. The anecdote brought the house down, Penny included. And there was no bolt of lightning from above.

(Fair Lady, 11 December 1996)

We are notoriously bad at paying our respects to our sporting stars when they retire: if administrators are not actively harbouring grudges against them at the time, they can usually expect little more than a hastily painted portrait of themselves, a gala dinner (to which only a few of their former teammates can make it, what with the season being in full swing), and the odd visit to the commentary box in the years to come. But death is quite another matter; and few sporting obituaries have had as superb a final line as Phuthi Lesley Manyathela's.

Eish, farewell, Slow Poison

Fikile-Ntsikelelo Moya

The Orlando Pirates star showered immediately after the match, as he usually did. He jumped into his car and off he went. It was the last time that his fans, friends and teammates would see him alive. That was almost 39 years ago, when Pirates all-time great Eric Bhamuza 'Scara' Sono died in a car accident in the Free State. This week Pirates lost Phuthi Lesley Manyathela. For older Pirates supporters and the South African sporting fraternity, that sickening feeling crept back.

Manyathela was said to have been tired after returning from France the previous day. Similar talk of tiredness was bandied about after Sono's accident. He had played in an encounter with Avalon Athletic at the Indian Sports Ground on Saturday, and kicked off in a friendly against Dobsonville Rangers in Soweto the next day. It would be unfair to compare Sono and Manyathela. For starters 'Scara' gave Pirates and South African football its foremost talent in his sons Matsilele Ephraim 'Jomo' Sono and the talented yet eccentric Julius 'KK' Sono.

To Pirates he was far more than just a player, having being responsible for the recruitment of a spindly Kaizer Motaung and the tricky Percy 'Chippa' Moloi. Manyathela may not have recruited anyone to the club, but his contribution to its recent glory is unquestionable. His 18 league goals, the most by any player last season, won the club the championship. In fact it was his goal, coming at the death against Wits University in Phokeng, Rustenburg, that saw the club being crowned South African champions in May. With that goal he had also fulfilled the promise he had made to club boss Irvin Khoza that he would score at least 22 goals (18 in the league and four in cup games) for the season, to match the jersey number he wore.

No great wonder that the club is considering retiring the number. If it does, it would be the second jersey number that the club will stop printing because of a road accident. The first was Clifford 'Tough' Moleko's number 13 jersey. 'Tough', who was on loan to Cape Town-based Seven Stars at the time, died in 1998.

Although Manyathela's mercurial talents have been praised all round – albeit posthumously – there were times they did not seem obvious to everyone. After setting the amateur scene alight for Shayandima Arsenal in Musina, Limpopo, Manyathela joined then first division team Dynamos on loan. Pirates director of youth development Augusto Palacios spotted him when Palacios was scouring the country looking for suitable players for the under-20 national team he coached at the time. At the same time Kaizer Chiefs scouts had got wind of the youngster's talent. The battle for his signature ensued. Pirates won the day over Chiefs, partly because they offered the youngster's parents more money and – unlike Chiefs, who wanted him to go through their youth team for a season – the club promised him jersey number 22 in the first team.

In July 2000 he made his debut for Pirates in the Vodacom Challenge and created a goal. His detractors could argue that his was a simple tap in, but it was that instinct for being in the right place at the right time, and doing the basics, that would make him stand out among his teenaged peers. But if he thought that that, combined with his tendency to come off the bench and score vital goals, would ensure he would get a regular run in Gordon Igesund's championship-winning team of the 2000/01 season, he was wrong.

It was only with the arrival of Frenchman Jean-Yves Kerjean during the 2001/02 season that Manyathela's immense potential shone through. In that time, scoring seemed to come naturally to him: he was the chief goal-getter for the under-20 and later under-23 teams he featured in.

Manyathela was certainly the lynchpin and the crown jewel in a Pirates teeming with youthful exuberance. Now he is dead. Pirates have lost exceptional players in their prime such as 'Asinamali' Metseeme in the mid-1960s and, more recently, Moleko.

But with Slow Poison, *eish* …

(Mail & Guardian, 15 August 2003)

Pushing the limit

Tom Eaton

IT all began with Madonna. Had she not performed at the Melbourne Cricket Ground in the summer of 1993, and had her devotees not trampled that magisterial paddock into dust, and had the shameful conditions not wrecked Brian McMillan's knee, Gary Kirsten might not have played his hundred-and-first Test this week and signed off as the premier South African batsman of his generation.

Of course it is easy to say with hindsight that Kirsten was destined for international cricket with or without the intervention of the material girl, but fate can be particularly arbitrary where selection is concerned. In the end it was his brief designation as a temporary stop-gap allrounder that won Kirsten the trip to Australia: with perfect timing he had burgled a five-for

for Western Province with his innocent off-spin just as McMillan's joint gave way with the sound of a falling redwood.

That the selectors should have felt compelled to defend their decision by talking up Kirsten's extremely limited use as a bowler was an early sign of what was to follow, the curious brand of slander that has been practised for the last eleven years and which will no doubt be enshrined as lore in the inevitable tributes and biographies that his retirement should trigger. They couldn't take him to Australia as a specialist batsman, the feeling seemed to be, because he simply wasn't one. Great team player, lovely guy, but not by any stretch of the imagination a thoroughbred.

The left-hander, the crickerati quickly concurred, had been passed over when natural talent was being handed out to the Kirsten family. But all those runs for Western Province couldn't be overlooked, and so it was announced by the court wordsmiths who shape so much of South African sporting thought: Gary Kirsten was a fighter who played very well within his limitations.

It was a phrase permanently grafted to Kirsten's game, irrespective of his form or fortunes, and for a decade it went unchallenged by editors or journalists who failed to see its deeply patronising origins.

But 2 000, then 5 000, and finally 7 289 Test runs later, one had to wonder just what those limitations were. There were no shots he couldn't play, and more tellingly, some he wouldn't play. His concentration was tangible. If Jacques Kallis plays in a bubble, Kirsten batted in a bomb shelter. And when technical problems infiltrated his game – pushing away from his body, chopping deliveries onto his stumps – he simply made them go away.

To those spoiled by the baroque elegance of Daryll Cullinan or the ascetic deftness of Andrew Hudson, Kirsten's trademark square drive would have looked like someone swatting a mosquito with a Wellington boot, and perhaps this contributed to the faulty assumption that hard work was a substitute for ability.

His pedigree thus denied, his groundbreaking batting was soon taken for granted by the public who saw it as his job, an attitude partly encouraged by his modest statements about the role of senior professionals. When Hansie Cronje or Cullinan thumped a pyrotechnic one-day century, they were lauded as showmen. When Kirsten helped himself to 188 against the United Arab Emirates in the 1996 World Cup – the third highest one-day innings in history – he seemed merely to have satisfied expectations. After all, if the senior pro isn't going to hit the rubbish, who is? Anything under 150 would have seemed a failure. A compliment and a curse.

By early 1997, still playing within his limitations, usually off his pads over wide long-on, he was rated the second best one-day batsman in the world behind Sachin Tendulkar, and the fourth in the Test rankings in a list that included the Indian, Brian Lara and Steve Waugh. Two centuries in the Calcutta Test drew a distinct line under a four-year period in which Asian wickets and attacks had confounded South African batsmen, and while Kallis and Herschelle Gibbs have since made merry on those dusty strips, it was Kirsten who evaporated the mystique of the turning ball.

It is no coincidence that Kallis, Gibbs and Graeme Smith all started their first-class careers with Kirsten at the other end. Gibbs especially has fed on the left-hander's resolve, and their mid-pitch conversations were private batting tutorials held in public, the eternally worried-looking Kirsten perhaps making an undemonstrative observation about the usefulness of chasing wide outswingers or charging a spinner one has just hit for six.

By late in 2002 it was time for Kirsten to move. Smith had taken the opening berth by the neck, beaten it senseless, and dragged it back to his cave, and so the options were clear: move down or move out. Kirsten moved down.

The demotion down the batting order is one of cricket's more gentle traditions, a sad and often understated moment in which an ageing star is allowed to squeeze in another handful of Tests relatively safe from the indignity of being outpaced or outfoxed by younger bowlers. Occasionally there is a last hurrah. Usually there is a wheeze, a cough, and a press conference.

Well aware of his weakening bones and fading eyesight, Kirsten decided the best thing to do was to play within his limitations, and scored 7 more Test centuries. Statistics can be wicked, but if cold numbers mean anything, Kirsten's last 18 Tests yielded two centuries more and a higher average than Graeme Pollock's last 18.

It was fitting that in the end he went beyond his own limitations and allowed himself to cry as he left his Test career behind him.

Real batsmen, of course, don't cry. But then Kirsten was never a real batsman, was he?

(Mail & Guardian, 2 April 2004)

The champion who never was

David Isaacson

When Mzukisi Kenneth Sikali engaged in his most vicious battle, he was outside the ring. The boxer was drinking at his flat and an argument started with other tenants. It soon turned into a full-blooded free-for-all, with the boxer in the thick of it.

Somebody phoned a friend of Sikali's to come and restore order. By the time he arrived, hulking men of 100 kg were cowering outside, while inside Sikali was scything his way through the block.

All 50 kg of him!

It's the stuff of legend, but it's perfectly believable when watching Sikali box. The first time I saw him – defending his SA junior-flyweight title against Job Tleru in 1996 – shivers ran down my spine.

He dismantled the challenger inside of five clinical rounds, breaking his nose in the process. Sikali was the epitome of controlled fury that night, avoiding blows and counter-punching with brutal accuracy. All the while he sported a menacing smile.

I knew immediately that I had witnessed someone special; a pugilist with the brain of a boxer and the heart of a street fighter.

Sikali went on to win three peripheral world titles in the junior flyweight, flyweight and junior bantamweight divisions. But in a fortnight, on Easter Sunday, he challenges for a bona fide world championship.

Sikali, 33, takes on International Boxing Federation (IBF) flyweight champion Vic Darchinyan in Sydney, Australia. If he wins, he will join Baby Jake Matlala as the only SA boxer to hold four world titles.

I still remember seeing Sikali at the press conference after his annihilation of Tleru. A journalist tapped him on the shoulder and Sikali spun around with a hard expression better suited to a dark alley.

I was nervous about interviewing him one-on-one. But when I arrived at his small house in Port Elizabeth's New Brighton township a month or so later, I was greeted by a mild-mannered man whose eyes smiled as widely as his mouth.

He had bought a cold drink so he had something to offer me. My apprehension was unfounded; we hit it off and have since become good friends.

During our chat he told me a story common to the fight game. It all began in the streets of Langa township near Uitenhage, when he would pick on other children at every opportunity. What was unusual is that he targeted bigger children. 'I love being under pressure,' he explained.

When he was introduced to boxing at the age of 16, he instantly fell in love with it. 'I couldn't wait to go to the gym after school every day,' he recalls.

His desire to box, mixed with the thrill of victory, are probably the ingredients that make him one of the most courageous ringmen in South Africa.

In an early fight, his top lip was so badly cut that a piece of flesh was hanging loose. When he returned to his corner at the end of the round, he told his then trainer, Tembile Shushwana, to cut it off. Shushwana reluctantly obliged with a pair of scissors.

Many boxers get nervous before a fight, but not Sikali.

'I think about fighting my fight. I don't worry about what my opponent might do. If he catches me, then he catches me. Why worry?'

One of the few times Sikali got nailed, by Pongsaklek Wonjongkam of Thailand nearly eight years ago, he offered no excuses for his first-round stoppage defeat. 'He caught me with a punch I never saw.'

Admittedly, Sikali's need to spend every day in the gym has waned. He moved to Johannesburg in 2000 after fight offers dried up – he was below the radar in the Eastern Cape.

And he needed money, having lost his house in a failed venture as a taxi owner. In spite of possessing a basic mechanical engineering qualification, Sikali has seemed incapable of buying a vehicle that doesn't break down.

In Gauteng Sikali quickly earned the reputation of being a slacker, albeit a brilliant one.

He was hung over one Monday morning when he got an offer to fight two days later – against wily veteran Daniel Ward, a former Commonwealth champion. Sikali was out of shape but, needing the cash, he accepted.

He knew he couldn't go beyond four rounds, so he went into the ring and bombed out Ward in two. It was the quickest stoppage loss of Ward's career, and the fastest of Sikali's.

Around that time, in 2000, he also briefly trained under Nick Durandt, whose policy of blood, sweat and tears didn't suit Sikali's habits.

The fighter would arrive for early morning runs still reeling from his nightly escapades in Hillbrow.

Sikali joined Harold Volbrecht late that year and the pair clicked.

'If I tried to lock Sikali in a cage, it would kill him. He needs some freedom,' says Volbrecht.

Sikali's lifestyle is not ideal, but that's how some of the great champions of the early 20th century lived.

What Sikali's critics may not realise is that when he does train, he cleans up his act. No drinking, no smoking, no parties.

He transforms into a professional. Although in the gym he's under the supervision of Volbrecht and assistant Thami Lukhele, he's alone at home, where he is meticulous about road work and watching his diet

While heavyweights traditionally reach their peaks in their 30s, lighter fighters have shorter careers. For sheer talent and lack of previous opportunity, Sikali deserves to win the IBF crown.

As it is, he has beaten two bona fide world champions, both World Boxing Organisation junior-flyweight titleholders.

Hawk Makepula, a 1996 Olympian, was a former champion when he first fought Sikali in 2002. Argentina's Juan Cordoba, a points loser in 1995, went on to win the title in 1998.

But at some point Sikali's lifestyle and advancing years will catch up with him, probably sooner rather than later.

Since I met Sikali nine years ago, the collection of scars on his face has grown, although the minority were sustained in the ring.

Some seven weeks before his first bout against Makepula in 2002, he was attacked from behind, getting cracked on the head with a monkey wrench – leaving him unconscious and with a chunk of his right ear dangling by a thread.

The fight should have been postponed, but Sikali refused. Even with his training schedule disrupted, and weak from loss of blood, he scored a narrow points win.

In a rematch the following year, a full-strength Sikali tore Makepula apart with a barrage of head punches inside of four rounds.

It was after that second bout that the public finally saw a glimpse of Sikali's impish sense of humour.

When Makepula lost the first bout, he complained of leg cramps. After the second fight, Sikali quipped: 'This time he had head cramps.'

Sikali has always had a keen sense of humour. When he was in Thailand in 1996, he shared a sauna with a local boxer there. Both men were naked and unable to speak the same language.

The Asian pointed at Sikali's groin and, by gesturing and grunting, asked: 'Why so big?'

Initially taken aback, Sikali retorted in similar sign language: 'Why so small?'

Although considered a hell-raiser in Johannesburg, he is a family man in Port Elizabeth; a man of love. The heart that makes him a great warrior beats hardest for his kin. That's the Sikali I know.

He helps his separated parents financially from time to time. Following his first Makepula victory, he beamed for minutes after putting down the phone to his mother, Nozizwe.

'Hey, she told me she is so proud of me,' said Sikali, who later got 'I love my mom' tattooed on his left arm.

And when he can afford to, he spoils his two children by different women, daughter Siphosethu, 12, and son Mzukisi jnr, 4.

'I don't care about myself; I care only about my children,' he told me over a glass of wine one day. 'I don't care if I have no money for myself, but I don't want people saying that I didn't look after my children.'

He wants them to inherit more than his legendary tales of battle.

(Sunday Times, 13 March 2005)

This piece from Drum *marks the brief intersection of two iconic lives: Nat Nakasa, the rising star of South African journalism (the first black writer to work at the* Rand Daily Mail*); and the troubled heavyweight fighter Ezekiel 'King Kong' Dhlamini, whose life and death inspired 1959's hit musical, 'King Kong' (Todd Matshikiza, father of* Mail & Guardian *columnist John*

Matshikiza, wrote the music and some of the lyrics). Barely 22 when he wrote this profile, Nakasa was refused a passport to study in the United States, and eventually went into exile in New York. He took his own life in Harlem in 1965. He was just 27.

The life and death of King Kong

Nathaniel Nakasa

Ezekiel 'King Kong' Dhlamini – that rugged, ever-unkempt giant with the iron muscles of a Durban rickshaw puller – is back in the limelight. Within two years a legend has emerged round the man who threw himself into a dam rather than face the gray sameness of prison life.

That is as he would have wished. That the whole land should remember his death. That the whole land should remember the strange, fabulous incidents that crowded the 32-year life of 'Lightning Marshal'.

Right this moment, here in Johannesburg, King Kong's gorilla face is on red posters pasted on to walls, his name splashed in the papers and pasted on to car windows. A musical elephant-size job with over 50 men and women on the stage is being made on King's life. The estimated cost of the opera's production is £6,000.

The 'Spice Smasher,' the 'King Marshal' – Mandlenkosi Dhlamini if you want to be official – met his first boyhood days in the district of Vryheid, Natal, around the year 1925. After showing up, fairly regularly, in a Roman Catholic school for two years, King Marshal turned his back for the last time on a classroom.

Only about 14 then, according to his brother Elliot, King Kong went to work in Vryheid, herding a white family's milk-cow and keeping their little garden in lookable condition. There wasn't much in the way of pay. But what a pleasure to be away from his father's whip in the family fields!

Only a few months hurried by and King Kong was gone. Nobody had any idea where he was. The next to be heard of him was when he wrote – at least supervised the writing of a letter to his mother – reporting that he was in Durban. But Durban was too quiet for his tall, Tarzan-youth.

So without much waste of time, King Kong took his exit from Durban.

Off to the wild, stabbing, over-populated Johannesburg. Much, much further away from his parents, and his three brothers and two sisters, all his juniors.

Not bothered for one moment about getting himself a job and a boss, King Kong tried his big hands at gambling with cards and casting dice – just to knock together some kind of a living. It was a gambling argument that landed the King in jail after a man had been battered to death. King was acquitted, and swaggered straight back into his old life.

In those days he used to visit places like training gyms and singing or dancing hangouts since he had tons of time on his hands – which 'won't work' hasn't? He found his way to the sparring rooms at the Bantu Men's Social Centre – a den with hard-hitting boys under the famous hand of William 'Baby Batter' Mbatha.

Those who tell the story of King's first day in the gym have now turned it into a joke for entertaining guests at the township parties. He is said to have laughed himself sick at the sight of people fighting with 'cushions' round their fists.

'Why don't they use bare fists, these chaps?' King is said to have asked.

To King Kong the whole thing looked silly. He told the boys he could lick them all in a row, gloves or no gloves on. What's more, when he was shown the trainer, he repeated his words: 'I can lick your boys any time all in a row, including you their boss.'

The trainer laughed it off and went his way. But when King insisted, getting more insulting and aggressive, trainer Mbatha got into a pair of gloves and flung two to King Kong. In two or three rounds Mbatha sent this Goliath to the ground, proving his point.

But this didn't stop the King from being stubborn. In fact, the defeat made him angry as a wild beast. Yet some sense had been knocked into his head. The defeat made him want to take lessons from Mbatha.

After some time, results began to pop out. In many a tournament King was awarded a walk-over win since there were no opponents in his division – the heavyweights. Promoters told the black giant: 'Your trouble is that you are too heavy. Try to reduce.'

King listened to the advice, and the trick seemed to work. In 1946 King was matched against Joe Maseko, then a seasoned amateur boxer in the middleweight shelf. King lost on points to Joe, just like everybody had expected.

This, of course, meant a serious grudge against Joe Maseko. For King

Kong always had a grudge against anyone who got one up on him.

Then came a big moment for the King, when he was matched against Gilbert 'Kwembu' Moloi, a respected and thoroughly feared boxer from Joburg's Sophiatown. King Kong was fresh throughout the night, and put Kwembu down every round, to win the fight on points.

King Kong showed plenty of this unorthodoxy that night. Every time he dropped the humiliated Moloi, he would refuse to go to his neutral corner. He stood over Moloi with his fists clenched, ready to pummel him to the ground should he get up.

In a South African Amateur Championship Tournament down in Durban that same year came King's next tussle in the ring. The opponent was Durban's sleepy-eyed heavyweight, Nat Mngoma. When the King lost this fight, it only meant one more creature's name in the long list of those he was going to 'fix up one day.'

Mngoma should have counted himself among the lucky guys because King Kong did not run after him in the streets challenging him to a return fight. And King could have done this without any persuasion.

The story has been told time and again how King Kong once cornered one of his challengers at the Durban Railway yards. Here's how it goes: A light-heavyweight in Durban, Sam Langford, said something which sounded like he was keen to face King Kong. The King heard of this, so he took a single ticket to Durban – 400 odd miles from Johannesburg – just to see this boxer who dared challenge him. The poor fellow was busy sweating away a day's work when King Kong confronted him at the railway.

'Are you the chap who wants to fight me?' King inquired impatiently. 'Let's get going now.'

'But how can we fight here in the yard at work?' Sam protested. 'These things are done through promoters and managers and trainers. And it must be in a ring.'

'Listen, boy,' King cut in. 'You said you can beat me any time, any day of the week and twice on a weekend. Now what are you scared of?'

King Kong was already weaving and bobbing in the yard when a third party – a fellow worker of Sam's – intervened. Some sense was spoken into the King's head, and he walked off satisfied that Sam was a damn yellow guy.

Round about September 1951, King got a fight for the Transvaal heavyweight title against John Sullivan – roundly hailed as a tough in the boxing game. The BMSC hall in Joburg was packed to the roof, that night.

Famous for his unfailing stamina, King chased poor Sullivan round the ring from corner to canvas, piling face-tearing punches with the speed of a flyweight. King would stand hands up or rubbing his tummy while Sullivan landed feeble punches all over the giant's front. After a few rounds King got to work again, giving Sullivan the powder that brought the fight to a sudden end.

The next step in the King's programme was to become the South African champion – to beat every heavyweight in the game here. And he got what he wanted. That's when he beat Joe Mtambo in Cape Town.

But then again King Kong found himself without opponents. It got so bad, this lack of opposition, that the King landed up doing barefist fighting on Sunday afternoons. The boxing bug was in him. He had to exchange blows with some willing victim.

For weeks on end he would travel long distances to Pretoria and the mine dumps on the Reef. Pedi tribesmen would pay his fare and offer him stakes if he came to their open-air, barefist fights. The lonely champ would line them all up and knock them out one by one. Even at these fights the South African champion wore his maroon and blue 'King Marshal', 'Spice Smasher' gown.

Not satisfied with these barefist goes, King Marshal would occasionally show up in Johannesburg's busiest streets – all gowned up for exercises. Stunned shopping crowds on hot summer days would watch this oversized six-footer shadow-boxing on the pavements and on street corners.

It was during these eccentric times that King Kong's last fight – against Simon Greb Mthimkhulu – was clinched. Greb was a real good and tough boxing man. But nobody really expected to see him beat King.

There was big confusion when the King failed to show up on time. But still the crowds waited on him. In the meantime the King was trotting the two-mile distance from Jeppe Hostel, the usual big crowds running behind and around him.

When he ultimately made the ring and flew over the ropes in his characteristic boastful style, he was soaked in his own sweat.

With a 14-pound weight advantage over Simon Greb, King Kong toyed around with his opponent. Two friendly jabs and a slap on the face sent Greb breathless on to the canvas for a short count. It became a foregone thing the King was going to crush Greb any time.

But then King Kong started dancing about, swinging his arms like a policeman during a drill session. What's more, he left himself open for any attack.

It happened in the third round. Greb rushed in with a stinging right to the tummy and pressed home a butchering left on the King's jaw, sending the champion to an immediate, peaceful sleep. The King lay flat on his back, his fans shocked.

This was to be a turning point in King Kong's life. From then the great King Kong lost some of his glamour. He wouldn't have anyone look or laugh at him. 'What are you looking at me for?' he would ask. 'What's so funny about me?'

Yes, his reputation had been injured. But his strength and skill remained with him. He could have easily beaten Greb had he not done those ballet gimmicks in the ring. But his end in boxing was near. It came in a secret sparring session in Johannesburg with the white man-mountain, Ewart Potgieter.

Potgieter sent the black giant twice over the ropes. The King got so hurt that doctors urged him not to fight again for some time. King Kong himself felt he was getting weaker and weaker each day, but still he had one more fight.

'He used to grumble a lot to me,' says Elliot, his brother, who is in Johannesburg. 'He used to tell me that some doctor had given him an injection that reduced his strength. He always said wildly that he would kill that doctor if he found out who he was.'

That was the end of the King's ring career. But even a King must live, so the man with the strength of ten began operating as a bouncer in gangster-infested dance halls.

With his change of occupation came new kinds of trouble – with the law. While bouncing one night he stabbed a troublesome knifeman to death. He pleaded self-defence, and was let off.

But the big conflict – with the law and with himself – was still ahead. It is a night in 1956 at the Polly Centre Hall. The King was out with his only known girl, Maria Miya.

King suspected that the girl had been unfaithful to him for some time. So when a misunderstanding came up between them, King stabbed her to death. While a shocked crowd muttered around, King himself ordered them to 'call the police'.

The police came, to find the giant standing in the hall, a knife in his hand. 'Drop that knife,' the police ordered. King refused. They warned that they would take action if he did not drop the knife. King still said 'No'.

With the hall all tensed up, the police opened fire on King Marshal. Three bullets went through his body and hit two policemen behind him. Everybody thought his end had come – but the King lived on. He was taken to hospital, where he stayed, only a short while. Before he had recovered, he was taken to The Fort jail at his own request. A rather strange choice. But he was granted his wish.

The peak of the drama in his life was now near. After a few months he was in the Supreme Court, tried and sentenced to 12 years in jail. Even the trial of King Kong was not to be without its touch of the fantastic: he begged the judge to give him a death sentence instead of jail.

A reporter who spoke to him before he was locked up says King Kong had this to say: 'I have nothing to say. I'm not bothered at all about my girl's death. My only worry is that by the time I come out of jail I will be too old to fight.'

If there's one thing King Kong never feared, it was jail. Those with him tell that he had a royal time in the cells. Neither the guards nor the fellow convicts wished to be involved in a brawl with him.

It was the dull, disciplined life of jail he must have hated. In the outside world he was constantly surrounded by crowds of people. People who talked about his fame and his might. This admiration was a part of his life. Not the grim-faced crowds, like the bunch of hard-labour convicts who saw him hurl his life away; who saw him drown himself in a dam at the Leeuwkop Farm Jail on April 3, 1957.

The King had himself granted his death plea to the judge.

(Drum, February 1959)

Allan Donald was so much more than That Run-Out. For almost a decade the champion fast bowler kept South Africa in the hunt, first with his back to the wall as an inexperienced and notoriously brittle batting lineup battled to come to terms with international cricket in the early 1990s, then finally with a cush-

ion of runs behind him and a cordon off safe hands in front of him. But the slips were the least of his concerns when he was in the zone and cruising in off his 20-yard approach and made the ball talk: a monstrous inswinger to knock back Sachin Tendulkar's furniture; vicious movement in of the seam to castle Mike Atherton; two raw and ugly half-hours when he did his best to kill Atherton and Steve Waugh. And then there was Edgbaston in 1999. It's not how we remember AD. But it's hard to forget …

Just one run!

Allan Donald

Our dressing-room was very quiet that night at Headingley. We were still in the World Cup, we had got to the semi-final due to our satisfactory net run rate, but the chance to eliminate Australia had gone that day. At least we'd have another go at them in four days' time. As luck would have it, Australia versus South Africa was to be the second semi-final, on my home ground of Edgbaston. Would that be a lucky omen for me and my team? We would know the other finalist before our game, because Pakistan were up against New Zealand the day before, at Old Trafford. What a time to get revenge against Australia! We had beaten them many times before in one-day matches, but rarely when the chips were down, when it really mattered. A World Cup semi-final really mattered – not least to Herschelle Gibbs. Understandably, he was very down after Leeds, and the papers went to town on an alleged remark from Steve Waugh when he spilled that catch. It was reported that Waugh said to him, 'Congratulations, Hersch – you've just dropped the World Cup,' and although some of our fielders confirmed that, Hersch said he hadn't heard it. He was too busy cursing himself for his over-confidence, but it's the sort of thing that Waugh would have the bottle to say to him. One of these days I'll ask Steve Waugh about that.

Hansie Cronje and Bob Woolmer did their best to gee up Hersch in between Leeds and Edgbaston, telling him he mustn't brood about it. 'Go out and put it to bed,' Hansie told him, and I must admit that Hersch and the rest of us practised very hard and effectively in the build-up to Edgbaston. We had one day off, when we played golf, and after that we were very focused, watching videos of the Australians, planning how we could maximise our strengths to negate them. We felt that it was good to have the chance so soon to hit back at the Aussies, that Steve Waugh couldn't do it again. Our time was now.

On the morning of the match, our team bus was very quiet as we headed towards the ground. Headphones on, no one spoke, we were all in our private thoughts, fully aware of what faced us. Our warm-ups on the outfield were tense, yet committed, lacking our usual high spirits – but if you can't get edgy before a match of this nature, when could you? We knew the Aussies would be feeling exactly the same. We felt hugely encouraged by the overwhelming support for us on the ground. Everywhere you looked, there were green jerseys, with hardly a peep from the Aussie fans. It was a special Edgbaston atmosphere – a packed house, a glorious June morning, with the adrenalin pumping overtime. This is what you play international sport for. I felt it was going to be our day.

It went very well for us early on, after we had stuck them in on a slow pitch which helped the seamers and didn't do much for strokemakers. It wasn't a particularly good pitch for such a big occasion, with a few deliveries stopping on the batsmen, so it was hard to judge how good their score of 213 was. They had recovered from 68 for four through half-centuries from Michael Bevan and, inevitably, Steve Waugh, but Shaun Pollock and I hit back at the death, taking nine wickets between us. As I walked off the field, at the end of their innings, I thought, 'We can't complain at needing 214.'

We started very well. Gibbs and Gary Kirsten put on 48 for the first wicket, seeing off the dangerous Glenn McGrath. Soon it was 53 for three, as a truly great bowler took the game by the scruff of the neck. Shane Warne came on, well aware that he had to do something special – and quickly. He did. Three wickets to Warne in the space of eight balls. The one that got Gibbs in his first over really started the alarm bells ringing, as Hersch's off-stump was hit by a ball that pitched outside leg-stump. It wasn't a great idea to try working that delivery through legside, but it turned a mile, and this great bowler for the big occasion was off and running. He was lucky to get Hansie Cronje – given out, caught at slip when the ball hit his boot, not bat – but Warne was superb in that first spell. Darryl Cullinan's run-out stemmed from the pressure and soon we were 61 for four.

I couldn't stand the tension in our dressing-room anymore, and I escaped to a room occupied only by the fourth umpire, Roy Palmer. I stayed there for the next 33 overs, praying that I wouldn't have to walk out there and bat. Surely the Aussies weren't going to do us again? But Warne had to come off after bowling eight overs, and they had to mix their part-time bowlers up. Jacques Kallis and Jonty Rhodes calmed our nerves by adding 84, and it looked as if we were getting there as we entered the last ten overs with 70 needed and six wickets left. We might not even need Klusener! But then Jonty got himself out for 43 and, when Warne returned for his last two overs, we needed 61 from 48 balls. Just see off Warne, and we're home! His last over went for fifteen – including a majestic six over long-on from Shaun Pollock. But Jacques tried to play him through extra cover with an inside-out drive and he was caught for 53. Pollock and Mark Boucher then went soon after, and at 196 for eight, I was beginning to realise I might be needed.

Lance Klusener was playing remarkably, though. The Aussies took a chance in keeping the deep mid-wicket area open, and Lance plundered that part of the ground. He smashed 23 off his first twelve balls, and yet he never looked in any trouble. There was no sense of panic, he just picked his spot calmly. I was dreading having to bat. What if it came down to me, with Lance helpless at the other end? How would I remember where all the fielders were? What if I got one on my legs, I tried to guide it down to the fine leg boundary, and I just hit it straight to a fielder? How do I get Klusener on strike when all the gaps are plugged? No one was talking to me at that stage in the dressing-room because the hope was that I wouldn't be needed. Everyone else was too busy cheering on big Lance, as he smashed the bowling around. Steve Elworthy was out there with him – a vastly experienced cricketer, a highly competent batsman, the ideal person for this sort of situation. All Steve needed to do was support Lance, and I wouldn't be needed.

But Elworthy was run out, going for a second run that didn't need to be attempted. We were up with the required rate, Warne was bowled out, and a few more blows from Klusener would see us through. This isn't meant to be a criticism of Steve, because I soon showed what pressure can do to an experienced cricketer – but I reckon we would have won it if Steve had stayed in, rather than go for that second run when it was bound to be tight. All this is being wise after the event, though, because my pulse was racing as I picked up my bat and gloves and went out to join Lance Klusener. I can't remember anything the boys said to me as I left the dressing-room. I suppose there wasn't much to offer, really. We all knew what I had to do – give it to Klusener and run when I was told.

Lance was unbelievably calm when I joined him out in the middle. On the way out, the din from the crowd was remarkable. No packed ground in England generates more atmosphere than Edgbaston, yet it seemed to calm Lance, rather than intimidate him. I was close to panic, with fifteen needed, but he just said, 'Don't worry about it, we'll be fine,' as if it was a benefit match! Over the next few minutes, he showed an amazing big-match temperament, and I'm still in awe at his calmness as I think about the bedlam out in the middle, and the stakes that we were playing for.

The penultimate over was bowled by Glenn McGrath, a guy perfectly capable of dismissing Klusener, never mind me. His fifth ball was clubbed by Klusener for six over long-on, but through the hands of Paul Reiffel, as he back-pedalled towards the rope. It was a desperately close thing, but you wouldn't know from the look of Lance. You could see the heads of the Aussies drop as Reiffel threw the ball back, and when Lance took a single off McGrath's final over to get the strike, they looked down. Klusener now looked in complete control. All I had to do was just stay there, and hope I didn't have to face another ball. There was nothing really to say as Lance and I met between overs, we just had to look at the lack of confidence in the Aussies to tell it was going our way. I just wished my partner good luck and went back to the non-striker's end, waiting for Damian Fleming to start the final over. Nine to win, one wicket to fall, six balls left.

The first ball was smashed through the offside cordon to the extra cover boundary, beating the sweeper out there by three yards to his left. I don't think I'd ever seen a ball hit harder. Until the next delivery. This one travelled at a rate of knots to the right of Mark Waugh at long-off, and it raced over the ropes. What an amazing shot – what nerve! I threw up my arms in delight at that second boundary, convinced we had won it now, and the crowd's excitement was deafening. I looked around the Aussie fielders, at Shane Warne with his hands disconsolately on his hips, at Steve Waugh clapping his hands, trying to shout something positive – and I thought 'We've got them!' One more run needed, four balls left.

Waugh then showed his experience and tactical shrewdness, although I didn't think so at the time. Fleming had been bowling reverse swing and to the left-handed Klusener; that was ideal for the batsman, because he was just hitting through the line to deliveries that were starting on middle and moving away to the off. So Waugh told Fleming to go around the wicket and try to tuck up the left-hander. Amid all the hubbub from the crowd, I thought it was just a delaying tactic to see if they could prey on our nerves, but I had complete faith in my batting partner. One more ball from Fleming should do it, I thought. Wonder if he'll smash another offside four to end it in spectacular fashion? The third ball did cramp Lance for room, and he jabbed it out to Darren Lehmann at mid-on. He made a great diving save to his left, and as I raced down the pitch, I was sent back by Lance. As I turned, I realised I'd be struggling if Lehmann hit the stumps direct with his favoured left-hand throw. The ball just missed the stumps. I'd have been out by a couple of feet if it had hit. Sprawled on the floor, my heart pounding, I thought, 'Thank God, we've got away with it. We'll be okay now.'

I walked down the pitch to have a word with Lance, but amid all the noise, it was a waste of time. He was wild-eyed, but calm. He still looked in control of himself as I told him, 'Pick your spot, and hit it out of the park.' Three balls to go, one run needed to win. Fleming bowled a yorker. Lance dug it out with the bottom of his bat and it bounced past the bowler. I was in the crease until the moment when the ball passed Fleming and only then did I start to run. I looked up at Lance, saw him rushing to my end, and so I started to run as well. My legs felt like jelly, as if I wasn't making any headway at all down the other end. I heard the Aussies shouting 'Keeper! Keeper!' as I tried to get my legs moving properly. It was a dream-like sequence, almost in slow motion. I ended up dropping my bat, and was run out by ten yards at least. The Aussies fell into each other's arms and my world just fell apart. The match ended in a tie – with both sides all out for 213 – but they went through to the Final on net run rate. We knew that would be the case if the scores were level, so we had no one else to blame but ourselves. Or more particularly – me.

I couldn't bring myself to watch that final over on video until a few days later. I then pieced together the elements of that final ball. Was I right to stay in my ground until the ball had passed the bowler? I think so. After all, that narrow escape from Lehmann's throw off the previous ball had shown how risky it would have been to charge down the pitch too early. Yet I should have run instantly the ball beat Fleming because although Mark Waugh was very close at mid-off, he would still need time to get down to the ball, pick it up and get it back to Fleming. Surely Lance would have been home at the bowler's end in that space of time? But I was too slow in getting out of the blocks and Fleming had the time to gather Waugh's throw, under-arm it down to the wicket-keeper's end, leaving me stranded. It looked terrible – amateurish, panicky, the sort of thing you see on the village green every Sunday. Not in a World Cup semi-final, featuring a guy who has played for his country for more than a decade. Nothing you do in your career can prepare you for a moment like that. I had let down my batting partner, my team and my country.

Along with most of the boys, I was in tears in our dressing-room. I just felt worse as the night wore on, as Jonty Rhodes came to console me, followed by Hansie Cronje. Both told me it was bad luck, but I knew that wasn't the case. I had blown it. I was still in a state of shock when Lance came over and apologised. 'For what?' I asked. He said, 'It was my fault, I should have left it, there were two balls to go after that one. We still had time.' We spent the rest of the night trying to take the blame while absolving the other, but it served no purpose, I suppose. I couldn't be consoled by anyone. In the end, Hansie called us together for a group huddle. He thanked us all for our efforts, that it just wasn't meant to be. The more I apologised, the more I was told it wasn't my fault, but the boys were just being kind. Then Bob Woolmer stood up to thank us all for supporting him down the years. That's when it dawned on me that Bob had coached us for the last time. He had decided to finish after the World Cup, and that was now for South Africa. Bob broke down, and we all started to cry again. It was horrible, just horrible.

We sat in the dressing-room for at least two hours, stunned, emotional and inconsolable. Many of our supporters waited for us outside to cheer us, and that made it even worse. One wasn't quite so understanding. He shouted, 'Why didn't you f*****g run, Donald?' and he was quickly led away by a security official. I wouldn't have been able to answer that question myself. I went home to Harborne that night – just ten minutes' drive – and it was like entering a different world. It did my heart good to see the smiling faces of my two children, to give me some perspective on what had happened. They still loved their daddy, no matter what happened in the final over of a cricket match. Next day, I went to the team hotel, to say goodbye to the boys, and pick up my kit. I looked at the newspapers, and the pictures of the despairing South African supporters at the ground brought it all back to me again. Forget my anguish – what about all those folk who had paid so much to come over and see me throw it away with one moment of panic?

You could put it down to human error, but an experienced international froze at the crucial time. And that was me.

Over the next few weeks, I was heartened by many kind messages from South African supporters. There were just a couple of abusive messages, and I couldn't have complained if there had been hundreds of them. Friends at Warwickshire and my family were marvellous to me for the rest of that English summer, but I couldn't get the events of that Fleming over out of my mind. I watched the tape over and over again, and just felt annoyed at myself. In my last World Cup, I had contributed to the biggest disappointment of my career. Bob Cottam, our bowling coach at Edgbaston, said to me one day, 'Al – you look terrible. You need some time off.' It's true that I was emotionally drained, and very tired. I wasn't sleeping very well, my mind still pored over that daft moment. Warwickshire were very understanding, and gave me a fortnight off. It took me at least four months to get that match out of my system. Having worn out that video tape, I never want to watch that run-out ever again.

My nightmare summer in England didn't improve all that much after that semi-final. When I returned after licking my wounds, my ankle problem flared up again. I broke down five times over the next ten weeks, and I got through a few one-day matches for Warwickshire, but with no great comfort nor success. I didn't take a single wicket in the championship, and by the end of the season, I knew that some influential people at Edgbaston were wondering if I was finished. Could they take a chance on me and offer me another contract, when there was no guarantee that I'd last a full season? I could fully understand those views, but no one could have been more depressed or worried than me. I had to fly out to South Africa during the championship match at Durham, after I broke down again – and I was a very worried man when I went to see the specialist Dr Fief Ferreira. I realised that an operation was the favoured option, but that would probably put me out of the forthcoming Test series against England, due to start in two months' time. A satisfactory recuperation from such an operation would normally take around four months, and there was no guarantee that it would rescue my career. I told Dr Ferreira and the South African cricket team's physiotherapist Craig Smith that I preferred taking a chance on a scan and injection, rather than an operation. They agreed to give it a go. They found some inflammation in the ankle, but not an excessive amount of damage. An injection at last hit the spot. It was agony, but we felt it would do the trick. Two days later, in the middle of September, I flew back to Birmingham, under strict instructions to stay off my feet for as long as possible. My career was still alive, but I knew I had been lucky. The upcoming series against England meant so much to me as I advanced on my target of three hundred Test wickets. I needed another 35, and couldn't contemplate falling short.

I also owed it to Warwickshire to prove the doubters wrong. Everyone was so generous to me during my benefit, and yet I couldn't repay so many kindnesses. First I was away until the middle of June on World Cup duty, then my depression took me out of it for a fortnight, and finally my ankle gave way. And all the while, the collection buckets were going around Edgbaston, various functions were being handsomely supported. My good friend Ernie Els attended a marvellous golf day at the Buckinghamshire Club, just before he played in the Open, while my book launch dinner was graced by Jack Charlton, Ernie Els, Gareth Edwards, Francois Pienaar, Michael Lynagh, Rory Bremner and all the South African cricket team. So much goodwill from so many people left me rather embarrassed at my lack of success on the field in 1999. I owed it to many to get back into the thick of things and start taking wickets again. It was time to stop feeling sorry for myself.

(From Allan Donald, White Lightning: The Autobiography, 2000)

Small moments

Donald McRae

IT was cold in Cardiff. Old women bowed their heads, scarves flapping irritably, as they dragged their Tuesday-morning shopping behind them. The men pushed their hands deeper into their coat pockets. They also picked up the pace, hoping to stamp some of the griping rawness from their feet. As we turned left towards the stadium, we did the same. The concrete outline of the main stand could barely be seen through the cloud. It was a sky so low and so grey that, searching for a Celtic streak of brooding romance, I said it might be carrying the whitest snow.

I didn't sound like a velvet-voiced Richard Burton growling a line from a Dylan Thomas story. I sounded like a South African in Cardiff. Two teenage girls skipping school shivered and laughed. But they hadn't even noticed us. They took turns to throw thin and drooping chips at each other outside the nearest burger bar to the Arms Park.

We both thought it might have been different. I guess I had been hoping that we'd be recognised. I would've loved it if some wizened old wing three-quarter had come scuttling across the pavement. 'Welcome to Wales, boyo!' he'd say. He would pump James Small's hand, congratulating him on taming Jonah Lomu in the previous year's World Cup final. Then, he'd cast a mildly bemused eye my way, wondering if I was a prime example of those beefy but deceptively mobile Springbok loose-forwards with a strange Afrikaans name. 'Welcome to rugby country!' he'd chortle. 'I'm off for a pint of Brains with JPR – fancy comin' along?

James Small's expectations were more realistic. 'Fuck it,' he said, 'I never thought Cardiff would be this freezing! We should be sipping cappuccinos in some cosy café instead ...'

But we were so close that we pressed ahead. Cardiff Arms Park, only months away from demolition, suddenly looked huge and grand in the surrounding silence. We hesitated at the bottom of the first row of cement stairs leading to the ticket office. They were still advertising seats and standing room for that Sunday's match. 'Wales v South Africa (World Champions), Sunday, 15 December 1996' ran the message on the blackboard outside the turnstiles and on the damp posters plastered on the adjoining walls. It would be the last major international at the Arms Park. I thought the match would have sold out weeks before. But we had moved twenty years on from the last glittering age of Welsh rugby.

'Oh sure, it's not quite the same anymore,' the smiley gatekeeper told us, 'but it'll still be packed by kick-off. We've only got four or five thousand to shift now ... and they'll go. You fellers over for the game?'

Small nodded and looked up at the high curve of the arena as it towered above us. He knew that, in less than three years, a new stadium would host the 1999 World Cup final. James Small would be thirty years old then. In the unforgiving terrain of international rugby, even for a wing, time would be drawing in on him. He'd already said that he could count the seasons he had left on one hand. Small put up a thumb and then a finger. He grinned and added a third digit, which he half-cocked and then straightened. '1997 … 1998 … 1999 …' he counted, reminding me again that the modern rugby player measured his seasons in years rather than just winters.

The sport had changed drastically in the eighteen months since the World Cup. Rugby, having turned fully professional, had become even more draining. It demanded speed, strength and stamina at a new and brutal pitch of intensity. It tested men relentlessly, even if it paid them well. The game's star performers trained and played for eleven consecutive months, criss-crossing the rugby world with dizzying impact. Their rate of burnout had quickened.

'But James,' I argued tentatively as we searched for a way into the ground, 'maybe you'll hit your peak at thirty …'

Small laughed throatily. 'Maybe …'

'And then what happens?' I asked, tempting him to say that he was already dreaming of scoring the winning World Cup try, against the All Blacks, in Cardiff's Millennium Stadium Final.

'Who knows?' Small shrugged. '1999 seems a long way off right now.' He pointed to one of the gates. It was slightly ajar. 'Let's go through here.'

Inside, we crossed the main concourse and wandered past the lines of steel shutters which would be rolled back that Sunday to reveal bar after bar. Although he'd never been to the Arms Park before, Small's rugby instinct took over. He could tell that the dressing-rooms were on the other side of the ground. It was enough for us then to walk through a darkened entrance, over a narrow stretch of paving and onto the field.

We were quiet as we looked around. The sky above seemed lighter and higher than it had been outside. Our gaze moved across the pitch and up the steep banks of seating along both touchlines and behind the right-hand posts. To the left, where people stood, the stand was less imposing but, still, Small whistled gently.

'Quite a place,' he nodded. 'Imagine it full, with all the singing …'

We walked across the green and springy surface. Small stretched out a few feet ahead, looking right towards the wing he'd patrol on Sunday. By the time we'd reached the halfway line we stopped again and stared at the old cathedral of rugby. In the Tuesday hush, we seemed far from the drone of the city centre. We looked at each other. It suddenly hit us. We were in Wales, standing in the middle of the Cardiff Arms Park.

'Sometimes,' Small said, 'you get goosebumps in a place like this. I grew up in the '70s when there were all those great Welsh sides. We used to be a little in awe of them. They were better than us then. Y'know, I've never really been a student of the game but, man, some players and some teams just stay with you. For me, the Welsh were always special. I loved JPR and the way he ran with the ball – wherever he caught it.'

We began moving again, reminiscing further with every step. 'JPR, Gareth Edwards, Phil Bennett and all those Welsh guys were always there when we were little,' Small remembered. 'I was five years old when I first stood on my father's shoulders at the old Ellis Park. The Springboks against the Lions in 1974, the year they really fucked us up. It was the last Test and people were screaming all around me. The Lions ripped us – especially the Welsh. That's my first memory of rugby ...'

Small shook his closely cropped head and lifted his sleeve. 'Look, goosebumps, bru.'

He was right. The tightly chilled flesh on his muscled arm rose up in bumpy little rows of emotion.

'To be here now,' he murmured, 'twenty-two years later, to be on this pitch, knowing that we're playing Wales on Sunday. Jeez, who would've believed it?'

The groundsman for one. 'Oi!' he shouted angrily, waving his arms at us as he thundered across the field. 'What you playing at?'

I explained that we were engaged in a respectful pilgrimage to the home of Welsh rugby – not long before its destruction and even closer to the moment when the Springbok number 14 ran across the sacred Arms Park turf.

'Fuck off!' the venerable keeper snarled. 'I don't care who he is. Nobody walks across this pitch today. Go on! Both of you! Off!'

Sheepishly, we trudged away, wondering if every last rugby sentimentalist in Cardiff had been similarly numbed. Perhaps Cardiff was not even much of a rugby town anymore – an idea which sounded absurd as soon as it left my mouth. If we had taken a similar walk near Ellis Park, we'd have cast an eye around for knife-sharpening killers rather than ghostly images of Cliff Morgan or Barry John slicing through the Springboks. No one thought of Johannesburg as some cocooned rugby citadel. Rather, moving with the South African times, it had since become 'The Murder Capital of the World'. Cardiff's own transition from rugby mania to ordinary British city life seemed more sensible, if less startling.

We went for a drink before lunch. I had abandoned my search for the Welsh heartbeat of the game and so, inevitably, they found us. 'You one of the Springboks?' a tough old boy asked Small as we ambled into a pub across the road from the stadium. There was a soft gurgle when Small told them his name.

'You marked that Lomu feller then, didn't you?' one of the others remembered, as I silently took back everything I had said about the loss of Welsh rugby fervour.

'What was that like, then?' another man asked.

'Well,' Small said, thinking of Lomu as he took a sip of his Coke, 'it doesn't feel like you've tackled an ordinary guy when you try to stop him.'

'I'll bet!' the first old boy chuckled. 'But you'll fancy your chances this Sunday.'

'We haven't seen too much of your guys,' Small answered diplomatically, 'but we know you've got some good players …'

'That little Robert Howley …' a woman sighed.

'Our best scrum-half since Gareth,' the leading man stressed.

'Scott Gibbs, too,' Small added. 'All those guys who've played rugby league – especially Gibbs. He's got a real physical presence.'

'That's Scott Gibbs all right,' the Welshman agreed. 'But it won't matter on Sunday – you'll have a romp. It'll be one-way traffic.'

It was then that I showed my own crashing variation of the Scott Gibbs crunch. Reaching over to make sure that my recorder was capturing all this sweet off-the-cuff rugby banter, I swept my jug of Brains from the counter. We watched in horror as it smashed on the bar-room floor. Small lifted his brow sympathetically as the Welshmen cracked up.

'I reckon that's what you South Africans are going to do to our boys …'

'The long hard fall of Welsh rugby,' another voice cackled, 'again …'

Small looked at me quizzically, wondering if I was drunk already. But, before I knew it, he had bought me another beer. He was very different, I decided, to the player I had read about in countless articles. This was not the man who, some said, personified the title of his favourite book, *No Beast So Fierce*.

A bearded man moved in at Small's elbow. He needed a few photographs.

'Sure,' Small said, with an early crack of a smile for the camera.

'A couple of shots outside?' the man suggested hopefully. 'Y'know, just you actin' casual, gettin' in the mood for the game.'

Small nodded. He turned to me, a vision of flying glass still hurtling through his head 'Have a drink,' he advised, 'and then we'll go somewhere quieter and talk ...'

'Cheers,' I said.

After a pint of Welsh bitter, my reasons for travelling to Cardiff seemed clearer than ever. James Small was the first Springbok I had ever met. When we shook hands, I'd felt a strange sensation, a sudden and heightened sense of everything the Springboks meant to me. Even when South Africa made me despair, even when I knew what they'd symbolised in 1974, in 1981 and in 1992, I'd always loved them. It was a helpless constant. They were part of me. They belonged to the worst days; but they'd come back for good on the best, on that June Saturday in '95.

In moments of the purest rugby, I could be entranced by the All Blacks or the Tricolores. I could forget everything in a fraught World Cup quarter-final between England and Australia. I could thrill to a free-flowing Five Nations exchange between the French and the Welsh in Paris or Cardiff. I could enjoy provincial rugby in the southern hemisphere, and club rugby in the north. But the Springboks transcended rugby.

Small believed that even more than me. He had lived through the conviction longer than anyone else in the Springbok team. And, still, he seemed to feel it more deeply. At the Arms Park, I had sensed the emotion coursing through him, the fervour which made him say, 'I would die for my country on the rugby field.' If someone else had said it, I might have raised a dubious brow or simply covered my mouth to hide the smirk. But not with Small; for, even with professionalism running rife through rugby, it didn't matter. He really meant it.

So I thought of Small whenever I heard older fans, whether they were in Cape Town or Cardiff, grumbling that money eroded the heart of rugby. They feared that the fat salaries, the very turning of rugby into a profession rather than a passion, would destroy the game. They couldn't understand why rugby's young bucks should fly first-class from one international hotel to another, or why they should have the choice of any car or home they fancied if they hit the big time. Rugby players were not meant to act like footballers. For the traditionalist, they were supposed to hold down a steady job in the day, practise hard in the evenings and then enjoy a few beers after Saturday's game.

Rugby, however, had become a career – even if the stringent physicality of moneyed rugby made it a short burst of a working life. So there was cynicism in professional rugby. There was disloyalty; too, as players veered towards the dosh, making the most of a honeyed life off the field. They would go for it, as long as it lasted. They would train, rest, play and earn a large pile of cash. Rugby players, finally, had become professional sportsmen.

But, even from the outside, I could see how many disparate types of men made a living through rugby. Some were conceited or complacent, and some were just very dull. I liked another kind of rugby player. I wanted to meet the guys who played as if they lived for rugby and yet, at the end of a game, still had lives which existed beyond sport's narrow borders. With someone like Small, I knew that a lunchtime conversation would quickly wander past the next match in Cardiff and end up somewhere more unexpected.

Yet he was a man who shivered inside when he pulled on a Springbok jersey and caught sight of its colour. I wasn't especially interested in nationalism but, when the Springboks ran out onto a field, fifteen green shirts blurred the present and my past. It did something far more to players like Small, opening up emotions buried too deep to be affected by money. The black jersey, even more so, spread a jolt of feeling across the face of every New Zealander who wore it. Perhaps because it was so hard and visceral, rugby brought such raw softness to the surface.

Some rugby truths would always stay the same. But so much else about the game had changed. Cardiff, so representative of rugby from the 1950s and '60s and '70s, seemed an oddly appropriate place to consider the shock of the new. In the distant southern hemisphere, especially, conventional links had been sharpened to a bright edge by the introduction of two very different competitions. The Super 10 provincial tournament had grown into the glistening Super 12 championship. For the first three months of the season, between March and May, five teams from New Zealand, four from South Africa and three from Australia produced some rollicking rugby. The pace was cruel, but it created wild levels of entertainment. Rugby had become a serious business.

There had been further expansion. For the first time in one season, the 1996 Tri-Nations saw Australia, New Zealand and South Africa play each other both at home and away in furious back-to-back internationals. The

All Blacks and the Springboks then contested three additional Tests in South Africa – a series as gruelling and profound as anything previously seen in world rugby.

In the northern hemisphere, the wheel of revolution spun more slowly. But it was quick enough to have transformed the sport in Britain, Ireland and France. If the administration and marketing of rugby still seemed amateurish in comparison to their brash equivalents down south, the clubs, coaches and players had embraced the concept of professionalism with diligent enthusiasm. It was, inevitably, an idea centred on the hope that there would be enough money to make everyone feel that they were suddenly rich. In England, in particular, there was a naïve belief that rugby could follow football's reinvention of itself as a multi-million-pound enterprise. The crucial difference, however, remained that football was the national game. Even professional rugby would never be able to compete at that level. It would invariably occupy a more specialist enclave, only breaking out during a phenomenon as rare as 'Lomu-fever'.

Yet in New Zealand and white South Africa, rugby was still locked into collective theories of national identity and cultural significance. In those countries, it didn't matter that rugby described itself in newly commercial terms – its true power resided in the enduring passion it elicited from ordinary people. A similar vigour had once energised Welsh rugby but, at least amongst the Cardiff kids we saw that week, there was the odd sight of as many red shirts marked by a Manchester United badge as a green dragon.

Ironically, the spread of professionalism threatened to open that divide between the mid-'70s and the mid-'90s into an end-of-century chasm. The Tri-Nations and the Super 12 had given southern-hemisphere rugby even more impetus. Yet, even in that tight band of three, a gap had emerged. By the end of 1996, South Africa's aura as World Champions had begun to fade. New Zealand, instead, had become the dominant force.

Auckland, captained by Sean Fitzpatrick, won the inaugural Super 12, beating James Small's Natal in the final. Even more historically, South Africa then suffered the unthinkable. Under yet another new coach, Andre Markgraaff, they lost their unbeaten record in a home series against New Zealand. A magnificent All Black team also beat the Springboks and the Wallabies in all four of their Tri-Nations matches. They played South Africa five times in 1996 – and only lost the last 'dead rubber'.

The Springboks' World Cup image as a unifying social force had also begun to curdle. Having lost an ill Kitch Christie as coach, and inexplicably discarded their inspirational manager, Morné du Plessis, Springbok rugby had been in retreat all year. Markgraaff had dumped Pienaar, replacing him as captain with the quieter and less politically flamboyant Gary Teichmann. While Teichmann was respected and liked within the game, Pienaar's leadership seemed sacrosanct, bolstered as it was by his friendship with Mandela. But Pienaar was out, seemingly forever. It marked the start of another painful period in South African rugby.

Small had never been far from crisis himself in 1996. There were some great achievements, such as the way in which he ended the Super 12 as the tournament's leading try-scorer ahead of Lomu and Wilson. His reputation as South African rugby's most fervent star had been reaffirmed. But, continuing a pattern established years earlier, Small was dropped against the All Blacks for 'disciplinary reasons'. After he'd performed brilliantly out of position at full-back in the first Tri-Nations Test in Cape Town, Small was spotted by a journalist the following Thursday night. He was in a nightclub. Although he argued that he was merely pursuing his growing interest in photography at a fashion show, Small had broken the team's 10.30 p.m. curfew. It was a familiar scenario.

In a curious way, the man and the team seemed the ideal fit. For each, chaos perpetually followed triumph. The Springboks could replace their 'One Country, One Team' World Cup ambition with a gloomy collection of political gaffes. They could lose Du Plessis and Pienaar, but it seemed as if they would never shake their infamous president, Louis Luyt. They could win a World Cup against the All Blacks and then, in their next meeting in South Africa, build an 18–6 lead, before collapsing in the crush of twenty-three unanswered points.

But, for both Small and the Springboks, in every forlorn moment there would be a more hopeful undertow. The Springboks always promised to improve, they always intended to escape the shadows of racism. Small, meanwhile, was the lone survivor from the first Springbok team to have emerged in the wake of apartheid, in 1992. Four years later, according to the All Blacks, he was still the best wing in South Africa. Yet in terms of being dropped, fined and suspended, Small was already the most-reprimanded Springbok in rugby history. At the same time he neared two more long-standing records – for the most caps and the most tries scored in a green-and-gold shirt. As he neared those more exalted Springbok marks,

I could sense Danie Craven turning slowly beneath our feet. If Small provided a link between the country's variously dramatic recent eras of rugby, he was not reminiscent of any Springbok from the bad old days. He was even unlike some of his newer contemporaries.

While the selectors excluded Small for 'bad behaviour', they chose to play Henry Tromp at hooker against New Zealand. In 1993 Tromp and his father had beaten a sixteen-year-old black employee to death on their farm. They were both convicted and served a short sentence in prison. And then, three years later, Tromp made his Springbok début in a team missing Small, described as 'South African rugby's naughty boy supreme'.

In a radio poll in Johannesburg, 13 000 callers voted that Small should keep his place while a thousand went the other way. A stranger forum of support for Small came from the conservative Zulu Inkatha Freedom Party. Their spokesman, Ed Tillet, said that, if Small so wished, tens of thousands of Zulu impi warriors could be mobilised to take 'the necessary action on the streets of Durban' to ensure that he was not wrongly persecuted.

The Tromp turmoil, the dispute between Markgraaff and Pienaar, and the news that the country's Minister of Finance, Trevor Manuel, had supported the All Blacks rather than the Springboks, were more serious signals that South African rugby's old wounds of division had reopened.

Rugby had always been an inherently conservative sport. In South Africa, however, there were players and spectators who still assumed that the word 'reactionary' was the highest possible compliment for a tight defence. So when a character like Small sauntered along, brimful of attitude and chock-full of emotion, they trawled through rugby history's books. It was no use. Small was without precedent.

In their attempt to define the way in which Small had changed the once rigid iconography of Springbok rugby, the South African press turned regularly to British football. Without any obvious comparisons in either their own game or their own society, they had tagged Small as 'The Paul Gascoigne of South African Rugby' and 'The Eric Cantona of South African Rugby'. Beyond the Premiership, and in even more entrenched rebel territory, he was also known as 'The James Dean of South African Rugby'.

Small had always interested reporters working outside of sport. He made news and elicited overblown national reactions irresistibly – whether it was his admission that he had smoked dope or the sight of him crying bitterly after missing a try against the All Blacks and, again, after he became the first Springbok to be sent off in a Test match.

With his magazine looks and TV commercials, his love affairs and break-ups, his reputation both on and off the rugby field turned him into a soap-opera-style celebrity. The liberal and un-sporty *Weekly Mail* decided, as far back as 1992, that 'James Small is the closest thing we have in this country to a superstar'.

I knew, too, that Small was troubled by something which made him as compelling as he was confusing. While it caused him no end of unease in his tangled life, it also drove him on in the harsh arena of Test rugby: He did not have the natural brilliance of Jeff Wilson or Christian Cullen, the sheer *élan* of Jeremy Guscott or Thomas Castaignède, but Small had the bravado and resilience to compete at even that exalted level.

By the end of 1996, Markgraaff recalled him for the tour of Argentina, France and Wales. He was immediately back in the Test side, inspiring South Africa to successive victories over the Pumas and the Tricolores, scoring two tries against the French.

Markgraaff resorted to that footballing short-cut when he considered Springbok rugby's strange new standard-bearer. 'James Small is the Eric Cantona of South African rugby,' he explained once more to those who had yet to hear it. 'But Cantona has worked hard to improve his discipline and has won much respect for it. We hope that James Small can do the same ...'

I preferred the words of Harry Viljoen, an intelligent coach who had worked with Small in both Transvaal and Natal. 'If I've got fifteen James Smalls in my side,' Viljoen said, 'I'll take on anyone else in the world ...' But, being a rugby man who knew Small as well as anyone, he paused. 'I've just got to teach him not to be so emotional ...'

Cardiff, Tuesday, 10 December 1996

There was so much feeling in James Small that, facing him across a table, I made a silent decision to write this book. We sat in Cardiff's only Mexican restaurant. It was raining outside but, inside, the Small passion burned. It scorched through those preconceptions which link all professional rugby players to the conservatism of the game's institutions – from Ellis Park to Twickenham. After Small, it was easy to look beneath just the scores and the competitions, to move beyond the unity of teams and the nationalism of countries. Rugby was also about individual men.

It helped that we had been put together by James's oldest friend and, in the Small vernacular, his 'cultural guru', Josh Georgiou, whom I had just met in Johannesburg. It also meant something that we came from the same place, that we were both still reeling a little from having grown up as white South Africans in such a strange time.

'You know how it was in South Africa then,' Small said as he stirred his third Cardiff cappuccino and I drank my umpteenth Belgian beer. 'We felt so isolated. We felt so insecure about our own culture. Everything was geared to this "overseas dream", to getting the hell out of Johannesburg and seeing how different life could be in London or Paris. I became very bitter. I'd be preparing for a match in Pretoria or wherever when I'd get a postcard from someone in Paris. I'd wonder if I'd ever see what they saw. And fuck, now, the irony is that because of rugby I get to travel the world. So last week it felt like some kind of circle had been completed.'

Three days before, Small had stood in the Parc des Princes in Paris. 'On Saturday, just before the start of the French game,' he said, 'the noise and the colours in the stadium were incredible. I looked up towards the seats where I knew my mom and dad sat. It was unbelievable. I thought then: "This is it! No amount of money anywhere in the world can ever buy a moment as pure as this. I'm in Paris. And, way up there, my mom and dad are watching me play my thirty-fifth rugby football international."'

'Moments like that drive me on. It'll be the same this Sunday. I'll think of all the shitty grounds my dad's watched me play at, from school onwards. He'd always sit on his own. He'd get worked up because he supported me like crazy. My old man's got into fights with other spectators because they've always liked to diss me. But on Sunday we'll have made it all the way to Cardiff Arms Park. That moment is just not purchasable.'

Earlier that morning, perhaps an hour after we'd met, James Small had told me about his parents. He did so almost in passing, but there was a tiny echo in his voice. Like so many apparent 'bad boys', the very idea of an unbroken family both inspired and haunted Small. He was exceptionally good-humoured in Cardiff – and mainly because his parents and sister were about to follow him from Paris. They were a family again.

The divorce, which had happened when he was young, hit him hard. Since then, he had hardly ever seen his parents together in the same room; so to have them sitting side by side in Paris, of all cities, had opened him up.

'My mother always provided the stability during my rockiest moments,' he explained, 'but the rugby passion began with my dad. In 1956, Vernon Small played soccer for South Africa. When I was a kid, that always meant a huge amount to me. It's always been a passion for me, to follow in my father's footsteps and play for South Africa. Sometimes he even let me wear his Springbok shirt. It was all I wanted.'

'When you were that kid,' I wondered, 'did you ever feel that the Springbok shirt also represented something else?'

'To be honest,' Small said, 'I never really thought about that. It was only later that I began to put everything into context. That first Test of ours, back in '92, against the All Blacks, was very emotional. There had been a lot of pain and isolation. And I'll never forget voting in the first election in 1994. We were on tour in New Zealand and so we were probably the very first South Africans to cast our vote. That was a special moment. But, before that, as a kid, I was just sports-*bevok* [fucked]. Nothing else mattered. Soccer, rugby and athletics ruled my life. Later, when I was around seventeen, I got suspended from soccer for headbutting a referee. That was when I got totally involved with rugby instead. We would have rugby practice on Tuesday and Thursday and games on Wednesday. I was absent from school most Fridays ...'

While I'd been disdainful of Afrikaners, Small was less judgmental. 'I grew up in awe of a lot of Afrikaners,' he explained. 'And the more I played rugby, the deeper that feeling grew. The higher the level of rugby, the more surrounded I was by Afrikaners. I made it to Craven Week [South Africa's provincial schoolboy tournament] with Transvaal. That was unbelievable. In those days, the main Transvaal school side was supposed to be all-Afrikaans. The "A" team for Craven Week would be all these hulking guys from Monument Hoër Skool [High School] and the "B" team would include a couple of token English guys. And I ended up making the South African Schools' side that year – which was almost unheard of. They kept saying "Who's this fucking *sout-piel* [salt-cock]?" and they've kept saying it ever since!

'When I hit provincial level there were guys like Piet Kruger and Andre Skinner – great characters of South African rugby who were also hardcore Afrikaners. In 1992 the only two English guys on the Springbok scene were myself and Evan Speechly, our physio. And when it came to the Saturday night after a game, when the players were put in charge of the team, I would get fucked up. I was fucked up every Saturday night for two straight years.

It was my initiation into Afrikaans rugby at the highest level – but, because I was this English *oke* [guy], there was a bit of seriousness in the beatings. I was singled out because they were asking, "Who is this young Englishman? Who the hell does he think he is?"'

'And now?'

'Well, things are different. Our captain, Gary Teichmann, is English-speaking and there're a lot of English guys on this tour. But it's not really an issue. I'm rooming with Jacques Olivier who's Afrikaans and he's a friend of mine – like a lot of the guys. Yet one of the best moments of my rugby career came just after my first Springbok Test in 1992 – at the after-match function this Afrikaans guy in a Northern Transvaal blazer comes up to me. I can see his face right now. And he says to me, in this thick Afrikaans accent, "James Small, I have to say something to you. Listen, we *okes* had all written you off. But we were wrong. As a rugby player you're okay. You deserve to be a Springbok." Then, it was unusual for an Afrikaner like him to even talk to an English-speaker like me. But for him to say that I was as good as the rest of the team – those are the memories that stay with you …'

'As I guess', I murmured, 'do the tears …'

In South Africa's opening post-isolation Test following Mandela's release, against New Zealand, he faced the formidable Inga Tuigamala. Small showed an immediate affinity for international rugby. He made tackles of astonishing bravery and ran with commitment and pace as the Springboks fought back from a disastrous start. In the end, the enduring memory for most was the image of Small knocking on with an open try-line only metres away. If he had held on and scored, South Africa might have completed a shock victory after a decade in the wasteland.

'Oh boy,' Small laughed softly, 'I just bawled my heart out afterwards. I was inconsolable! But, after a while, I was able to look at the whole match and realize that I had done well. They said I couldn't stand up to Tuigamala. He was this hundred-kilo Tongan winger in a black shirt who had been running over everybody. People were calling him the best wing in the world. They said I had no chance.

'I'll never forget the Friday afternoon before the Test. I was with my sister in this pub in Johannesburg, The Moosehead. We were getting something to eat at the bar and these four guys behind us were discussing the team. It was a huge moment in South African rugby – our first Test in years. These guys went through the whole side, player by player. And I was the only guy they didn't want. I went over to the loudest guy and said to him, "Give me your business card and I'll call you after the game!" And he started stumbling, "Oh shit, I'm sorry, I didn't know you were there." I said, "Fuck that! I heard what you said. Give me your card and we'll talk after the game."

'That night I couldn't sleep. My first Test for South Africa and we're playing New Zealand. I was so nervous. I just kept walking round and round the hotel in my Springbok shirt. I eventually went to bed in that jersey. And I thought about what those guys had said about me. The next day, quite early on in the game, there was an opportunity for Tuigamala to steamroller me. He got the ball in their 22. I was hanging deep for a kick but he decided to run. He had a clear thirty yards in front of him to pick up speed. I don't know how I did it but I hit him, knocked him down, got up and ran up the sideline with the ball. And on Monday morning I phoned that guy who had dissed me and I said, "There – fuck you!" and put down the phone. That's how I feel my whole life has been – proving people wrong.'

'But not everyone thinks of you as a martyr,' I pointed out.

'No. You've just got to look at the World Cup.'

'Yeah, you and the rest of South Africa against Lomu ...'

'Well, with a name like mine,' Small grinned helplessly, 'I was always destined to face a guy as huge as him. And in Johannesburg, my old home town, in the World Cup final. The Springboks against the All Blacks! The whole nation, from Nelson Mandela down, is rocking. You can feel this longing for us to win. But, to be honest, I'm shitting myself.'

A laugh, as sharp and dry as Small himself, slipped out. 'Jonah Lomu's awesome. He's standing tall at six-foot-five and clocking in at 120 kg. I'm five-ten and sitting pretty on the same wing at 85 kg. And the whole fucking country is saying, "Go on, James, go get him, boy!"'

He shook his head in disbelief. I remembered how, just before the kick-off, Mandela had stopped in front of Small. The President offered the green-and-gold number 14 a curious smile, as sweet as it was grave.

'And then,' Small said, 'Mandela laughed. Very gently. You could see it in his eyes. He was thinking, "Shame! This poor guy is marking Lomu!" Mandela took my hand and said, "You've got a big job to do today, Mr Small!" I'd only seen Lomu once before. It was the Dubai 7s and I didn't know who he was then. He was huge. I thought, "Who's this brute of a lock?" And then I heard he was a wing. I thought, "Oh shit!" He had this walkman on but the headphones were so massive that it looked like he had two orange soccer balls on the side of his head!

'Before the final, it was eerie. On the way to the ground, on the bus, I had my own little walkman on. I was listening to this song, *Hymn of the Big Wheel*, by Massive Attack. It's this beautiful song, with a slow and hypnotic beat, and this high voice sings this one line over and over ...' Small and I, respectively full of caffeine and beer, and similarly high on excitement, sang that very line, in the aching falsetto of Massive Attack's Horace Andy, the great Jamaican vocalist: '*and the big wheel, keeps on turning* ...' I am not a singer, and I don't think James Small is either, but I have the tape to prove it. For a moment we were Horace Andy and Tricky singing for Massive Attack in Cardiff. I was ready to repeat the line again, as it goes on record, but Small was sensibly back on the bus to Ellis Park.

'I'm playing this song over and over again,' he said, as if he'd already forgotten our poignant duet. 'And I could see people walking to the ground, carrying the new flag and these banners which all seemed to have a "Small" name printed on them – telling Jonah Lomu that he had a "Small problem". Time seemed to slow down. I got those goosebumps again. Like the song, it felt like I had come full circle – after all the heartache, I was back on top again. The wheel had turned.

'But, on the day itself, there were other guys who took on Lomu as well. I had a lot of support. Before we went out, Chester Williams said to me, "You just hold him, James, and the rest of us will pull him down." Kobus Wiese also said, "Just cling on to him and I'll fuck him up!" Chester hit him, Kobus hit him, Japie [Mulder] hit him, Joost [van der Westhuizen] hit him, I hit him ...'

'And how does it feel,' I repeated, 'when you tackle Lomu?'

'When you hit him hard,' Small said after a thoughtful pause, 'it's like hitting a wall. But I got his attention. Jonah's very aware of me on the park. He knows what I bring to the party. I'm this psycho-kid who's not going to stop at anything. He knows I'm capable of going a little ballistic. So we've had some good battles over the last year. And I think I can safely say that there's only one game when he got the better of me – in the Super 12 final, when he scored two tries. Apart from that, I've held my own against him. But I would never class myself as a great player. I'm just a worker. But a very hard and a very committed worker.'

'Are "hard-working" and "committed" also fair descriptions of the

Springboks? The All Blacks might have had more flair …'

'But we had this incredible desire to win. I don't want to sound philosophical or even religious, but it was down to something deeper. This will sound strange coming out of my mouth but I truly believe that it was South Africa's destiny to win the World Cup. It was almost as if there was divine intervention, that God wanted South Africa to share in some joy, that elation, after so much shit over the years. It was like he was saying, "Okay, South Africa, here's a month of pure enjoyment and togetherness for the whole country – this is yours." And to have Nelson Mandela there, on the day, well, that was just the sweetest moment.

'When we attended the State President's function for winning the World Cup, Mandela comes up and says, "James Small, my son has posters of two white men all over his wall. One of them is Francois Pienaar, which I can understand. But, for some unknown reason, the second man is you!" He laughed but it made me think – jeez, even the President knows I'm supposed to be the bad boy!'

Small often played up to his unhinged persona – for he thrived on the enduring intensity of his role as the country's most controversial rugby player. '*Ja*,' he drawled, 'and the image also pays off sometimes. The media love that "bad boy" thing. And, of course, a lot of the Afrikaner players aren't that media-friendly so I get all this attention because I'm different.'

As early as August 1993, the Small saga had already turned down a bumpier track. As he offered to work alongside Adèle Searll, an anti-drug campaigner in Cape Town, the papers revisited his own past. While everyone knew that most South African kids had rolled a couple of joints by the time they were sixteen, Small's indulgences were printed with a breathless puff of shocked revelation.

Charlene Smith's *Sunday Times* feature began with these words: 'Rugby hero James Small used to be the terror of Johannesburg's northern suburbs – a *dagga* [dope] smoking drop-out whose future looked bleak.' Smith did her best to write a story of redemption. Although she went into astounded detail about the teenage Small smoking a joint on a golf course, she was relieved to announce that there was a happy ending.

In celebration of the fact that he had not smoked for the previous two years, a local company had pledged to pay the Adèle Searll Drug Rehabilitation Centre R300 for every try Small scored. 'Managing Director Angelo Peros', the man coughing up the anti-dope dough, told Smith that he had seen Small 'talking to sixty teenagers. He is the perfect anti-drug symbol for young people. He is incredibly charismatic and great with kids. They gave him a fantastic response. It has taken a lot of courage for James to take the stand he has …'

But, the following year, Small was attacked on New Zealand television by Murray Deaker, a glibly provocative TV personality. The theatrical Deaker described Small as 'a danger to all around him'. Freeze-framing moments when the camera zoomed in on Small's typically fierce match face, Deaker declared grandly that 'this absolute nutter' was 'obviously still suffering the effects of his dope-smoking'. After so many decades of abysmal publicity under apartheid, the nervous Springbok management refused Small permission to take legal action against Deaker.

Small's frustration escalated. Later that year he was involved in a 'nightclub spat' with a Springbok water-skier, Ian MacLeod. The 'aggro', as MacLeod characterised it on television, began when a girl 'pinched Small on the bum'. MacLeod's girlfriend, Adèle Hattingh, denied that she was the cheeky culprit. On the front page of the *Sunday Times*, as the country tussled with issues of democracy and murder, a cheesy rugby headline appeared: 'I didn't pinch James Small's bum – Adèle!'

The *Sunday Times* reported that 'the attractive second-year university student said that, unlike other women, she did not find James Small irresistible'. Meanwhile, another student at the club, twenty-year-old Melany Jackson, claimed that she definitely belonged to the broad church of 'other women'. Speaking in Afrikaans, she was quoted as saying that, when she met Small, she 'was in seventh heaven. He has the softest lips and the hardest body a girl can dream of. It was heaven just to meet him.'

Back in hell, and dropped for the UK tour at the end of '94, Small was less ecstatic. His exclusion from the Springbok team felt like 'someone had reached in and pulled out my heart'.

But Small soon won back his spot in the World Cup squad. Afterwards, in the following weeks of national euphoria, images of Small kicking a ball around the townships seemed the perfect symbol of 'new' Springbok rugby. Photographs of Mandela and Pienaar together at countless functions provided the political seal to bind the entire country to rugby. Yet Small was a little closer to ordinary life. He was still one of the boys on the street.

'I'd say it's been pretty much an even spread of ups and downs over the last nine years,' he reflected. 'At the start of each season I think, "This is gonna be a good year for me, this is gonna be a peaceful year." But then, somehow, I self-destruct or get made an example of. There've been times when I've been in the depths of despair. You know all the incidents. But a lot of those things were blown out of all proportion. The drug thing just got turned inside out and I ended up having to talk like I'd been some sort of junkie. It was ridiculous. Then that Murray Deaker guy in New Zealand rolls these clips of me playing rugby. I'd be about to ruck a ball and Deaker would say, "Look at the maniacal frenzy in James Small."

'Morné du Plessis, our old team manager, would always tell me – "James, you have to be more careful. They're making a big thing of this because it's you … they wouldn't care if someone else did it." After a while, you just say to hell with it. I'm happy with my image. It sells and, also, it forces people to give me some space. A lot of them think that I'm going to turn round and deck them!'

But, in Cardiff, Small was intent on discovering a more cultural side to his already complex personality.

'How do you feel about all the Gazza and Cantona comparisons?' I asked. 'When I was compared to Eric Cantona,' Small enthused, 'I took that as my biggest-ever compliment. If I had just an ounce of the skill Eric Cantona has in his left foot, I'd be a happy man. But Cantona also has that immense intelligence.'

Small looked me straight in the eye. He reached for his wallet. He found the neatly folded set of words. 'To achieve happiness,' he read aloud, 'sometimes you have to go through the worst depths of despair. Genius is about digging yourself out of the hole you have fallen, or been pushed, into. Failure makes you succeed.'

The Springbok tyro looked up slowly and confirmed the truth. 'That is a direct quote from Eric Cantona.'

'But James,' I replied, sounding as if I had lived in England too long, 'you support Liverpool!'

'*Ja*, but I love Cantona! You remember what he said about journalists and seagulls …' In true Cantona fashion, Small tore away on a deeper artistic jag, telling me about Iceberg Slim's gritty American novels before skidding down to talk about John Hiatt, Robbie Robertson and the other artists he featured on a compilation album of his favourite songs, *A Small Collection*.

Small also detailed his next venture. 'I've just done this deal with a company called Mr Price. We're gonna do this range of underwear. I've been buying all kinds of samples in London and Paris – I've got a suitcase packed full of everything from boxer shorts to ladies' teddies.'

He chuckled again, as if he could imagine hiring Jonah Lomu for a Calvin Klein-like underwear ad campaign. 'We've got the perfect name.'

'What's that?' I asked.

'Well, it just had to be "Smalls"!'

We were still laughing when I called for one more beer and, adhering to his new discipline as a reformed rugby player and exotic underwear entrepreneur, a sparkling glass of water for Small. 'The thing is,' he suddenly broke off, 'I'm not just that one-dimensional guy they write about. I don't just want to be known as the nut who got kicked out because of a fight in a nightclub. I want to be known as someone who did some interesting things off the field. But, maybe most of all, I want to be known as a great competitor, as a guy who is good to play with and hard to play against. I'm twenty-seven years old now and I've only got a few years left to set the record straight.

'I know that the hardest thing for any sportsman is to give up the game. Who knows how you react when you're no longer "The Business". You not only lose the fame and the money that comes with it – you lose the chance to do something you do best of all. You're just an ex-player. This is my ninth season as a full-time rugby player. So I've had a good run, I've had a long run. And, sure, there are times when you get *gatvol* [fed up] and you don't feel like going away on another tour or to another practice on a Monday morning. But, now, I'm happy. That's a big thing for me to say. Because I'm a very negative person most of the time. Y'know, I don't like flying because I believe I'm destined to die on a plane.'

I could have mentioned that this made him the 'Dennis Bergkamp of South African Rugby' – but his distress was real. 'I always have this feeling of impending doom. If it's not that, it's another thing. I'm always waiting for the bomb to go off. It's as if I can't believe good things can last.

'But, now, life feels good. I'm playing for my country in Buenos Aires and Paris and Cardiff and it feels great. My family are around me. I've got some fantastic friends and a lot of wonderful opportunities outside rugby. It feels like things couldn't be better. I'm going to try hard to live for this moment, to just enjoy it and see if I can put something special on the field next to everything else that has happened off it.'

It was the perfect moment to turn off the tape. I called for the bill. We sat for a few minutes and spoke about our plans for the year ahead.

Christmas was only ten days away and it felt like a new beginning awaited both of us. And then the phone rang. As James reached for it in his jacket pocket, I made a slurred crack about how a Welsh Lolita must have tracked down his mobile number. He winked, and then nodded hopefully.

But it was his father. It did not take long for the mood to change. The hurt spread slowly across James Small's face. I looked down, trying to appear fascinated by each and every number printed on our bill. The conversation continued while I worked on my mental arithmetic. Then, I did the right thing. I went for a walk.

Eventually, when I returned to the table, James ran a hand across his cropped head. His eyes glistened. 'That was my dad,' he said. 'He's on his way to the airport. He's not going to wait until Sunday. He won't see me at the Arms Park.'

I hesitated, not quite sure how best to respond. But, as he pushed back his chair and stood up, James Small said the words before I could. 'I'm sorry …' He walked towards the door and then turned and shook my hand. He said it again. 'Sorry …'

Cardiff Arms Park, Sunday, 15 December 1998

The weather was still miserable. But the green-and-gold shirts shimmered through the gloom. Our eyes were on James Small all afternoon. We were with three older Welshmen who were unfailingly humorous about South Africa's supremacy. It was not the result they wanted, a 37–20 Springbok cruise, with Joost van der Westhuizen scoring three slashing tries. But they took us out to a crammed pub afterwards and told us about the glorious, if dipping, history of Welsh rugby. They lamented the fact that the Cardiff crowd hardly sang anymore – snatches of *Why, Oh Why, Delilah!* and *Bread of Heaven* were all they'd heard that afternoon. We told them about James Small.

In the match itself, Small was injured early on, cracking a rib, but he played on with his usual fire. We cheered every time he touched the ball or brought down a red jersey. The night before, Alison and I, and her brother, Tim, an Englishman living in Cardiff, had gone to visit James and his mother, Vaughn, at the Springboks' hotel. It was an ordinary Saturday night in Cardiff and so the four of us had a few glasses, while James guzzled his water instead.

He was happy again, as I was too, as we stressed to Alison and Tim how sorry we were that the Welsh were about to be thrashed in their last big match at the Arms Park. His mother laughed and told us stories about James as a kid, and how it was not the easiest thing to live in South Africa when your son kept hitting the headlines as often as Nelson Mandela – if not for the same reasons. 'Ag, Ma!' James would say.

But it was the night before his last game of the season and so, after an hour, we said goodbye. He walked us to the door and put his arm around my shoulders. 'I want you to have the shirt I play in tomorrow…' he said.

Twenty-four hours later, even though I still did not believe it, Alison and I swept through those same revolving doors. The foyer of the hotel was packed, but there he stood. James Small had a beer in one hand and a cigarette in the other. It was the end of another year, and his life felt sweet again. He came towards us with his arms opened wide. 'Howzit!' he shouted.

A minute later he stretched over and gave the jersey to me. It was wrapped in plastic. The mud of Cardiff Arms Park glinted darkly through the shiny surface, already just a memory from a famous ground. I only told him later what it meant to me, that shirt, how the green and the gold had echoed through my life, how it reminded me of everything that was so powerful and unforgettable about South Africa. Then, I just grinned at him, thinking of the moment when I would lift the muddied number 14 shirt out of its glossy wrapping and hold it in front of me, turning only to say to my English girl, 'I love these colours …'

(From Donald McRae, Winter Colours: Changing Seasons in World Rugby, 1999)

The night Kallie Knoetze became a man

Gavin Evans

A man stood weeping, bitterly asking of no-one in particular: 'Why did he lose? Why did he lose?'

On the other side of a high fence which separated boxers from public at

Mmabatho Stadium, hundreds of fans jumped up and down in delight, hailing the demise of Kallie Knoetze as they chanted 'Big John Tate'.

The man who cried – and many thousands of others who stood or sat in stunned silence – was white. The jubilation came from black people.

Knoetze, so often crude and boorish in his public pronouncements and labelled a symbol of racism because of his policeman past and his shooting of a black schoolboy in the leg, had finally taken his comeuppance.

He had brought his legion of fans across a line on a map to fight a big, black American in what, officially, is not part of South Africa – and lost.

The fight, in the capital of Bophuthatswana, was before a mixed audience. But one was hardly aware there were blacks in a predominantly white crowd of more than 40 000 – until Tate won.

Through Friday night cars arrived in a steady stream. By Saturday morning the road to the stadium was jammed.

Kallie's faithful had travelled hundreds of kilometres to see him take the penultimate step to the world title.

The beautiful and the rich stepped out of luxury cars at the Mmabatho Sun, the less beautiful stumbled out of buses into the veld around the stadium, clutching two-litre Coke bottles, laced, presumably, with stronger beverages.

By the time the boxing started there had been the usual, senseless, fights in the stands which seem to be standard before major South African rugby and boxing matches.

Three convincing South African wins in the preliminaries set the scene for the big moment. And when Kallie launched his terrifying, savage 'bombs' in the first two rounds, Tate ran away. The American looked decidedly unhappy, if not frightened.

The crowd bayed for the knockout blow. But it never landed. And it was Tate who turned executioner, tearing apart Knoetze's minimal defence with clinical, controlled punching.

When it was all over after eight rounds, Knoetze was staggering against the ropes in wide-eyed desperation. Only raw courage had kept him on his feet. A white South African hero had been destroyed.

Or had he?

The boxers had to make their way down a fenced-off passage through the crowd to caravans in a corner of the stadium. Tate sparmate Dwain Bonds was a frenzied cheerleader as black spectators raced from the stands to squeeze against the fence, driving guard dogs to distraction, and chanting the name of Tate.

Knoetze made the long, painful walk to his caravan accompanied by the derision of the fans, drenched hair clinging to his head, his face a puffy swollen mess.

Surrounded by ashen-faced handlers, he disappeared into the privacy of his caravan.

Then came the moment when Kallie Knoetze showed he was a man, in the old-fashioned, heroic sense.

He came out of his caravan, and on still-unsteady legs lurched 50 m to Tate's caravan. There he shook the hands of each of the American's vast entourage and climbed the steps to congratulate the man who had ripped his reputation to pieces.

On the way back to his own caravan, Knoetze stopped as though struck by a thought. He shouted, 'Hey, Colonel (to Tate's manager Ace Miller), there's still another South African' – Gerrie Coetzee, Knoetze's own bitter rival, who fights Leon Spinks in the other half of the title elimination series in Monte Carlo on June 24.

Then, with a slight smile, he walked across to a journalist and said: 'I am a bigmouth (*grootbek*) and I am still a bigmouth. The better boxer won.'

Kallie won many points for a show of sportsmanship which matched the courage he showed in the ring. But there was more to come.

First, though, Tate had his turn. The man labelled 'The Fighting Machine' appeared at the after-fight cocktail party. As always when Tate appears in public, even though this was a small gathering, his 'heavies' swept through the room like presidential security men and Tate was whisked to his place behind a table.

Tate is a mumbler. He is certainly not articulate. But he showed a flash of humour when he picked up the microphone, saying 'testing, testing, this is the world's number one heavyweight'. And followed this with a huge grin.

Tate mumbled answers to questions. But when he became technical about the sport which earns him his keep, a light seemed to go on, and he rattled off details about left jabs, right uppercuts, combinations, tactics. A whole lot of boxing knowledge has been fed into the man programmed to win the world heavyweight crown.

The press conference over, Tate stopped not even to swallow a victory drink before his bodyguards cleared the way for him and he was out of the room – and soon on his way back to Johannesburg.

Knoetze arrived at the cocktail party and endured the jostling and the questioning, refusing to make an excuse and repeating time and again that the best man had won.

When the cocktail party ended, one felt the South African had taken his defeat with honour. The evening, however, was far from finished.

Later, at the Mmabatho Sun's lively Mine Bar, Knoetze walked in. He was recognised by the band and called to the stage. He rounded up five friends, armed himself with a brandy and Coke, and sang 'Cottonfields'.

Kallie, his left eye almost closed by an ugly bruise, became the life and soul of a superb party. He sang, he danced – with a black woman at one stage – and he paid tribute to the boxing ability of John Tate.

By the time the party ended, no fair-minded observer could fail to pay tribute to Kallie Knoetze, a man with a big mouth – and a big heart.

(Rand Daily Mail, June 1979)

Morné, born to lead the Boks

Dan Retief

Morné du Plessis, captain.

That seemed always the one certainty about the Springbok trials.

Yet, four years ago the mere mention of his name threatened a split between Western Province and the rest of South Africa.

He probably found the simplicity of the announcement gratifying.

An inherently shy and modest person, Morné du Plessis can do without the fanfare which surrounds the naming of a Springbok captain.

He would have been pleased to know that finally he was just Morné du Plessis, rugby player. Captain of the Springboks, yes, but not the subject of heated and overtly political debates.

It was not always the case.

He was once the man who would never captain South Africa because he was a Prog.

Du Plessis's succession to the throne vacated by Hannes Marais was the subject of a frenetic media and public debate.

In the Cape he was worshipped, and north of the Hex River Valley he was castigated.

Initially, these arguments centred on his ability as a rugby player. Unorthodox as a player, and adventurous as a captain, Du Plessis was bound to raise the ire of the regimented men of the North.

It was inevitable that a brief sortie into public politics would eventually be used to discredit him.

Rumours were rife that the selection panel, headed by conservative Johan Claassen, would hold Du Plessis's support of Dr Van Zyl Slabbert against him.

Both Du Plessis and Claassen disagree that there was an attempt to paint him 'pink'.

Du Plessis doesn't believe his captaincy was ever threatened because of the statement he and cricketers Eddie Barlow and Andre Bruyns put out in support of Dr Van Zyl Slabbert – certainly not from within the selection panel.

'It was all fabrication,' said Du Plessis over an early-morning breakfast in Johannesburg. 'Claassie and the guys would never have done it. And they never did. In the long run they were proved right. They picked me, didn't they?

'I really believe that in rugby circles, as far as the choosing of players is concerned, there is no political interference. I think they always pick the best man.'

Johan Claassen, a paternal, dignified figure who now presides over sports activities at Potchefstroom University, let out a rumbling chuckle when asked whether politics played a part in the selectors' alleged disapproval of Du Plessis.

'It was cheap sensationalism,' said Claassen. 'Newspapers who wanted to could easily have fabricated those stories. Morné, because he was a controversial individual, was open to them.

'Our only concern was whether he was ready for the captaincy; whether he had reached the level of maturity to be trusted with the job. Morné and I had many discussions. He will tell you we talked about many things, some of them very personal, but we never talked politics."

Morné du Plessis is the embodiment of Dr Danie Craven's theories on genetics. The belief that Springboks breed Springboks.

He was born to be a Springbok. And, if you will, born to be a captain.

When, on June 15, 1975, he was named as the 35th Springbok captain, he became the first son of a Bok captain to emulate his father. The occasion was the short French tour of South Africa.

Felix du Plessis led the Boks in three Tests against the All Blacks in 1949.

Morné's mother, Pat Smethurst, captained South Africa at hockey, and his uncle, Horace Smethurst, led the 1947 Springbok soccer side to Australia. Another uncle, Eric Smethurst, also played soccer for South Africa.

This was not the only thoroughbred bloodline in Du Plessis's sporting pedigree. His connections with Springbok rugby go even further back, for Felix du Plessis's uncle, Nick, was a Bok in 1921 and 1924.

With this background, it was hardly surprising that the young Du Plessis had an aptitude for sport.

Rugby, however, was not his first love.

Du Plessis, born in Krugersdorp on October 21, 1949, excelled at all games, but showed the most promise as a cricketer at Grey College, Bloemfontein.

In Standard 9 and 10 he made the Free State schoolboy side, and in his last year won an SA Nuffield cap.

Du Plessis's present ball-playing qualities can be attributed to the fact that he was a fullback and centre at school. He played alongside Dawie Snyman in the backline, but eventually was moved to lock, 'either because I had become too slow for fullback, or because they needed a tall lock – probably both'.

At about this time, Felix du Plessis got in touch with Dr Craven to tell him he was sending his son to Stellenbosch.

Du Plessis was billeted in Dr Craven's hostel, Wilgenhof, and came under the influence of Stellenbosch's under-20 coach, Jannie Krige.

Krige recalls that he quickly recognised leadership potential in the young

Du Plessis. 'He stood out from the others. There was a certain authority in the way he adapted to different playing conditions. We made him the captain of our under-20 side, and he also captained Province under-20.'

Krige remembers that the young Morné was not near his peak as a youngster. 'You know some players are phenomenal under-20s, but then they level off. The advancement of Morné as a rugby player has been a steady process of improvement.'

It was Dr Craven who finally turned Du Plessis into a loose forward after he had spent much of his early days at Stellenbosch alternating between lock and flank.

Morné recalls that Doc made the change the day before he was to play his first senior game for the Maties. 'Doc had been away, and when he returned he asked to see the team. He took a look and said: "No ways. This guy can't play lock. He is a loose forward." So they changed the team. I went to flank, and eventually made my debut for Province in that position.'

Du Plessis won his first Western Province cap against Griquas in Kimberley on June 13, 1970. Province were beaten 22–18.

One hundred games later, Morné returned to Kimberley. That was late last year, to lead Province in the Currie Cup semi-final against Griquas. The match was as hard as rugby can be.

For much of his century-making game, it seemed Griquas would spoil the occasion, but in one of his finest displays of leadership, Du Plessis managed to inspire his men to victory in the dying minutes, 20 points to 15.

After only nine games for Province he was appointed as one of the youngest captains in the Currie Cup. It was not a generally popular choice and he made mistakes, but to their credit the Province selectors persevered with him.

They benignly refused to comment on some of the more adventurous excesses as their youthful captain formulated his philosophy on the game.

At the age of 21, Morné, already the target of some unfavourable comment in the North because of his penchant for linking with the backs rather than playing it tight, was made a Springbok in the side to tour Australia.

It was hoped to develop his play, but a serious injury to Tommy Bedford meant Du Plessis was thrown in the Tests as No. 8 to the illustrious pair of Piet Greyling and Jan Ellis.

The first big controversy in Du Plessis's career would soon burst and send his Western Province supporters into a frenzy of indignation.

The Gazelles were to tour Argentina, and Du Plessis seemed the obvious captain. Instead, the position went to Griqualand West's Jannie van Aswegen, a man with no record of captaincy.

Claassen says that Du Plessis's play had deteriorated after the Australian tour.

It was during this period that Du Plessis won a Western Province cricketing cap as an opening bowler.

Du Plessis made the first two Tests against the 1974 Lions, but was not really in line for the captaincy after the selectors had prevailed upon Hannes Marais to come out of retirement.

The crushing defeat in the second Test against the Lions at Loftus Versfeld was one of the darkest moments of Du Plessis's career. Dugald Macdonald, who was at No 8 that day, with Morné on the flank, told of how the two closeted themselves in their room that evening 'to drown their sorrows'.

Both knew that they would be dropped for the third Test, but it is to Du Plessis's credit that he shrugged off the bitter disappointment to win back his Test place later in the year on the tour to France.

Ironically the man they called the 'scrum inspector', because people in the North, particularly the well-informed and influential journalists, felt he steered away from the hard forward exchanges, was made the Bok captain in 1975 soon after throwing a controversial punch which felled Kleintjie Grobler during a Springbok trial in Bloemfontein.

Many felt that Du Plessis's sudden aggression won him the captaincy, because it finally rid him of his 'cissy' tag.

Johan Claassen does not go as far as to confirm this, but then he also does not condemn Du Plessis. 'We all saw what happened that day,' Claassen told me. 'No one would not have retaliated. No one blamed him for defending himself. Kleintjie Grobler himself admits that he got what was coming.'

In October 1977, Du Plessis suffered another embarrassing incident when he was sent off the field with Stellenbosch forward Schalk Burger during the Western Province Grand Challenge rugby final at Newlands.

Does that make him a rough player? Or is rugby turning into an excuse for a brawl? Du Plessis says no. 'Not at all. Last season was the cleanest I've played in. It was the hardest, but absolutely the cleanest. There was very little dirty stuff and I honestly believe that referees and coaches and everyone concerned with rugby are in a big effort to keep things clean.

'It only takes one bad game for the chaps to take stock and decide to sort things out. The England–Wales match was not as bad as it was made out to be, but look how clean the next few games were.

'But there is no defence for what I did. One shouldn't go around hitting guys or being sent off the field. I deserved what I got. Even when there has been provocation, you should control your emotions and not let it get to you. It took me a long time, but still ...'

Do you see yourself as a hard player, I asked him: 'Not really. You know I'd never be able to play lock, for instance, because I'm not hard enough. And I wouldn't enjoy it. I've got to be able to play with the ball or be involved where the ball is. I'm there to do a job as an eighthman, and if I have to be hard to do the job, then maybe I am hard.'

In spite of the fact that Du Plessis was named captain of the Springboks on June 15, 1975 – almost five years to the day that he made his debut for Western Province – and that the Springboks won the series 2–0 against the French, he was again faced with a political row a year later when it became time to pick a Springbok side to take on the All Blacks.

The *Sunday Times* ran a front-page lead story that there was a *verkrampte* plot to remove him as the captain. Afrikaans newspapers joined the squabble, but the *Sunday Times* was adamant that they were on the right track.

It all dated back to an incident when Du Plessis had just left university. He and cricketers Andre Bruyns and Eddie Barlow attached their names to a statement in support of the new Prog candidate for Rondebosch, Dr Van Zyl Slabbert, who had played a few games for Western Province and was friendly with Du Plessis.

Though Du Plessis has modified his views on getting involved in politics – perhaps because of the trouble it caused him – he is not your average rugger bugger.

He sets great store by honesty and is not afraid to speak his mind on issues. He admits that 'one has got to be blind and deaf not to be aware of the politics of South Africa and Rhodesia, but long ago I made a decision that I'm not cut out to be a politician.

'I decided that it wasn't my role to be publicly involved. I would like to set an example through my actions and by being completely honest in all situations.

'I don't think I want to use my position as a rugby player to influence people. I believe it would be wrong for me to take advantage of my prowess as a rugby player to influence people because I am not involved enough. I'm worried about my life and my actions, I don't want to change other people.'

Another hurtful incident in the Springbok captain's life and times took place on a warm Transvaal winter afternoon at Loftus Versfeld on July 30, 1977.

Shortly before the end of a dramatic Currie Cup game against Northern Transvaal, the Western Province captain dropped out of the sky in a thudding smother tackle on little Naas Botha.

The crowd erupted. The next day Du Plessis spoke of quitting rugby.

Du Plessis is forced to plot a difficult course between a responsible job as marketing manager for Adidas, his responsibility to his wife and baby son and the problems which accompany being the Springbok captain.

The status of being Springbok captain is something that worries him. Du Plessis believes that you are only the captain once a series starts.

Du Plessis has recently made himself inaccessible to the casual telephone caller. His secretary blocks most of his calls and he has an unlisted number at home.

He has no choice. He cannot allow his domestic life to be invaded by rugby fans and at work he has a job to do. To his credit he will always return a Press call though he feels the media sometimes 'tend to get a little hysterical about rugby – especially this year'.

Du Plessis's biggest worry about his coming series is that the mental pressure exerted by the Press will get to his players.

'The pressure that gets put on these guys that they are not used to could be disadvantageous,' he told me. 'Take the two world title fights we've just had. The pressure that was put on those two guys by the South African Press … you know, about the importance of winning and winning for South Africa. They went into the ring with a crippling load, whereas the other guy … he's a true professional. His involvement with the Press is purely a joke. To gain publicity. If he loses, he's just been another boxer. So he fights with a free mind. I just hope the same does not happen to our players this year.'

Du Plessis believes the problem for the Springbok rugby players of handling the off-the-field pressures is going to be greater than what the Jaguars and the Lions can throw at them.

'You take Kallie Knoetze, for instance,' he says. 'He openly admits that everybody expects him to be a 24-hour fund-raising machine. He's got to go round the country, do this, do that. You know, one does expect a sportsman of a certain standard to do his bit for society because they build him up to where he is, but there is a limit to what an amateur sportsman should have to do.'

A feature of Morné's sports career is that he has always viewed himself as an 'amateur' sportsman. And as an amateur he has known that he can take it or leave it whenever he chooses.

'You see, that is the beauty of being an amateur sportsman,' he said. 'Perhaps that is the only advantage of being an amateur. The codes are a little different. You find a little less nastiness in amateur sport. I don't know. But gee, it is a hard amateur sport we play. But the one thing that there's a price on, for me, is that you can say: "Well, thank you very much, I've had enough", or, I want to start again, or whatever the case may be.'

Does he feel rugby players get too little in return for the vast amounts of money they generate? 'I think that in the short term we get much too little back, but I think in the long term a player gets a lot back, especially a Springbok player. You can get it back, but it's not there on a plate for you. You've got to work for it whoever you are.

'You know, I used to beat a loud drum about what we got out of it. But these days I'm not interested about where the money goes. The beauty of amateur sport is perhaps not to worry about where the money goes. I can't complain about the rewards I've got out of it. Everything I've got are memories.

'Sure, I've got a big job. I suppose I might never have got the job if I hadn't been the Springbok captain. But I don't keep the job because I am the Springbok captain.'

How does he see his life after rugby? 'That's a difficult one,' he admits. 'I'll have a big hole to fill. But what I really would like to do is coach an under-20 side, where winning and losing is still not that important. Perhaps that way I'll be able to help some other guys, through the little bit that I know, to enjoy the game.'

Du Plessis revealed that he has no ambitions to hold an office in rugby administration. 'I'm a terrible administrator. I've just got no patience for it,' said the man who eventually gave up the dual Western Province captain–coach role because it became too much of an organisational job.

Morné has two big disappointments in his life – the fact that he was never able to play representative rugby in Britain, and that he has not been in a side that won the Currie Cup outright.

He attended the England–Wales match at Twickenham a few weeks ago, but admits that he would rather 'have arrived in a bus and gone into the ground through the tunnel'.

In the off-season, Du Plessis is a running nut. He runs every day and last season realised a personal ambition by running a marathon, in the impressive time, for such a big person, of 3 hours 20 minutes. He believes running is a form of meditation and recommends it for everyone.

If the Springbok captain could pick a pastime away from the madding crowd, this is it: a holiday by the sea in Hermanus, a long run along the coast, and perhaps a game of golf.

He goes into the coming series with the faith of a nation resting on his shoulders.

Instead of asking how can we play that Girronkey (because they said he played like a donkey and looks like a giraffe) they are pleading: What would we do without Morné du Plessis?

(Rand Daily Mail, 17 April 1980)

And then there was Naas …

Forget Republic in 1961: if anything split white South Africa down tribal lines, it was the blond Northern Transvaler whose teeth gave Leon Schuster a career, and whose boot threatened to turn rugby into a game of ballistics. North of the Vaal he was revered. South of the Karoo he was reviled. Afrikaners crowed over their boytjie with the nuclear kick; English-speakers mourned the end of civilisation as they'd known it. And black South Africa didn't give a damn either way … The following, appearing in the distinctly unsporty Weekly Mail *in 1986, is in English and is unflattering. These two facts are not unconnected.*

The death of the running flyhalf

Sinned Lebur

Armchair critics around the country are reeling in the wake of the startling switch in rugby tactics since last summer when the army went into Sebokeng.

Last rugby season witnessed an unprecedented upsurge in spectator interest, both live and televised. In spite of barely raising a sweat in crushing the Sri Lankans and a club team from Buenos Aires, the national team was touted as the strongest in the world – and could well have been so.

The days of glory last season revolved around two individuals – Naas Botha and Errol Tobias. Unlikely superstars both of them were: Botha was a hero because he was not here; and Tobias because he was not white.

Botha, sidelined in professional pursuit of the Great South African dream of fame and fortune in America, was pivotal in the resurgence. When Nasie was playing, SA rugby was dominated by eight behemoths from the SADF in Pretoria, plus the Boy Wonder himself.

Nasie's great strength, as everyone knows, is his kicking. The Ray Reardon of the rugby world, he can boot the ball from any point to any point on the field. Without this gift, Nasie would not even make the average club team.

In front of the machine-like Botha and his emulators (such as De Wet Ras and Robbie Blair) entire teams had metamorphosed. Loose forwards no longer needed to get to the ball because it went straight from Nasie into touch; instead they became taller and bigger, indistinguishable from locks in fact (Stofberg, Mallett). The front rows got fatter because all they needed to do was stroll up and down the touch lines to the next lineout. Weight rather than strength or speed became their chief attribute.

One former 'Springbok' prop boasted that he had gone an entire provincial game without touching the ball or raising a sweat. The French had a joke: South African rugby players are all the same. They all have big ears and weigh 100 kg. The fatter ones are props, the taller ones locks and loose forwards, the shorter ones scrumhalves, if they can kick the ball 50 m they are flyhalves and full backs and if they can run a bit they are centres and wings.

Nasie's supporters claim that he does run with the ball sometimes. And so he does – straight across the field, crowding his centres and wings.

To get to the top in this type of rugby, the three-quarters underwent their own natural selection. The stars were no longer elusive runners but human bulldozers who spent more time training in gyms than on the field. Danie Gerber and Ray Mordt became in the eyes of young fans what Mannetjies Roux and Jannie Engelbrecht had been to their fathers – but the new generation of stars were three stone heavier than the old.

Suddenly last season all was different. Nasie was in America learning to speak the language and our second hero appeared.

UDF-niks sneered when Errol Tobias, a 50-year-old coloured bricklayer from Wellington, was chosen as a flyhalf in the national team. Window dressing, they said. Is this the best flyhalf in the country? Tokenism of the worst kind, they said.

Well, they were right – and wrong. Our Errol was chosen because he was not white and he fitted in with new directions towards tricameral parliaments, international hotels and domination of a more subtle nature. The selectors, operating from their own view of what the complete modern flyhalf was, missed only one thing – our Errol was the best in the country. Fast and unpredictable (not least to his own teammates) he *ran* when he got the ball. More importantly he ran straight and left space for clever three-quarters to out-think their opponents.

That our Errol's team won against mediocre opposition was no surprise. That in the process they produced rugby that was at times breathtakingly exciting was a revelation. Overnight, everybody was running the ball.

Northern Free State (where the hell is it anyway?) emerged as one of the top provincial sides and announced that they would play their 'traditional running game' against Northern Transvaal – and lost by four tries to two.

The finest back line in the country was claimed by Free State itself, who had in previous years shown their disdain for back play by fielding an eighth man in the scrumhalf position. Even Transvaal and Northern Transvaal, the homes of the hyper big forward prototypes, edged towards the new age. Both teams began to lose consistently, largely because they were too big and too slow.

Natural selection began to run in the other direction. Speed was the keynote for loose forwards as more play broke down on the wings; locks and props also had to get there eventually, and slimmer versions emerged.

Scrumhalves began to have more function than simply a long pass to a deep-lying flyhalf, and exciting young players appeared (Thabo Thomas).

The fans were ecstatic. Rugby had again become the most exciting ball game in the world. No one was sure that the new team could beat a full All Black or Lions side but, by golly, here was a team to support!

What happened?

Sebokeng was unable to be pacified by the police. In other words, banging heads was no longer achieving results. The army chiefs knew that military involvement in domestic unrest would not look good. It is as if we are saying we have a civil war on our hands, some said. A fist smote a desk somewhere. *Kêrels, ons is in die army om te wen. Niks anders is van belang nie.*

The rest is history. The SADF invaded Sebokeng. The South African Rugby Board changed the rules of the International Rugby Board to let Nasie back into the game. That the two events happened simultaneously is no coincidence. Two fists banged two tables – one belonging to the rugby board and one to the SADF – and the army moved into both the national rugby side and Sebokeng.

Now no one doubts Nasie will be chosen against the All Blacks, together with 14 others with big ears and 100 kg on their stomachs. The game is there to be won.

Our television screens will be filled with endless lineouts intercut with endless lines of 18-year-old national servicemen in dusty townships, one facing inwards, one facing outwards, one facing inwards.

Can no one rid us of this troublesome ethos?

(Weekly Mail, 21 June 1985)

HANSIE CRONJE

'Gee Hansie 'n kansie' the placard begged in 1991 as the young Free State batsman sat on the fringes of national selection, battling for a place in the team against rival youngster Jonty Rhodes. More than a decade later, his life cut cruelly short, Cronje's supporters are still pleading with us to give him a break.

His critics have never understood the fervour of this lobby and point to an average captain, a threadbare batting technique, rapidly dissolving consistency in the latter half of his career, a wilful and often spiteful streak in his nature, and then the final catastrophic revelations about his betrayal of the nation's trust.

His admirers will hear none of it. To them, Cronje remains a symbol of everything that was young and hopeful and successful in South Africa in the mid-1990s. He was at the forefront of an Afrikaner cricketing resurgence. He was a Christian, a husband and a sportsman. His fall from grace is forgiven as a human error, and his premature death is mourned as a family bereavement.

But whatever one's feelings about the man, his decision to use his position to enrich himself degenerated into one of the country's most sordid and avidly followed controversies, and did almost irreparable damage to the sport he had worked so hard at. The following is just a tiny sample of the plethora of articles that the match-fixing scandal – and his subsequent death – elicited.

A dossier of decline

Telford Vice & Neil Manthorp

Why did he do it? That question is well on its way to being answered. He lost focus and concentration, reaching the optimum level of '*gatvolness*' before deciding – in the words of a senior former team-mate – 'to do something for himself and to hell with everybody else ...'

The former captain then over-indulged in what started as an interest, became a hobby and then an obsession: making money. He thought he could get away with it. He thought he could get away with anything. Wouldn't you if these events had happened to you?

1992 – April 20

On the third day of South Africa's historic re-entry to the Test arena against the West Indies at Kensington Oval in Barbados, Brian Lara treads on his wicket attempting to cut.

Lara, on 51, and Keith Arthurton are rebuilding a West Indian innings that had slipped to 68 for three with a first innings deficit of 83. Then square-leg umpire David Archer says he was unsighted and Lara is therefore not out.

All but one of the South Africans bear the injustice stoically. The exception is Cronje, who shrieks in indignation all through his desperate sprint to the wicket from his position on the long-off boundary. His unbridled anger is clearly heard in a ground that is more than half empty because of the Anderson Cummins boycott.

Neither Archer, colleague Steve Bucknor nor match referee Raman Subba Row act officially over Cronje's outburst for fear of ruining the 'occasion'. But several of the South African team admit to feeling 'embarrassed' by Cronje's behaviour, which also includes complaints from the 22-year-old about having to stay in the same hotel as 'supporters and the press'.

Nothing is said by anyone from the United Cricket Board.

1994 – November 7

Cronje is given out caught behind down the leg side by umpire Wilf Diedricks in the second innings of a Castle Cup match for Free State against Natal at Kingsmead.

The pitch had assisted the bowlers throughout the match, and Cronje had spent almost an hour on 21 after almost three hours at the crease for the same score in the first innings. Free State had begun their second innings 110 runs behind, and Cronje's dismissal reduces them to 39 for two in a match they would eventually lose by nine wickets.

Cronje's protests are of such force that umpires Diedricks and Karl Liebenberg report him for dissent. A disciplinary hearing duly finds him guilty, but his fine is a paltry R500 – an amount which deeply disappoints Diedricks and Liebenberg, who feel Cronje should have been dealt with more severely.

The UCB initially does not make the fine public and then, when Cronje's fine is uncovered by a Durban newspaper, a statement from Ali Bacher is prepared and sent to the South African Press Association but not to any of the international agencies that had requested it. The first, clear attempts to protect the new captain from any adverse publicity have begun.

1997 – December 16

An Australian television station reveals exclusive 'footage' (!) of Cronje standing on the ball and rubbing his spikes over one side of it during the first World Series match played against Australia 12 days earlier at the SCG.

Cronje is very, very clearly seen looking around for cameras, dropping the ball on the ground, turning it over with his boot until it is in position and then standing on it with all his weight. Cronje denies any intention to 'ball-tamper' and describes his actions as 'absent-minded' and 'innocent'.

The UCB, however, go on the offensive with Bacher positively raging about the 'so-called scoop' being 'below the belt', before adding that the UCB might pursue the matter further. 'Hansie is known to be a man of integrity and absolute honesty and we feel nobody in South Africa should question that. We feel there has been a deliberate attempt to defame Hansie Cronje ...'

Three senior South African players, contacted by *SASI* two weeks ago, all concurred. 'We had no doubt at the time, and have had none since, that what Hansie did was ball-tampering and therefore cheating,' said the most senior of the three.

1998 – February 3

Infuriated by Mark Waugh's 'escape' on the final day of the third Test in Adelaide, Cronje slams the sharp end of a stump through the umpires' changing room door at the end of the match.

Bacher is contacted by an Adelaide journalist on the team's return to SA and denies any knowledge of the damaged door. A day later Bacher admits that 'a door was damaged by a South African player' but declines to name the player and says an apology has been accepted by the ACB and the incident is now closed.

Australian television then confirms that only Pat Symcox and Cronje were pictured leaving the field with souvenir stumps. An aggrieved Symcox proclaims his innocence.

A week later Bacher says he has decided it is in everyone's best interests to 'bring it out in the open'. Cronje says he did not know it was the umpires' door and that it was a 'moment of madness'. Bacher says 'Hansie is human and he erred,' before adding that another apology has been accepted by the ACB and the matter is closed. Again.

No action is taken. An ACB official tells SA journalists: 'I am staggered ... I cannot believe that a player, let alone a captain, would get away with anything remotely like this in any other country in the world. It's unbelievable.'

1999 – January 18

Incensed by Bacher's comments immediately after completion of the famous 5–0 whitewash of the West Indies at Centurion Park, a furious Cronje orders Herschelle Gibbs to drive him back to the team hotel.

Following another disastrous meeting between Bacher, Cronje, Bob Woolmer and several of the players at 10:00 a.m. the following morning, at which Bacher reiterates the Board's policy of sending a team 'of colour' to the World Cup, Cronje shakes Woolmer by the hand, wishes him luck, empties his one-day kit onto his hotel room floor, drives to the airport and flies back to Bloemfontein; resigned.

Bacher does everything in his power to prevent the situation from becoming public and, along with the Rhema Church's Ray McCauley, spends a frantic and tense 24 hours talking sweetly and persuading Cronje to change his mind.

No action is taken against Cronje for leaving the team without permission, in breach of his contract.

1999 – May 12
Three days before SA's first World Cup match against India in Hove, Cronje tells an English newspaper he'll 'see them in court' if they print allegations that he flew home to Bloemfontein when he did.

1999 – September 24
Two weeks after being reappointed as captain for just the first two of five Tests against England, Cronje admits to being 'on the brink of concluding' a two-year deal to coach Glamorgan County Cricket Club in the English county championship. He describes the deal as a 'golden opportunity to spend six months of the year with my wife and prolong my career' but admits 'I haven't spoken to Dr Bacher yet'. The deal would have left Cronje unavailable for the forthcoming tours of Sri Lanka (July) and Australia (August).

Bacher launches onto the attack again, but not against Cronje. He describes Glamorgan's approach as 'inappropriate' and talks of using 'proper channels'.

No action is taken against Cronje.

2000 – April 11
Cronje phones Bacher at 3:00 a.m. and admits to 'not being entirely honest' and 'accepting some money from an Indian bookmaker'.

Bacher, as the routine predicts, launches a broadside that may yet signal the end of his international career in cricket politics. Despite laying actual charges and not idly speculating over Cronje's involvement, the Indian police force's allegations are described – on radio – as 'scandalous and libellous' by Bacher.

In the days afterwards, the subcontinent's cricketing bodies unite in their anger against Bacher, who compounds his predicament by telling an Australian journalist 10 days later that he has evidence that two World Cup matches were fixed and at least one umpire has been bribed – a thinly veiled reference to Pakistan's Javed Akhtar, who presided over SA's defeat to England in the fifth Test of 1998 at Headingley. Former Pakistan captain Imran Khan calls for Bacher's resignation from the ICC unless he can substantiate his claims.

If Cronje was the great captain and leader of men that we all liked to believe, then why did he need so much protection? Perhaps we are all to blame for refusing to peer below the surface and question what was before our own eyes.

Ali Bacher can be criticised as an over-protective and overbearing figurehead, but there can be no doubt that his motives were honest and honourable. The problem, perhaps, with an autocratic and all-powerful leadership style is that one becomes too close to the subject to see it.

If Cronje 'cracked' under pressure, then former vice-captain Craig Matthews can understand why. 'Being captain of a national side is hard enough, but being captain of South Africa, during the time he was, was the hardest job in cricket,' the recently-retired Matthews told *SASI*.

'It was made even harder – if that's possible – by his desperate, desperate desire to win at all costs. That sounds strange now, but it's true. He was obsessively driven to win. I remember several times having to talk to him on the field to calm him down.

'He is a temperamental man who needed talking to, whether it was by me or someone else. Maybe he wanted to win too badly … and I have to say he may have crossed the line of rationality sometimes in trying to win,' Matthews said.

At the beginning of the 1997 season Cronje captained an 'informal' SA VIII in Hong Kong for a 'Sixes' event. Being an informal tournament, Cronje told the eight members of the squad before play began that individual prize money – notably the R6 900 up for grabs to the man-of-the-tournament – would be kept by the individual instead of being split between the team pool and the player. All agreed.

Unexpectedly, unheralded Derek Crookes was named as the prize winner. Cronje accepted the cheque, cashed it, and shared out the money equally – R862,50 each. When the bewildered squad asked Cronje what had happened to their agreement, he replied: 'Tough. I changed my mind'.

A long-time colleague says: 'He is obsessed with money, and has been for as long as I can remember. He has also done very, very well, too. He is a successful "trader" with shares and stocks and bonds and, whenever I've heard him speaking to his broker, he's been talking about moving units of R100 000 here and there.'

Provincial colleagues at Free State mention how Cronje spends his time reading the financial pages of the newspaper and commenting with delight at how the price of a particular commodity had just risen another two points.

But it wasn't just in business that he was obsessed with money.

'The subject of money was never far from Hansie's thoughts. Whether he was just fooling around or being serious, he was pretty much always talking about how much he was making from a deal, or how much something was costing. He was always doing deals,' another teammate said. 'I think he had a moment of weakness one day, whenever it was, and took some money. When he didn't get caught he tried it again and then he just got in deeper and deeper. I think a few of us had our suspicions but we just didn't want to believe it,' a senior player said. 'He could be really odd about it [money]. Even though he was earning a fortune, he'd go to McDonald's when we were on tour rather than a nice restaurant. He'd say "I'm not wasting my money in there, money is for saving." It was very strange, we couldn't understand it,' another teammate said.

Cronje changed enormously during the near-six years of his captaincy, appearing to grow increasingly fond of the finer things in life. Two years ago he was made an honorary life member of the country's most exclusive would-be golf and country club estate, Simola, in the Western Cape. He was immensely proud.

When the project went bankrupt, Cronje quickly investigated the possibility of joining the country's most exclusive existing club, Fancourt, also in the Western Cape, and moved there earlier this year in a house reputed to be worth R3,4 million.

A year ago he started wearing a thick, solid gold bracelet while his leisure clothing and suits bore the unmistakable mark of an Italian cut. Cronje was a man doing well and he didn't mind it showing, which is a far cry from the modest, humble, jeans-and-T-shirt man who took charge of the national team late in 1994.

(SA Sports Illustrated, June 2000)

Death brings outpourings of forgiveness and love to our flawed hero

Colin Bryden

Death brought into sharp focus Hansie Cronje's good qualities, of which there were many.

Nelson Mandela and Thabo Mbeki mourned him, as did millions of ordinary South Africans, but no epitaph was more moving and succinct than that proclaimed by his widow, Bertha, at his funeral.

'I wanted to tell the world, I wanted to shout it out, I wanted to explain to people that, even though Hansie made a mistake, he was still the same Hansie, a kind and loving husband, a genuine friend and an honourable man,' said Bertha, who went on to tell of the 'wonderful realisation' in the days following his death that the public shared her recognition of his special qualities.

Bertha captured the public mood. Hansie was an inspirational leader of cricket teams and a man able to communicate easily at many different levels, whether having lunch with Mandela or interacting with underprivileged youngsters in townships.

What made him especially fascinating was that he was flawed. The word 'mistake' was used many times in the past week, among others by his brother Frans, and by Peter Pollock in his eulogy in Bloemfontein.

It is a generous understatement of what led to Cronje's fall from cricketing grace.

To his own eternal credit, Cronje himself did not trivialise his wrongdoing, which took place over a period of years. In his last interview, with John Maytham of Cape Talk Radio, less than 24 hours before he died, he said he was not proud of what he had done.

'It would be foolish to think it never happened … I knew I would have to live with this for the rest of my life,' he said.

In the emotion following his death, a conversation between his father, Ewie, brother Frans and lawyer Leslie Sackstein led to Sackstein sending a fax telling the United Cricket Board that they would not be welcome at the funeral. Initially, too, there was talk of the media being unwelcome as well.

The message was rescinded after it was discussed with Bertha. When he spoke on the Extra Cover TV programme, Frans Cronje seemed relieved that eventually all had been welcome to share the family's grief and that the service had been broadcast to a wide audience.

The reality was that the UCB had no choice but to ban their former captain for life and the media were duty-bound to respond to public interest by recording every painful detail of the saga of the bribery scandal as it unfolded.

Contrary to what seems a general perception, Cronje was not the only cricketer punished for associating with the wrong people. Two other international captains, Salim Malik of Pakistan and Mohammad Azharuddin of India, have also been banned for life.

Where Cronje was alone, however, was in admitting his faults. In the past week more than one international cricketer will have had a pang of guilt at the realisation that they managed to hide their own misdeeds while South Africa's captain admitted his.

He leaves memories of greatness on the sports field. No South African captain before him had a record of success that was remotely comparable, and it will take an exceptional leader in the future to match his standards.

His life, his rise and fall, captured the imagination of millions. His death was a graphic reminder of the reality and unpredictability of mortality.

Because he was a man of great qualities, yet prone to human frailty, his premature passing has given us all cause to consider our own good fortune and to examine our consciences.

That in itself is a remarkable legacy.

(Sunday Times, 9 June 2002)

Hansie Cronje Superstar – the man who meant too much

Luke Alfred

Despite the temptation to imitate in miniature the USA and South Korea's 1–1 draw earlier in the day, my eldest son and I played cricket on our back lawn last Monday night. Sam played with his Hansie Cronje bat, the one with Hansie's signature. Strangely, the bat's splice and handle were working free from the bat's blade as we mucked about, and soon – I realised – the bat would be passing into memory, just like Hansie himself. Come the summer and Sam and I would be buying another bat with another player's signature on it and to Sam, all of eight years old, Cronje would be so lost in the past that his name might as well have been Donald Bradman.

Later that night I was thinking about how in bedrooms across the country the Hansie posters would, if they hadn't already done so, be peeling at the edges and fading on the walls; the sentimental, confused front pages would be sinking a newspaper lower on their pile in the pantry. The memory of Hansie would be seeping into the memorialised past we call history, there to be picked at for meanings which elude us today but which might become apparent with the passing of time.

The one meaning which stares at me at the moment concerns the idea that with Hansie's death we have passed into a different age. It is as if we have passed from the Victorian into the Edwardian or from the Middle Ages into the Renaissance. We have passed from Hansie's age into an age which has yet to be named. Hopefully it will be an age with fewer temptations for our international sportsmen and -women; correlatively, it will hopefully also be an age in which our sporting public are a little wiser, even a little bit more sceptical in the way that they are prepared to adore and idealise their heroes. Would it be too much to hope for to call this an age of normality rather than an age of transformation?

In taking over the national captaincy from Kepler Wessels when he was the youngest member of the national team in Australia in 1993, we all assumed that Hansie was more vitally attuned to the needs of the age. Unlike Wessels, whose loyalty to this country was always compromised by his loyalty to another (he played Test cricket for Australia), Cronje was young enough to never have played for anyone else. His was the face of change, of the future, of a South Africa we could proudly be rather than the South Africa the rest of the world suspected we still were. And so, partly by accident, partly by design (one thinks here of Ali Bacher's Svengali-like moulding of Cronje), he became a human vessel for many of our hopes, many of them not even recognised as such. We were proud of Cronje but there was something defiant in our adoration. I might be mistaken but I suspect that for white South Africa at least, Cronje came unconsciously to represent the unrepentant fighting spirit – something akin to 'We may have been isolated from the world of sport for twenty-two years but we have not been affected, not in the slightest'.

As a result of who he was and his status, Cronje was required to wittingly and unwittingly carry the burden of a nation's expectations in the period after re-admission. These expectations were extreme, extreme in the sense that any nation that has been figuratively tarred and feathered for twenty-odd years has strong needs for acceptance. It also has some pretty strong needs to prove that it is worthy of being where it is, and often the two needs work in opposition rather than in conjunction. As a charismatic and photogenic man, Cronje became the focus of unrelenting attention.

Had South Africa experienced the sporting period 1970–1992 as an uninterrupted expanse of time, as a period continuous and gradual, stardom might have been borne more easily if only because there would already have been a pre-existing tradition of cricketing stars, but for Cronje, idolised in his community as well as the rest of South Africa, his status can't have been easy to fathom. Earning a vast salary, driving a flash car, having foreign bank accounts, even being able to command a cool R20 000 per throw for his public speaking engagements, Cronje swiftly became Hansie Cronje Superstar. While it is tempting to be cynical, even his choice of religion – the rousing sermons of the Rhema Church – tells us of his love for the theatrical, of his need to be large and larger-than-life. There was nothing self-negating or austere about Cronje's church. It is a big church, with a big relationship with God and, as such, it fitted Cronje perfectly.

But by the middle nineties, South Africa itself was changing. The political miracles of earlier in the decade were beginning to fade, sport was becoming re-politicised and the country began to get down to the earnest business of reconstruction and development. Change was in the air, with a black political and business elite beginning to flex their muscle. In response, white South Africa began to cringe slightly, to retire. As they did so, they began to re-invest the familiar with meaning. Cronje was transformed from ambassador for change (his former informal title) to a guardian of sport's sacred values, values such as merit over political interference or meddling. Cronje himself did nothing to suggest that he wasn't comfortable with his new role but, once again, here was a man who was being required to carry too much meaning, to be too significant to too many. As he had been in the period directly after re-admission, here was the man who meant too much.

Cronje in his final incarnation showed all the signs of being exhausted by the country in which he lived. The records tell us that it was here that Cronje's greed and evil reached their apotheosis. This they did. But through the nineties, Hansie Cronje's perspective, his moral compass, his centre of gravity had quietly leaked away. His descent into a heart of darkness conforms chillingly not to the careers of sportsmen – the one exception which springs to mind here is that of Diego Maradona – but to those in the self-destructive tradition of rock 'n roll – Jim Morrison, Jimi Hendrix, Kurt Cobain. Cronje even died the quintessential rock n' roll death as he and two others flew headlong into a mountain as he dashed through mist for a weekend with his beloved. Cronje just happened to be a cricketer but really he was an entertainer, a musician with a bat for a guitar. His, I would venture, was the most photographed South African face of the nineties next to Nelson Mandela's. In a culture not known for producing international stars, the adoration that was foisted upon Cronje was ultimately too much to bear and, finally, he was the man who was forced to mean too much.

(Hansie Cronje died on 29 March 2002)

ONE ON ONE

All writing about sport is challenging, each in its unique way. The formal challenge of match reporting is to write accurately against the clock; the formal challenge of previewing is to write authoritatively about a future event in such a way that the expectation of the event is heightened by reading the preview; the challenge of one-on-one interviewing is to allow the subject of the interview to speak – to allow a story to be told in his or her words.

This is often more difficult than it might at first appear. Sportsmen often comment on sport in a matter-of-fact, even clichéd way. It is the journalist's job to make them comfortable enough to get beyond the superficial banalities and into a realm that has more interest and currency for a reader. Sometimes this can be achieved by doing nothing more than asking exactly what it is that they do, how they prepare for a major event. Sometimes it is done by asking simple, intelligent questions; sometimes it is done by setting the subject at ease. Whatever the technique used by the journalist, if an interview isn't handled with care and thoughtfulness the result will usually be dull and predictable.

– Luke Alfred

Don King unplugged

Tom Eaton

This is how Nero listened. His eyes are almost closed, regarding the tablecloth with a slow-burning, unblinking intensity. Once he moves his lips as if rehearsing a pronouncement, and then resumes his distrustful stakeout of the salt cellar to his left.

Away from the cameras and the parades, the pre-arranged spontaneous displays of public adoration, he looks terribly tired. He looks like he hasn't slept since he was poor. A man like this doesn't sleep. He hibernates. Or he rests. If his name didn't transform it into a tenuous journalistic pun, one might mention the sleeping habits of heads that wear crowns.

He is resting now, despite the urgent murmuring at his ear and the documents being thrust in front of him. Once it was news of a rebellion in a far-flung province, some local ruffian naïve and bloodthirsty enough to challenge the hammer and anvil of Rome. Today it could be negotiations, logistics, unruly fiefs in this new southern province of Don King's empire; but these secrets of state are not for my ears. The muscled American in the white T-shirt pauses and looks at my Dictaphone.

'You're not tape-recording any of this, are you,' he says. It is not a question.

I am sitting opposite King in a booth in an upmarket Sandton steakhouse. He and his entourage have been in meetings all day, and a late lunch has been hastily arranged. My photographer and I have been literally jammed in. On my left are the imposing forearms of the man who could yet pop my Dictaphone like a tick. On my right Carl King, son and right hand, makes flamboyant and ineffective enquiries about starters.

'Prawns,' he says to the menu with an inflection straight out of the pulpit of a small wooden Baptist church in the Carolinas. Everyone but his father nods. 'Shrimps,' he says, and again all but one nod. 'Whatchew got?

Chicken livers!' The maître-d kowtows. 'Prawns,' says Carl, having established nothing but his ability to name hors d'oeuvres. He raises his glass of wine and peers into its ruby depths. 'Let's see what's hapnin' in the world today.'

It is King Senior who makes the arrangements. The starters are settled, and the muscles depart. He is playing with an unlit cigar: I've seen smaller redwoods. The eyes, a curious blue-black, are now half-open and it is time to talk.

There are questions one would like to ask. What's it like to beat someone to death? Why did New Jersey ban you last month from doing business in the state's casinos for a year? What would it take for you to punch my lights out, right here, right now? But one senses that the first two questions would answer the third, and in any case, one doesn't want to bleed on Carl's nice suit.

Besides, the interviewer facing Don King is not there to interrogate. His role is clearly defined by the man's celebrity. You don't interview Don King: you present him with cues, and clap when he runs out of breath.

The double-page features on his visit in the local media last week were an indictment of their authors' inability or unwillingness to critique the ease with which he is drawn into theatrical, incoherent lectures on the nature of everything. Most failed to ask whether what King was saying was worth listening to. Some presented acres of gabble as an invitation to their readers to indulge in smug eye-rolling at a visiting curiosity, ignoring the hypocrisy of fifteen-paragraph quotes. After all, you get paid per word.

But whatever their insight and motives, all those who have asked Mr King his views in South Africa must have experienced that peculiar feeling of whispering from the wings to a popular ham indulging an infatuation with method acting. His rumbling soliloquies no doubt model themselves on Jesse Jackson, Louis Farrakhan and Martin Luther King, but Al Pacino is also in there somewhere, being tough and noble, drowning the mind with a torrent of words for as long as the camera keeps rolling.

The cameras have stopped rolling now, and he rattles through his lines as if he is trying to find his place in a script. Where most people would draw breath, King says, 'Know what I'm sayin'?', quickly enough to turn it into a noise – nwadumsan?

'Madiba's the miracle-man of the century, nwadamsan?' he says, massaging his ring-finger and looking at Carl's wine. 'He's indicative, nwadumsan, of what is possible. He snatched the possible out of the impossible, he snatched victory out of the jaws of defeat.' His respect seems real, but he is struggling to hide his boredom.

He reanimates suddenly, picking up the cigar by its stern and jabbing it at me, when talk turns to boxing and Vernon Smith, manager of Corrie Sanders and object of King's wrath in last week's sporting press. Reports in local newspapers quoted a theatrically indignant King saying the unfortunate Smith had 'double-crossed' him and local promoter Rodney Berman. Was this real anger, or some perfectly timed showmanship to generate hoopla around his latest project?

'Not anger, just stating a matter of fact. He really double-crossed himself, nwadumsan?' I don't, but King joins the dots. 'We were just the steppin'-stone to his self-destruction.'

'He said I'd given Sanders a slave contract. But even at slave wages he gets more than just about everybody else.' There seems to be some logic here: most of the slaves I know earn only hundreds of thousands of rands, rather than millions. I am about to ask where I can sign up for a slavery contract when more wine arrives with fresh miscommunications over prawns.

Like all conscientious salesmen, King is resolute that his latest product, the Carnival City event, is the greatest of his career. 'You know each time I reach the epitome, I never cease to amaze myself,' he says. 'God steps in and makes another fight, one that eclipses the one before.' Nothing about Zaire or Manila ring any bells? 'Of course,' he concedes, 'the continent of Africa and the Philippines, with Frazier and Ali and Foreman, they set the tone for international relationships.'

With global politics thus covered, we move on to the great fighters. He begins with Ali, Foreman, Larry Holmes, but quickly accelerates until he and Carl are bouncing names off each other like an Ali right hook off a Frazier mandible. Julio Cesar Chavez earns special praise – 'he got the largest live date in history, 36 000 people, nwadumsan?' – but it seems that every fighter King has ever promoted is a pugilistic god.

Suddenly he seems distracted by the noise and bustle of the restaurant. His patter deserts him, and for a moment he gropes for words, quickly truncating a fresh hypothesis about the importance of his fighters to the Third World, where they 'bring hope to the hopeless'. Again he looks too tired to recite his lines.

What about purists' complaints that there is too much money in the fight game, and too many divisions and champions, mainly because of the machinations of people like King? 'I think that those people are ...' He pauses, thinking. The intense introspection of earlier returns, and I wonder if this is what Don King is like when he's brushing his teeth at night. 'Pessimists,' he decides.

'They just want to think about holding on to tradition and custom. The only good thing about the good old days is that they're gone.' He says it with feeling and flair, and we laugh. As quickly as his banter abandoned him it returns, and to illustrate a grim past in which a single boxing organisation called the shots, he declares that, 'on the island of the Cyclops, the one-eyed man is king.'

The bad old days aren't all gone, it seems. I ask King if he thinks his perceived persecution by the law and the criticism levelled at him personally and professionally are a result of racism. 'Yes,' he says emphatically. 'There are always people who say it's too much money for you to have, too much of everything, unless you're being obsequious, sweatin' when it ain't hot, scratchin' when it don't itch, laughin' when there ain't nothin' funny, nwadumsan?'

But it is not only black Americans and black American boxing promoters who are discriminated against, he asserts. His support for Jewish organisations in the United States, including the Simon Wiesenthal Centre, has been well documented by his acolytes; but his motivation is more candid than some minority lobbies at home might like.

'African-Americans don't hold exclusivity on slavery,' he says. 'They don't hold exclusivity on suffering and torment, on denial an' deprivation.'

Is this gung-ho political incorrectness or old-fashioned Republican rhetoric? It's hard to tell as King comes to the defence of his president and country. At least I think he comes to the defence of his president and country. If this is fence-sitting, it is fence-sitting of the most decisive variety.

'I support George Walker Bush. He's one of the strong, innovative, imaginative, creative presidents. I'll leave the foreign policy up to the diplomats, but if you can get to George Walker Bush, and you can show him the error of his ways, you can effect change.'

Bush should be applauded for advancing integration, says King. 'He put two blacks in the top of government, Condoleezza Rice and Colin Powell, and not in token roles either. He's bold, audacious.'

But Bush's most admirable trait, King seems to imply, is his absolute power. It takes some explaining, but it seems that Republican dominance of both the Senate and the House is a boon to democracy in the free world.

'You can get much more done if you can persuade them to be righteous,' he says. 'If you bring a new guy in, he's going to take four years to disassemble that machine and reassemble a new one, and by the time you've done that, the people are going to be screaming in the streets because they lost their jobs and the economy's finished.'

He launches an attack on the countries that want a 'share of the booty' in Iraq without having done any fighting. 'If you're going to criticise, then you gotta stay out, like Nelson Mandela who stayed out for 27 years. Though really, he stayed in for 27 years!'

The conversation ends when the food arrives. King hefts his still-unlit cigar again, and squints at it through one eye as I am encouraged to disappear. In his corner of the booth, marooned in a sea of chicken-livers, he is a solitary giant. On the island of the Cyclops, the one-eyed man is King. Nwadumsan?

(Mail & Guardian, 21 May 2004)

Most interviews and player profiles flit over assumed middle-class childhoods, taking for granted generic details of supportive parents, a small garden littered with balls and old sports equipment. But sometimes they don't …

Dewald Pretorius

Neil Manthorp

IN 119 years of Test cricket at Lord's, few men will have travelled a bumpier road to the home of cricket than South African fast bowler Dewald Pretorius. Englishmen rightly marvelled at Makhaya Ntini's passage from goat-herder to honours board on the first day of this Test, but they probably had no idea that Ntini's journey was lined with velvet compared to that of the Afrikaans boy from the dusty Free State town of Kroonstad.

That he emerged from an orphanage to fight and claw his way to the top is well documented but it is all too easy to compartmentalise his story in the 'romantic novel' section of our brains. Perhaps, now that he is successful and an inspiration, that is where the story is best kept but the stark details are too astonishing to ignore.

Pretorius's mother, Alba, came from a successful family but fell pregnant with Dewald by a rogue who abandoned her instantly on hearing the news: 'He worked on the railways and already had a girlfriend in a different town. He was gone,' Pretorius says passively.

Mother and son returned to the family home but her poor choice in men resulted in marriage, forced by a second pregnancy, to a man called Markus Killian. The next 12 years were filled with misery for Dewald and his younger brother, Sakkie. 'He never wanted to marry my mother and he hated us. When I say he beat us, I mean he really, really beat us. We kept running away but there was nowhere to go. I'll never, ever forget that feeling of sickness and terror we had in the bottom of our stomachs when we saw him coming home. We were naughty boys, no doubt, but we didn't deserve what he did to us. Nobody deserved that.'

A promotion for Killian resulted in the family being transferred to the Natal town of Pietermaritzburg, just 50 miles from the big city of Durban. And it was the downside of city life that gave Dewald his first taste of freedom. 'He was murdered by four muggers in Durban, they stabbed him to death for a hundred bucks.' Pretorius speaks slowly, aware of how his next comment might look in print. 'It was the happiest day of my life. I hated him with a passion. I'm sorry, but I was so happy.' But the nightmare was just beginning, not ending.

Alba returned with her two sons and two daughters to her parents in Kroonstad but a couple of months later the children's grandfather died and the boys' lack of discipline deteriorated further. 'Sakkie was sent to a Boys Town detention centre and my grandmother put me in a hostel because my mother wasn't coping. But soon after that a welfare doctor arrived to examine me and I was terrified – I didn't know who she was so I ran away, again.'

It must be remembered what kind of society South Africa was in the 1980s. Apartheid's racist legacy is one thing, but in many instances the regime dehumanised its enforcers more than its victims. Nonetheless, what happened next to Pretorius almost defies belief.

'Two policemen came into the classroom and grabbed me, one on each arm. They told me they had guns and would kill me if I tried to run away. They took me outside and put me in the back of a police van and drove out of town. As we were driving away, we passed my mother in the street. She hadn't been told I was being taken away. I was crying out for her through the bars, trying to call for her. Then she just sat down and cried.' That was the last he saw of her for five months. He was 13 years old.

'They took me to a place they called "Place of Safety" in Bloemfontein. They shouldn't call it that. There were druggies, murderers, prostitutes, everything. Terrible things happened there. You don't want to know,' he says with still eyes. And he's right.

After seven months Pretorius could have returned home but Alba felt a transfer to an orphanage would be in her son's best interests. She simply could not cope.

Alone, afraid and feeling abandoned, the young Dewald discovered cricket. Or rather, it discovered him. 'One day the teacher, Hannetjie Hendricks, and some other kids were playing cricket. They said "come and play – have a bowl". I wasn't interested. I didn't know the game. But I bowled a ball and suddenly there was a look on her face I had never seen before. I just bowled quicker than anyone else, it was natural.'

But it wasn't the game itself that kept him interested, it was a little simpler than that. 'I was able to stay outside, under the blue sky. I did anything to keep out of the orphanage.' His skill with a ball, however, brought him into contact with emotions he had never previously experienced: affection, respect, self-belief and even just plain friendship. Soon enough, Dewald and cricket were head over heels in love with each other.

Through his teenage years he developed a burning desire to succeed. Ambition was something new to him but he embraced it with all his might. One day Dewald and some of his colleagues from the orphanage were taken to watch a Free State match at Springbok Park. 'I told them I would play for Free State one day, that I would have a shirt with my name on the back. They just laughed at me. They all thought I was mad.'

Undeterred by the prospect of rejection, Pretorius gave up his first job after leaving the orphanage and walked into the Free State offices. 'I told them I wanted to be a cricketer and asked for a job. I told them I would do anything, and I meant anything. So they let me stay in a room and I helped the groundstaff. But what I really loved was being allowed to bowl at the Free State guys during net practice. They smashed me everywhere, no sympathy. But I kept coming back for more.'

Corrie van Zyl, currently South Africa's assistant coach, was player coach at the union when Pretorius arrived. 'I asked him if I could have a ball and he gave me one. I went to the nets at a local school and bowled for two hours a day, every day. Just me and the stumps – I was going to get better, I was determined. Ten days later I went back to Corrie and asked for another ball. He asked what had happened to the first one and I told him it had fallen to pieces. He gave me another one, and another one after that.'

His landmark achievements on the way to a Test cap were all marked by a debilitating attack of nerves but quickly repaired with success. 'I was belted on my 2nd XI debut but took five wickets in the next match. On my first-class debut against the touring Pakistanis in 1997 I started with a wide and a no ball, and then trapped Aamir Sohail lbw with the eighth ball of the over. I couldn't stop shaking and smiling at the same time.'

On Test debut against Australia two years ago, the nerves once again overwhelmed him, as did Matthew Hayden and Justin Langer. But he found himself gradually relaxing during his second Test, at Edgbaston against England last week, and now believes he can become as well adjusted to his career as he has to his life.

'Of course you can want something too much, and maybe that was the case with me. I wanted it so much I couldn't quite handle it when I got it. But there are no more days left that will be too big for me. I have played a Test match at Lord's. There are many things that I want to achieve in cricket but my dream has come true. I can stop dreaming now.'

Everyone does not live happily ever after in this dream, however. Despite his greatest efforts to help his mother and brother into his new world, he has now cut all ties with both of them. 'There is only so much you can do, only so much money you can keep giving. My mother is living with another waster and my brother is basically a hobo, a drifter. When they show me they want to be helped, I'll be there. But for now we have made our choices.'

Pretorius returns to the orphanage as often as possible with one simple message to the children: 'I tell them it doesn't matter where they come from, it matters only where they are going. I tell them never, ever to use the orphanage as an excuse for failure because you can be whatever you want if you are determined enough.' Dewald Pretorius is proof of that.

(2002)

Most international sportsmen learn their lines, and the interview passes pleasantly and pointlessly. But when people like Herschelle Gibbs start talking, scripts tend to go down the drain, along with political correctness. The ribald batsman was reportedly given a stern talking-to about this interview, his typically off-colour crack about Khayelitsha raising the ire of those who weren't quite sure how to deal with a 'black' player being racially insensitive.

Gibbs could yet be great

Robert Houwing

The long, sliding windows in room 1727 of the Sandton Sun have been pushed back fully, allowing a deliciously cool breeze to waft in, tempering the brilliant Highveld morning sunshine and maximising the view of some of Johannesburg's leafiest suburbs.

It's 9 a.m. and Herschelle Herman Gibbs is still beneath the bedcovers ahead of a day-night international at the Wanderers. He is watching a Sky Sports soccer update on satellite and his cell-phone, as ever, beeps every few minutes; he's never been averse to a good yak.

I feel a bit like a Rolling Stone reporter interviewing John Lennon during his famous sleep-in with Yoko, but am not in the least offended; we've had dealings over some eight or nine years and I've even felt the force of his squash forehand, every now and then, down at the Point gymnasium.

A half-full case of Red Bull energy-drink cans adorns the sideboard and his kit is in a shambolic heap in the corner. Heck, it's tough being an 'affirmative action' selection for the Proteas.

Straight back to the ghetto after the game, eh Hersch? 'Ja, straight back to my shack in Khayelitsha, brother,' says Gibbs with that staple, cheeky grin.

We all know, of course, that this Green Point-born, Bishops-educated, middle-class Capetonian hardly represents one of the fiercely prodded, rags-to-riches 'development' success stories so desired by those on the political pulpit, and that his presence provides a bizarre spoonful of credibility because of his off-pale contribution to the make-up of the 'rainbow nation'.

We also know, however, that when pressure groups' soup-of-the-day demanded a sprinkling of black pepper among the white mushrooms, Gibbs – hardly, at the time, matching in first-class runs what he possesses in ability – was handed an unorthodox lifeline back into Test cricket, albeit in the unfamiliar and taxing role of opening batsman.

Now a series average against the West Indies of 26.25 (210 runs from eight innings, with a highest score of 51) may hint at continued under achievement, but we saw enough in the form of sublime, Barry Richards-like stroke-play – not to mention some instinctive, reflex genius in the field – to suggest Herschelle Gibbs, who is just about to turn 25, belongs in the Test arena and will surely blossom in the months and years to come.

Supporting that belief is the knowledge that, similarly, it took Gibbs several seasons to realise his provincial potential, after a much-publicised baptism for Western Province B at the impressionable age of 16 in 1990/91.

Once he finally found his feet on the first-class stage, people far and wide saw what he could do – notably at Nagpur two years ago when, in a tour match for South Africa, he savaged the India A attack to the tune of an unbeaten 200 (his highest score to date) and second-innings 171 for good measure; not too many of our present-day batters have that sort of staying power. And yes, Gibbs's international acclimatisation was not helped by being overlooked for England last winter.

He 'would like to think' that a truly emphatic Test breakthrough is also imminent now after a lean start. 'I wasn't really sure in those first four seasons for Province where my cricket was going, but I can thank Duncan [Fletcher] for a suggestion that finally kickstarted things. He said I should start opening in the one-day stuff and go out and play the way I wanted to. People, as well as myself, then became aware of how I could play.'

Fletcher's brainchild at provincial level paid handsome dividends in international combat a few weeks ago when, opening for the Proteas at St

George's Park, Gibbs 'exploded' with 125 in the limited-overs series against the West Indies – almost quadrupling his previous best at that level of 35.

Now we keenly await a repetition of that watershed feat in the more attritional terrain of Tests.

'I've been playing for the Proteas in and out for the last two years or so and for a long time it was exactly the same; I didn't go out and play the way I could, simply because in some instances maybe the occasion was too big for me and I didn't handle it that well. I am a very nervous starter and when you're too nervous there's a lot of indecision and discomfort at the wicket. That leads to silly mistakes. I feel stronger now … I feel I have a foundation for things to come.

'And I'm especially happy about it considering a certain little tournament coming up in England. Hopefully in the next two or three months I can show exactly what I can do at this level. I think I've proved I can play at the top and maybe now I can take a couple of half-centuries a bit further. I've let go that indecision of the past. If I've wanted to hit the ball, I've hit it. Cricket's all about choosing the right balls. I've been more relaxed.'

In an ideal world, where would chief selector HH Gibbs place HH Gibbs the batsman in the Test-match order?

'I don't think I'd open [in Tests], to be honest, although I will bat anywhere as long as I can play. If you basically have a good technique, wherever you are asked to bat I'm sure you can do the job satisfactorily. I haven't done too badly at opening. For me it was just a confidence thing and it has given me that.

'I've been disappointed to get out when well set sometimes, but at least the confidence is there now. Sure, a 40 or 50 is better than scoring three or four but you should be really "in" at 40, so in many ways it's worse to get out at that stage! Ideally I'm probably a number four or five.'

It did not escape experts' notice that Gibbs got out more than once in the West Indies Test series caught at forward short-leg. Pleasingly, I would submit, this is not something he is losing much sleep over – charges of 'weakness' in a particular area are often swiftly formulated just because a batsman gets out in similar fashion over a period of a few matches. Due thought must be given for coincidence.

'*Ja*, it was more a concentration than a technical thing, I believe,' says Gibbs. 'Sometimes you premeditate … like when Merv Dillon came around the wicket to me at Newlands just before lunch. I thought perhaps it was in order to bounce me and sometimes you get into a position a bit early; your weight falls a little to the off-side.

'You end up playing away from your body and falling over and automatically you'll hit on the leg side. It's the first time it's happened to me; maybe I was premeditating, not concentrating. It's hardly happened before in nine years of first-class cricket.'

If Gibbs is not going to let charges of technical shortcomings get to him, he's certainly not fussed, either, by the whole affirmative action hullabaloo. 'I don't want to say it's ludicrous … but not that far off! I just made up my mind that once they'd chosen me, I was going to make the most of it and play my heart out. I knew there was a vacancy within the top six and perhaps it wouldn't come up again. I can't be bothered with this affirmative shit really.

'If people are talented and given the opportunity in life, it's up to them how they deal with that opportunity. Everything in life takes time; very few can just come in and cope with a situation and automatically come out successful. But this is a land of opportunity, and if you're the right colour these days, there will be opportunities that can make or break you. Seize them while you can; they might not come up again. That's my only message, really, to others in a similar position.

'As players, we can't really comment much about it but I'd like to think choice on merit is something that will never, ever leave the selectors' thoughts.'

Does Gibbs, when winter's chill beckons, ever yearn for a return to the No. 10 rugby jersey he last vacated some five years ago?

'No. That feeling was with me, ate at me, for the first two years out of the game. I would go to Newlands and sit there imagining myself playing for Province. But the style of rugby's changed a lot and I don't think I would have been that suited to the new style.

'It was a bitter pill to swallow because I enjoyed my rugby more than the cricket at the time, but my cricket enjoyment has picked up a lot in recent years. I'm happy with life. A bit of "touch" is the extent of my rugby now.

'Anyway, I'd rather face Ambrose than have to tackle Vidiri or Lomu.'

(SA Sports Illustrated, March 1999)

Fixed fights, a comeback, Ali: Mike 'The Tank' Schutte talks

Clinton van der Berg

Standing close to Mike Schutte, it's difficult deciding what to be more impressed by: his neck from hell or his great big belly laugh.

Then there's his size. He was always a big man (118 kg in his prime), but there's a lot more width to 'The Tank' these days. See him hold a Castle between his chunky fingers and it looks like one of those itsy-bitsy halfcans. And his guitar; straddled on his ample lap it looks far too small. He really is way, way above his fighting weight. But the humour, thankfully, remains the same.

'None of the Mike Schutte jokes were ever made up. They're all true,' he laughs, revealing the familiar gap-toothed smile.

'A bloke drives his car over a chicken. Carrying it, he goes up and asks Mike Schutte if it's one of his. No, says Mike, I don't sell flat chickens.'

Roaring with laughter, he tells another: 'What do you call Mike Schutte with an IQ of 27? A genius.'

But his comeback, now that's no joke. '*Ja*, in January I'm in the gym doing my thing. I'm waiting until the end of the year is over because it's party time now, you know.

'Ag, I know I'm big, but I love my meat. Two kilos at one sitting is nothing. I sometimes have chops for breakfast.

'If I'm fit, the guys today won't last against me. Imagine it. "The Tank" versus Kallie (Knoetze). Maybe we'll get it going, but I'd win because I was taught by the greatest. Alan Toweel was the best; we were like his children.'

Hindsight, says Schutte, has taught him that Toweel espoused fine virtues as a trainer and a mentor. 'He always warned me about women. He told me that boxers lead a lonely life, but off I went and got married – three times. My first wife couldn't handle it. Later on I had such bad luck with women. I probably should have listened to Alan.'

As a boxer, Schutte was enthralling to watch. Like during his fight with Gerrie Coetzee, whom he kicked when Coetzee was on the canvas.

There were, insists Schutte, mitigating reasons: 'As he went down, he kicked me between my legs. His head was in front of my foot, so I kicked him back.'

If that pleased 'The Tank' it was the only highlight of a fight that saw him dropped six times and later suspended. 'I took him easy. He couldn't beat me. Alan [Toweel] said to look him in the eyes. I was waiting for him. Then he threw this huge right that caught me on the neck. Whoof! Down. I'm out and my eyes are like windscreen wipers. He dropped me six bloody times, but I got up each time.

'After that, I was hitting his body. My head had cleared and I dropped him. He got up and I knocked him down again. Then he had to go and kick me …'

The two briefly squared off for a bare-knuckle brawl in the change-room afterwards but, claims Schutte, Coetzee wanted no part of it.

'I was rough, but never dirty,' he says. 'I never made one enemy because I could always *vloek* a guy, maybe swear at his mother or something, but we'd always hug and thank each other afterwards.'

Schutte was a master of intimidation, but always attached a touch of humour to his antics. Like the time he waltzed into George Labuschagne's room and tipped his bed over. 'Don't worry about getting sleep,' he taunted his challenger. 'I'm gonna put you to sleep.'

Even though he believes his career was unfulfilled, there's no question Schutte boxed better than most. Indeed, many fight buffs rank him second only to Coetzee and there's ample respect for the heavyweight with the highest KO ratio in South African boxing history.

In his prime Schutte beat a host of top fighters, including OB English (who had drawn with Joe Bugner), Bill Carson, Pat Duncan, Rodney Bobick and Chuck Wepner, who had knocked Mohammad Ali off his feet.

Talk of Ali reminds Schutte of the biggest missed chance of his 49-fight career. The two signed to fight in April 1977, but Don King's people haggled over accommodation of all things and the fight was later scrapped.

'That hurt,' says Schutte, who turns 46 tomorrow. 'Ali himself said he was gonna go to Africa and fight this Scooter guy. He said I'd have to get on my scooter to get away from him. Jeez, and to think I could have had him, could have made millions …'

As it is, Schutte never did get his big-money fight. His entire career only yielded R102 000 in purse money – before his manager, trainer and hangers-on took their slice of the action.

His biggest purse for a single fight was R16 000, but there's no telling the dough he made on the side for that one. In Terry Pettifer's forthcoming book, he reveals that Schutte was 'on the take' in his bout against Kallie Knoetze.

'He threw an uppercut and I actually moved away from it,' Schutte says of the phantom punch that 'KO'd' him in the second round. 'There's no way he could have beaten me.'

Perhaps the great irony of Schutte's boxing career is that he succeeded at all. Rolling up his sleeves, he reveals short, pudgy arms more suited for casual beer drinking than stiff jabs or looping hooks.

'I could never straighten them,' he says. 'I had extra bones put in both elbow joints and I remember getting injections for the pain before every fight. But it didn't matter; even with these short arms I often outjabbed Gerrie and the others.'

Schutte fought many of the contenders, and his views on the top heavyweights of his day are revealing. For instance, he doesn't consider Coetzee his best opponent. Far from it. He picks Joe King Roman ('a strong bastard'), but he concedes that Coetzee hurt him the most, while Knoetze 'cracked' the hardest.

'But the guy with the most potential, and remember, we had five wars against each other, was Jimmy Richards. Great left-hooker. He could have been a champion if he'd been properly looked after. The best fighter I've seen? It would have to be Pierre Fourie. What a master.'

Schutte seldom gets to the fights nowadays, but he knows what he likes. 'The heavyweights are a bunch of palookas,' he says. 'Fransie Botha's nothing. The boxers I like are the small guys: Kostya Tszyu – brilliant – and Phillip Holiday and that little guy, Baby Jake. I love watching him.'

Having been raised in Vanderbijlpark, a rugged town that inspired many old-time fighters, it's not surprising that Schutte still chooses to live there, among friends. Fortunately he's dropped the debt-collecting schtick that immediately followed his boxing days.

'It was *rof.* Besides, I was too soft. Guys would offer me money to kill. I took the money, but I refused to kill anyone. *Ag,* I gave a few *klaps* in my time – that happened a lot – especially when I was in a mood. But I had to get out. You know what it's like. Guys see an ex-boxer walk up to them and they feel threatened so they pull out a gun. Then you're in shit.'

But Schutte wasn't always mean and nasty. Like the time an old man spun him a sob story and Schutte assured him it would be sorted out. Indeed, he ended up paying the man's R2 000 debt.

Schutte's current interests are a lot less risky.

He works at a local scrapyard and dabbles in music (he plays seven instruments) and comedy, a natural outlet for his exuberance and spirit. He also does the occasional film, having starred in *I'm for the Hippopotamus* (with Terrence Hill and Bud Spencer) in 1977, a couple of Leon Schuster flicks and some local dramas.

'Me and Kallie did wrestling for a while, but now we're gonna team up and go on the road and tell jokes. We'll earn a fortune for two weeks' work in December. Me and Kallie are big mates. People like us together. We have an effect on them like no-one else.

'Once I did a show at Hartbeespoort. We were jolling guitar and telling jokes and then this *dominee* comes in. So we all got a bottle and some fish and chips and had a good *jol*. Those days are gone, for sure, but those were the days.'

(Sunday Times, 1996)

The eternal Normal Guy with the educated Cape Town accent and the big hair, Bruce Fordyce looked strangely out of place in the 1980s, jogging up Polly Shorts as Casspirs crawled up every other highway and township street. It is interviews like this one with Normal Bruce that remind one just how far away Normal really seemed back then.

Fordyce on running: from Comrades to chicken run

Gavin Evans

IT's been five years since Bruce Fordyce won his first Comrades Marathon while wearing a black armband to protest against the running authorities' decision to link the marathon to Republic Day festivities.

But he would don the armband again if the need arose.

The black armband caused the organisers intense embarrassment, but it did have a powerful effect. As Fordyce put it: 'They learnt their lesson – they won't do it again.'

It also caused a few headaches for SABC staff, who didn't know where to point their cameras when Bruce strode past – especially when he insisted on switching arms to prevent them from focusing on his 'clean' side.

Now, six Comrades victories later, Fordyce says the political views which inspired him to wear the armband have not changed.

'Actually I think the black armband was a bit of a compromise – to enable some of us to make our views clear, but still be able to run after months of training. When you consider that today big business is talking to the ANC, my wearing a black armband seems such an insignificant thing,' he said.

But at the time that certainly wasn't the way many running fans and officials viewed it.

'Afterwards I was very unpopular with a lot of people. I got quite a lot of abuse at races and things – for about a year,' he said.

Much of the public has forgotten the incident; Fordyce was soon able to reap the considerable rewards of sporting fame.

No longer a Wits University archaeologist, he spends much of his time on business activities. Fordyce's commercial endorsements require frequent appearances for the sponsors. He and other top South African sportsmen have formed a company to give talks on motivation to the management staff of different firms.

But he has not allowed his business success to alter his perceptions.

He describes the political situation in South Africa as a 'disaster', and adds that while he would love to see peaceful change, he is pessimistic about its prospects.

Fordyce, who calls himself a 'wishy-washy liberal', says he is determined to stay here. He calls South Africa a 'fantastic country', but one he would like to see 'properly democratic'.

What concerns him, he says, is that his withdrawal from the university environment, combined with the pace of his schedule, have left him isolated from political developments.

Fordyce says the thing that upsets him most is when he hears of people emigrating – something many of his friends are doing.

'I've decided I'm staying – whatever happens.

'I can understand it when people leave because of the army or go into exile for political reasons – but I'm talking about gapping it. It's terribly sad because unfortunately a lot of very highly qualified people are going – people we desperately need.'

Unlike local stars in many other sports, for Fordyce the pastures are greenest at home. Ultra-marathon distance running is not a major sport overseas, and the most prestigious race he can run is the Comrades. He is therefore able to look at the question of the sporting boycott of South Africa with a little more distance than can most local sportspeople.

'I've always found the question of the sporting boycott a terrible dilemma.

'I acknowledge it has done a tremendous amount of good and that it's been directly instrumental in the changes that have taken place.

'But the trouble is I'm one of the sportsmen. I know so many of them. Nowadays it's those people's jobs – not just something they do for fun.

'So I sympathise with the boycott on the one hand, but on the other hand I want my mates to be able to compete.'

Fordyce made the decision to abandon his academic career and cash in on his athletic skills a couple of years ago. He is now a full-time 'professional-amateur' who, like most other athletes, is able to retain his amateur status by placing his earnings in a trust fund administered by the running authorities.

He says today there is little alternative to running as a full-time professional unless you are working in a university environment or, like many of the black runners, your job is to run for a mining company.

'In a sense the runners you see are very much the élite. Running as a sport is a middle- and upper-class thing because you have to have the luxury to be able to do the training and the luxury to be able to spend money on something that at the end of the day only brings you a medal or a certificate.

'So you'll see a lot of top black runners because they're sponsored by the mines and because they have the talent to run exclusively, but you'll never see a great depth of ordinary black runners – people just doing four-hour marathons.'

He plans to expand his activities.

'I'm always going to be like a jack of all trades – doing a bit of everything – maybe some coaching, some TV commentary, some business interests here and there.

'I've got a fantasy that one day I'll be the manager in charge of the South African athletics team to the Olympic Games – when they've been readmitted. I don't know how long that will take. That's why I pick myself as manager – I'll be out of it by then.'

But for the next four or five years he intends to remain active. He plans to continue running the Comrades – even though he has already won it more times than any other runner and holds both the up- and down-run records. He also hopes to concentrate more on shorter races in the future – standard marathons like Saturday's Nashua Marathon, as well as shorter distances.

'People might say what does a 1 500m race have to do with the Comrades, but I'm doing that because I'm trying to improve my speed. I do the 1 500m in just over four minutes. In fact, all my times are about the same as Zola Budd's. I'd have a helluva race with Zola on the track.'

He is also tempted by the challenge of the standard marathon – a stiff order, considering the depth of marathon talent in this country.

'It's an irony in a sense, but South Africa is really the world's leading marathon country. We're the only country in the world with three two-hour, eight-minute marathoners. So to do well here you've got to be really good.

'I think I can run a fast marathon, but I've done 10 years on the Comrades and other ultras which are not good for your speed. Also I might have some mental barriers in my mind because I know what you have to do to run a two-eight – you have to kill yourself.'

Between running and business, Fordyce says he has little time for cultural interests or 'jolling' any more – something he is not entirely happy about.

Aside from the lack of time, he also avoids movies and theatre 'because – it sounds like I'm a hypochondriac – they're always full of people with flu.' But even though he watches his diet more than he used to, he still enjoys a beer or two; the sounds of *Born to Run* and other early Springsteen classics can still be heard on his expensive sound system; and he can still be spotted at the occasional nightspot.

On balance he says he has things pretty good.

'If it weren't for the political situation, I'd say I had almost a perfect life – I've really landed with my bum in the butter.

'I keep thinking: "Gee, it's great, gee, it's wonderful," and then I remember I've got this shadow in the background – the shadow of what's going on around me. That's how I see it.'

(Weekly Mail, 9–16 October 1986)

COMMENT AND ANALYSIS

Despite the best efforts of marketers and fans to deny it, sport exists in a real world, in which the better team doesn't – and shouldn't – always win. Don't mix sport and politics, cry a resolute band of romantics, holed up somewhere between 1961 and the 19th century; but one might as well say that economics and politics shouldn't mix either. The purist in all of us wishes that sport wasn't inextricably linked with big business and bigger politics, but reality can't be denied for more than 90 minutes at a time.

And it is here that the Bigger Picture specialists come into their own. Some are sports writers, others are followers of the game who happen to win Nobel Prizes for literature. Others still are social observers and commentators, their scope of expertise briefly overlapping with sport, not surprising in a country in which sport intersects with almost every aspect of society.

Together they provide a vital respite from the petty politics and fickleness of day-to-day sporting life. Sports journalism in South Africa has traditionally patronised its readers, providing either dumbed-down analysis or unsatisfying and sloppy discussions of current events. The junior sports journalist is too tired, too jaded, too drunk to engage his mind. He can't risk losing the patronage and insider status granted him by corporate godfathers and team bosses, and so he says nothing.

But step outside of this almost feudal journalistic environment, and you find writers and thinkers, devil's advocates uninhibited by the demands and politics of the profession. The result: a body of sharp, insightful, often provocative writing that is willing to risk being wide of the mark so long as it triggers debate, and forces that most rare of commodities – thought – into sporting issues.

– Tom Eaton

Outside meteorology, almost no profession relies as heavily on prediction as does sports journalism. From broad sweeping forecasts of teams' successes over a season, to cavalier pronouncements on minute details ('3–2 after 43 minutes, Thierry Henry to equalise in the 44th before being red-carded for head-butting a streaker ...'), scribes pin their colours to complete fictions, spur-of-the-moment thumbsucks camouflaged in impressive language. Naturally they get away with murder: readers rarely remember predictions (how can they when so many are made?) and dismal success rates go unpunished. One can't help wondering that if the weather bloke on TV got it wrong as much as sports writers do, there'd be a revolution. However, predictions do serve one valuable purpose: they show us, long after the fact, what we were thinking at the time; and Peter Davies' s predictions back in 1994 provide a curious – and revealing – snapshot of a country waking up to democracy.

2010 – a sports odyssey

Peter Davies

There's an outpouring of emotion on the terraces of the FNB Stadium – and on the streets of Egoli, where thousands have been watching the game on a mega 3-D screen, they've already begun dancing and dunking each other in the fountains of the Civic Centre.

Back at the stadium, Teenage Motaung, son of Chiefs' founder Kaizer Motaung, and scorer of the crucial second goal, bearhugs that famous gold World Cup trophy, while the world's media click their camera shutters and jostle frantically for a better view.

Chest thrust proud, Motaung points to the shape of Africa on the Cup and jabs one finger in the air. Number one. Africa. No doubt about it, on this continent beats the heart of world soccer. Pele's prophecies have come true. An African side has won the World Cup. Again.

And how apt that South Africa has claimed the world's most revered team prize by triumphing over Nigeria, our biggest rivals on the continent ... and on the planet. The foresighted five-year plans of former coach Clive Barker have borne the ripest of fruits.

It was just 15 short years ago that the sceptics laughed off suggestions that African soccer would one day show the rest of the world the way. Then, metronomic European discipline was in vogue, and African football was skilled but raw.

But in the last few years of the previous century, the 'beautiful game' was transformed on the dark continent.

In the 1970s the Dutch pioneered 'Total Football'. In the late '90s, Africa patented and proved that 'Power Football' was the pathway to glory.

It was a simple concept. Discipline and fitness grafted onto silky, natural skills. Result: an unbeatable cocktail of skill and strength, discipline and daring, tactics and technique.

Soccer shed the boring off-side rule a decade ago, and the 'game of the people' has become even more popular. More goals, more action, more money from sponsors dying for a slice of the action.

Corruption in the local game is a vague memory. Those stories of administrators lining their pockets in the bad old days are dismissed as exaggerations. These days, anyone caught with their fingers in the cookie jar is banned for life.

And those murmurings of refs accepting bribes, or giving dodgy decisions in return for a handful of gold? No longer possible. Not with three decision-makers hunched behind closed-circuit TVs. Strange that people were averse to technologically aided decisions all those years ago.

Most people believe sport today would wither without such nerve-splitting replayed decisions. They really get the fans on the edge of their seats. Those who worried that the games would be delayed have been proved wrong. Stop the clock, watch the action, stop some hearts, make the right decision – for all to see. Whingeing about the ref is immediately rendered redundant.

After all, South Africa won the rugby World Cup on a replayed decision in 1999, when Chester Williams was proved to have applied downward pressure to the ball behind the French line. The ref was unsighted amid the melee of falling bodies and boots that thundered over the line, and would have surely awarded a 22 m drop-out in the pre-TV judgment days. But after a minute or so of careful scrutiny, the green light flashed, and the Boks were in seventh heaven.

Since those halcyon days, the Boks have taken a step or two back – or perhaps other nations have taken giant strides forward. At least the off-field administration shambles and petty bickering about national symbols dissolved without trace soon after the nation became one in 1994.

Everyone still calls the national team the Springboks. I mean could you really have imagined the Kiwis and Aussies ranting in the pubs about the relative strengths of the All Blacks, Wallabies and … PROTEAS (or whatever whimsical nickname the politicos of the day had dreamed up)?

The problems these days are all on the pitch. It's a year to go to the World Cup in Fiji and Western Samoa, the new powerhouses of world rugby. But if the Boks' recent trip to South America is anything to go by, with that woeful defeat to Patagonia, then there's trouble afoot.

The Brits, Kiwis and Aussies have come out smiling since Union and League were integrated in 2001 following the inevitable decision to make Rugby Union professional a few years earlier.

Suddenly, South Africa had cause to regret the patchy state of their League code. It became obvious that the League players adapted quicker to the new laws which discarded line-outs, banned kicking inside the opponent's half, and strictly entrenched the use-it-or-lose-it rules in the loose. The new scoring system, of six points for a try, two for a penalty, and three bonus points to the side that concedes the fewest penalties for foul play, has also changed the face of the game. There's more rhythm and flow, and South Africa will need to inject some rhythm of their own if they are to win the World Cup for the second time in their history.

In cricket, the sport South Africa has dominated since the turn of the century, it will be our turn to defend the World Cup trophy we retained by beating Pakistan in the USA in 2007. The choice of the US as hosts was strange to some, given the fact that their side, mainly expatriate Asians and West Indians (those whose hopes of making it big in basketball had faded), only just managed to qualify for the 2003 World Cup in South Africa.

But the world has long since realised that money doesn't just talk, it screams like a banshee when such decisions are made. After all, a host's primary function is to entertain, and the Yanks sure know how to put on a show.

The wickets, even a year ahead of schedule, are being specially cultivated under hothouse conditions to ensure uniformity at all venues. Enclosed stadia will eliminate the chance of rain stopping play. Makes sense, and ensures that the all-important TV contracts, the lifeblood of world sport, can be signed with confidence.

The growth of soccer in the US after the 1994 World Cup was phenomenal, and, as so many world-class natural athletes took a liking to the game, it was only a matter of time before the Yanks started climbing the ladder.

And now they're trying the same with cricket. Starting to think broader, the Americans, not bad for a country that still calls its domestic baseball championship the World Series.

But back to the South African cricket side. The side has thrived under the inspired coaching of Jonty Rhodes and astute captaincy of veteran left-arm spinner Jacob Malao. Malao first made the headlines when taking three Australian wickets for the Nicky Oppenheimer XI (remember those games?) way back in 1994, and is still bamboozling batters, but there's doubt whether he will last another campaign at the top level.

Having trawled neglected townships for talent in the 1990s, and come up smiling, the South Africans have dominated the world stage the same way the West Indians did in the '70s and '80s.

The batting, typically South African, remains a touch wobbly, but with their bowling attack, who needs to score 300 every time?

The awesome pace quartet, affectionately known as the 'Moroka Muggers' (opposing batsmen fear grievous bodily harm when at the crease), put the fear of God into most opposition, and variety is provided by spin twins Malao and leggie Rasheed Booley.

Booley's rise to international prominence is legendary – so memorable it could have been lifted straight from the pages of a pre-teen sports comic.

The story goes that Booley developed his unreadable deliveries after sessions of sweat and toil trying to copy the action of Australian wrist-spinner Shane Warne (remember him?).

Warne had randomly picked Booley, then aged 13, from a crowd of development scheme kids at Eerste River township near Cape Town in March 1994, and shown him how to bowl a flipper.

There was no reason why Warne chose Booley, he just needed someone to demonstrate the action. But Booley neither forgot Warne nor the flipper, and worked long and hard on getting his fingers strong enough to grip and control the ball.

When Warne played against Booley at international level for the first time, in 2003, the Aussie remarked – with a rueful grin – how sorry he was that he'd ever let him in on the subtle mysteries of wrist-spinning.

Booley's better suited to the five-day game, but with that particular brand of cricket all but dead in these days of vision-phones and inter-planetary travel, Booley has had to adapt to the different demands of the one-dayers.

On the tennis courts, it's difficult to believe that umpires once told fans to keep quiet while the ball was in play. A visit to Wimbledon these days is like attending a 1990s rock concert.

Players are welcomed by a courtside announcer, who wades through a host of player stats in the way that ring-announcers in boxing (remember when that sport was still legal?) used to do.

Players are encouraged to wear the most colourful possible outfits (even the elegant grand old dame of the courts, Mary Pierce, got into the spirit of things by sporting a yellow and electric-blue bodysuit for her appearance on Wimbledon's hallowed astroturf this year).

Music from the boomboxes blaring on courtside appears to motivate players to even greater heights, and the compulsory mini-cameras secreted in the player's headbands provide for sensational angles on TV. Now, all South Africa needs to do is produce another decent player. We've had a bit of a drought since the days of Wayne Ferreira and Amanda Coetzer. There's a definite shortage of fresh talent.

Speaking of young blood, what about 16-year-old Kieran Kenealy, still at high school but already running 10,5 secs for the 100 m. Now there's a talent. He's already been signed by the IMG group, and will be financially secure for the next decade at least with recent endorsements for pimple cream and starting blocks. I suppose the next major decision he'll have to make is whether to enter the Drug-Free Olympics or the Enhanced Olympics. Whatever his decision, he must just go for it. Like golfer Ernie Els, winner of four Masters, three British Opens and two US Open titles always says, 'the harder I hit it, the luckier I get'.

Sounds like he borrowed and adapted Gary Player's old war-cry, but Els's words sum up his, and South Africa's, attitude to world sport in the first decade of the new century. No prisoners taken, no apologies for being the best.

Yes, as the shadows lengthen on the greatest day in the nation's sporting history, it's not just the spectacular sunset that triggers a warm feeling.

SA sport has never looked rosier. Former Sports Minister Steve Tshwete had the vision to implement academies and elevate sports to an unprecedented level of professionalism in this sports-mad country soon after taking up his post in 1994. In the bad old days, many rough sporting diamonds were left sleeping in the dark. But under Tshwete's guidance, a rich seam of talent has been unearthed, cut, polished and allowed to glint brightly.

The average South African sports lover – you and me – now basking in the glow of a World Cup victory, can thank our lucky stars for people with such vision.

(SA Sports Illustrated, October 1994)

A battle of witlessness 'twixt brawn and brawn

Sinned Lebur

The Currie Cup Final, the distillation of the rugby season, is an occasion when, as Trevor Quirk would say, only rugby is the winner.

Rubbish, say the fanatics on the terraces.

It will be played on Saturday, September 28 at Newlands. As usual, it will be contested by Western Province and Northern Transvaal.

And one or the other team will win, to the greater glory of either Pretoria or Cape Town.

Rugby is, of course, as the great French semiologist of the fifties, Le Comte, put it, a metaphor for Life.

(Of passing note to academics, a Stellenbosch doctoral thesis of the same era by PJ Germishuys attacked this idea and proposed the reverse – that Life is a metaphor for Rugby. This philosophy still unfortunately holds sway over large parts of the country – particularly Klerksdorp.)

As predicted, the past rugby season has been a miserable one. Naas

Botha's successful precision kicking has insidiously forced every other provincial team to re-examine their tactics. To a great or lesser extent, all have swung towards a similar percentage game.

When the rest of our national life is redolent with lies, bluster and clichés, it would be foolish to imagine that rugby, too, would be anything but a celebration of mediocrity.

Western Province, to their scant credit, have tried to maintain their 'traditional' running game. But their singular lack of imagination or flair, plus their persistent selection of eight heavyweight forwards, made sure that their rugby was almost as boring as Northern Transvaal's – just more scrappy.

One may be sure that Michael du Plessis will run the ball on Saturday, and he deserves praise for that. He will, however, run without an ounce of sense or imagination, probably will not pass – except off the ground – and is in reality Naas's alter ego: one is a selfish kicker, the other a selfish runner.

South African rugby is no longer a team game – and nor is South African politics. The State President (or Prime Minister) used to be thought of as an expression of the national white will.

Recently PW Botha, that dangerous solo runner, said plaintively, 'How can I sit down and talk to *geweldenaars* about the future of this country?' – as though political change were merely the art of convincing PW of the necessity of it.

The WP selectors, aided by a string of injuries (casualties?), have rung the changes recently in an attempt to find a winning combination.

Their latest purge saw the dropping of scrumhalf Francois Bonthuys, the only player left in the backline with a hint of grace and style. The team has, if anything, grown more confused.

If Northern Transvaal, a team of police and SADF, are uncompromising proponents of subdue and penetrate (head bang and rape), WP is in reality the team of Stellenbosch University.

As the ideological heart of Afrikanerdom one would have hoped for a lead from the intellectuals in 1985 – progressive ideas, willingness to grasp formerly taboo nettles, verve and initiative.

Instead WP has grown to look more and more like their brothers up north.

It is no coincidence that even without the 'benefit' of the Emergency the Cape's response to urban unrest looked remarkably like the Transvaal's –

with the possible proviso that it may have been more brutal and stupidly provocative.

Who can forget the pathetic sight in the last WP–NT game at Loftus Versfeld of Rob Louw, the fastest of the WP forwards, hanging outside the scrums, trying to run on to Naas as he got the ball. Even Botha, himself no twinkle-toes, by the second half was laughing at his poor attempt at pressure loose-forward play.

It was not unlike trying to stop a march on Pollsmoor – the ball was always somewhere else when Louw arrived.

No doubt Louw will be called on to repeat the comedy on Saturday: when tactics have not worked, do not change them. Just apply them with greater vigour.

And these are supposedly the two top teams in the country!

Ironically, the two form provincial sides are not contesting the final. OFS and Transvaal have both beaten WP recently and, while not exactly setting the world alight, have at times played interestingly. (At least their faster loose forwards encouraged the respective sides to keep the ball in play for longer periods.)

Would it be stretching the analogy to point out that the Transvaal and Free State Nationalist Party caucuses saw the first shuffles towards the centre by the ruling party this year?

If one compares WP and NT, aside from Naas, they appear evenly balanced. There are two sets of equally overweight front rows, two sets of lazy lanky locks, two sets of lanky slow loose forwards, scrumhalves who can pass, centres who can tackle, and a Neil Burger-Bulldozer versus a Ray Mordt-Bulldozer on the wings.

The game will be dour, no quarter asked and none given – which is known on the stands as boring. Naas should ensure victory for Northerns.

It seems we will have to wait until next year for exciting rugby – or negotiations with the ANC.

But you never know. Rugby is a funny game. The writer will be at Newlands on Saturday with a Kooler Bag of Oolies, for reasons of safety shouting loudly for the same team as the people on either side of him.

See you there.

(Weekly Mail, 27 September 1985)

The African Renaissance is super, but the Soccer World Cup is the Soccer World Cup! Continental unity took a fascinating dive in the last nerve-jangling weeks before the bid teams set off for Zurich in 2004; and Barney Mthombothi got away with rhetoric that would have earned most white writers a non-negotiable exit visa and a fatwa.

Arabs stand in the way of a successful South African bid for the Soccer World Cup

Barney Mthombothi

The country is waiting on tenterhooks, pregnant with expectation. The *i*'s have been dotted and the *t*'s have been crossed. Anything that needs to be done has been done. But South Africa can't take anything for granted. After all, once bitten, twice shy. We've been here before.

Four years ago most South Africans had thought it was all over bar the shouting. We were ready to be anointed hosts when Sepp Blatter came to the podium and shouted 'Deutschland!'

Some South Africans thought Deutschland was some form of greeting. It was a shock to discover it was all over. It wasn't fair. But Germany had won. Deutschland became a swear word. It was a terrible let-down.

It was a bitter pill to swallow. But to make it a wee bit palatable we were promised, or we were made to believe, our bid for the 2010 Soccer World Cup would be plain sailing.

Up to now South Africa has been clear favourite by a long shot. But now clouds are gathering. South Africans are optimistic but the disappointment of four years ago lurks at the back of their minds. Surely, Fifa cannot play another cruel trick on us.

The empty suits who run South African football have characteristically not been averse to some screw-up. It is a miracle that Sepp Blatter still stands by this country after they ditched him for Issa Hayatou during the election of the Fifa president. The same medicine was dished out to Ismail Bhamjee.

We are lucky some people do not hold grudges.

It is, of course, no accident that it is the Arabs – the Tunisians, the Libyans, the Moroccans and the Egyptians – all limb-chopping dictatorships, who want to deny us our day in the sun, our finest hour.

Most of them don't stand a chance. Their only motive for throwing their hat in the ring is to mess it up for us; to crowd you out of the way, thus allowing one of their number to streak ahead and take the crown.

The Arabs are therefore ganging up against South Africa. This is an African bid.

Arabs are only African when it suits them. It's a cruel thing to say – but true – they are in Africa but not of Africa. Their hearts and minds are with their Arab brothers in the Middle East. That is what moves their passion, their soul. Africa to them is backwardness, a waste of time.

Africans are only called upon to make up the numbers in international gatherings where votes are required. At all other occasions they regard Africans with nothing but contempt. But the lure of oil money is usually too strong for African leaders to show some backbone and call their bluff.

This much-vaunted unity between North African Arabs and the rest of the continent is and has always been a sham.

In Sudan for instance, the Arabs have been lynching African people in the south of the continent with the active support of the Egyptians and the Libyans. We may soon witness another genocide of Rwandan proportions in the Darfur region of Sudan where ethnic cleansing is under way.

Few voices have been raised to avert such calamity. The African Union, essentially the old OAU in new garb, is muted. Only Kofi Annan, conscious of his culpability in Rwanda, has raised an alarm.

Arabs have been our masters for centuries, long before the Europeans 'discovered' us. North African Arabs were trading in African slaves as early as the eighth century AD. They invented slavery. Europe and the Americas merely perfected the trade.

Morocco remains South Africa's main challenger, despite the Fifa technical report which seems to have dented its chances. The Moroccan government has been doing a good job dishing out dirt on this country. Crime apparently has reached unmanageable levels, and this country could soon be a terror target – this from a country that breeds terrorists by the bucketful!

The South Africans have been playing by the rules like true gentlemen. But gentlemen often come last in these sorts of contests.

Morocco has an interesting history. It left the OAU in protest because the organisation dared to challenge its conflict with the Polisario Front. At one point it even dabbled with the idea of applying for membership of the European Union. Maybe that's where its heart is – in Europe. And perhaps that's why it cites its proximity to Europe as its strong point.

Is that the only positive thing they can say about themselves? Maybe Morocco doesn't understand that this is an African bid, not a European affair. Two years ago the World Cup was held in Korea and Japan, half-way around the globe from Europe compared to South Africa.

Saad Kettani, the leader of the Moroccan bid, hammering on their so-called strength, said at the weekend that Morocco was a goal-kick away from Spain. It's also worth pointing out that Morocco is a bomb or two away from Spain.

And that is no laughing matter. In March this year, in perhaps the biggest attack on civilians in Europe, Moroccan terrorists planted bombs that killed 200 people and injured 1 500 on morning rush-hour trains in Madrid. A number of the perpetrators have already been arrested by Spanish police.

Last year 45 people were killed in Casablanca in bomb blasts carried out by Moroccans who are members of al-Qaeda. The Moroccan commissioner of police had this to say a few days ago: 'As far as I know a dozen dangerous elements are still on the loose. Of course attacks are always possible.'

An interesting addition to the Moroccan delegation to Zurich this week will be Senegalese President Abdoulaye Wade who has come out publicly in support of their bid. Maybe he's merely doing what Jacques Chirac wants him to do.

But Wade was meant to be a close ally of President Thabo Mbeki. The two, with Bouteflika of Algeria and Nigerian president Olusegun Obasanjo, were instrumental in putting together the Nepad initiative.

Has the relation between Mbeki and Wade soured? It should be interesting watching the body language between the two in Zurich.

Welcoming Wade's endorsement, Moroccan bid leader Kettani said at the weekend: 'He presides over a state which has a fine example of democracy and free speech.'

Pity he can't say the same about his own country. Morocco is ruled by an unelected monarchy. The present king, Mohammed VI, took over five years ago after the death of his father King Hassan, who had ruled the country with an iron fist for 38 years.

Whichever way one looks at it, South Africa should not be on the same planet with Morocco on this bid. It's streets ahead, be it on governance, human rights or infrastructural development. It's a no contest. It's a democracy that works, and it's African.

It is just as well that Nelson Mandela and FW de Klerk, the two key architects of our democracy, are leading the South African delegation to Zurich this week. Yes, South Africa has all the infrastructure. But it's at the emotional level where we will beat the rest.

We make such a compelling candidate because of the journey we've travelled. For the world to see Mandela and De Klerk holding hands at a time when wars and conflicts are tearing the world apart will be like a breath of fresh air. They point the way to a better future.

South Africans, despite all the myriad problems and disappointments that still confront us, have achieved a lot together.

Winning the bid to host the Soccer World Cup will allow us to invite the whole world to come and celebrate our achievements with us. It will be the icing on the cake.

(Cape Times, 13 May 2004)

Give our black players more game time, not gym time

Mark Keohane

The latest initiative to inspire black player representation is the most damning evidence yet that transformation within South African rugby has been a total farce.

This year, Springbok coach Jake White has put Cats prop Lawrence Sephaka on a strength gym programme to develop him into a test candidate for the 2007 Rugby World Cup.

Yet, by the time Sephaka was lauded as the symbol of black development at the 2003 World Cup, R100m had been spent in supposedly developing black players and turning them into Test stars.

Sephaka was then dubbed the R100m Bok because after a decade of pouring money into development and sending black players to gyms, all that made it to the 2003 World Cup was one black prop.

Two years later and Sephaka is back in the gym, bench-pressing 160 kg, while his Super 12 teammates experience four weeks of Australian and New Zealand rugby.

The ill-informed will cheer. Those with a bit more information at their disposal will doubtlessly cringe.

Sephaka, despite playing in a winning U21 World Cup final against New Zealand in 1999, is still being developed.

Sephaka, despite making his Springbok debut against Argentina A in Tucumán, is still being developed.

Sephaka, despite making his Test debut in 2001, is still being developed.

Sephaka, despite fronting up to an All Black Crusaders front row in the 2002 Super 12 for 70 minutes, is still being developed.

Sephaka, despite being voted the best loosehead prop in the 2002 Tri-Nations series by the New Zealand and Australian media, is still being developed.

Sephaka, despite playing loosehead and tighthead in the same game against England at the 2003 World Cup, is still being developed.

White has had to put Sephaka in the gym because his fitness is not up to standard. You want to know why he lacks match fitness? It is because no one plays the bloody guy. Everyone wants to put him in the gym. God alone knows why. His maximum bench press was second only to Cobus Visagie, of the Bok props tested. It is not his strength that needs developing. It is his technique, and you only do that if you play.

Sephaka's graph is linked to game time. When he plays he prospers. The 2002 season is the test case. Sephaka makes his Test debut in 2001. The instruction goes out that he must play in the 2002 Super 12. This happens. In weeks one to six he gets five, five, zero, 50, 40 and zero minutes, respectively. His selection is then forced on the Cats Super 12 coaches and he plays 40, 80, 70, 70 and 65 minutes respectively.

In his last four matches, all the Springbok selectors rate his performance and he is picked for the 2002 Bok squad. Sephaka starts against the All Blacks in New Zealand and is superb. He is subbed after just 28 minutes with the Boks leading 13–10 and the scrum not in trouble. The Boks lose 41–20. The coach is told to play Sephaka from there on in. He gets 50 minutes in Brisbane against the Wallabies, 65 minutes in Durban against the All Blacks, and the full 80 against the Wallabies in a 33–31 win at Ellis Park.

Come 2003 and everyone wants to again develop him in the build-up to the World Cup. Come 2004 and he is back in the gym being developed. Come 2005 and it was a fight to get him a Vodacom Cup game with the Lions. Now he is back in the gym.

Something is seriously rotten in a system when a 26-year-old black Test prop just cannot buy any game time, let alone be given some. We need to play black players, not pay lip service to transformation by sending them to the gym. Money, gym programmes and good intentions won't develop black players. Game time will.

(Business Day, 4 April 2005)

Let's play African soccer again!

S'busiso Mseleku

Imagine Doctor Khumalo collecting the ball on the right flank, performing a 'shibobo' to beat a defender, then a 'vaya' to get past another. He dummies around a third opponent, then crosses to Chippa Masinga, who goes up for the header – and it's a goal for Bafana Bafana!

It's the stuff which used to make soccer fans scream with joy. And if only our boys could have done it in France we would have cheered. It would've been a goal made in South Africa …

But this kind of African magic – the *shibobos* (pushing the ball through a defender's legs) and *vayas* (rolling the ball in a semi-circle with your foot) – was sadly missing in Bafana's World Cup opening games.

It has led to accusations that our national side has adopted a European approach to the game instead of sticking to the style that brought them glory – African-style soccer.

But what is this African style of play?

Drum spoke to the experts – and they all agree Bafana Bafana are at their best when they play the game they learnt in our dusty townships and villages – that unique brand of football we call our own.

Zacharia 'Computer' Lamola, a former Kaizer Chiefs great, says: 'Our natural style revolves around keeping possession. Our play is a slow build-up from the back. We don't rush, even if we have to pass backwards. As long as you are in possession of the ball your chance of scoring a goal is 100 per cent.'

When Lamola played for Preston Brothers, before joining Chiefs, players were taught to treat the ball as if it were their girlfriend.

'You don't let anyone mess with your girlfriend, so you mustn't let anyone take the ball from you,' he says.

'The current team loses possession easily because they seem to be in too much of a hurry to get the ball to the goals.'

Zimbabwean coach Shepherd Murape, who's been in South Africa for some years, agrees. 'The African style of play is similar to that of South America,' says the former Dynamos player who went on to coach his country, Namibia, and, locally, Orlando Pirates.

'In Africa we start our moves slowly from the back. As the ball reaches the midfield we get into second gear and move into overdrive as the ball reaches our forwards. A quick burst of speed opens up the opposition's defence.

'This lets African players save a lot of energy. They don't rush things the way the European players do.'

Murape says another advantage of African-style football is the close-ball control. It isn't taught – it's a skill learned at a young age.

'African players learn their soccer with either a cloth or plastic ball in a dusty street or backyard,' says Murape. 'It has no bounce, so our players learn at a young age to manoeuvre between defenders. That's why some of the world's most skilled players come from Third World countries. Brazil is a Third World country but it has the best players in the world.

'You can't tell me anyone taught Jomo Sono, Kaizer Motaung or Ace Ntsoelengoe to play the way they did. They learnt it as kids.'

After Bafana Bafana's 3–0 defeat by France in their opening World Cup match, coach Philippe Troussier came under fire from all sides for changing Bafana's playing style. Former Bafana coach Clive Barker believes the change in style cost us dearly.

'We gave the first match away,' he says. 'We didn't play our style. Anyone who coaches South Africa must know the feel of South African soccer. It must be somebody who's been in the townships and felt the emotions that accompany South African soccer.

'You can't change a Ronaldo, Maradona, Shoes, Doctor or Benni. These players possess natural talent that just needs to be nurtured. Nobody can teach them how to play soccer or change their game. We must return to our kind of soccer.'

Barker says a coach's role is to guide his players. Trying to change their style would be like a boxing trainer trying to convert born fighters such as Rocky Marciano or Mike Tyson into boxers.

Barker shares many soccer lovers' belief that Doctor Khumalo should have been used in the opening matches. 'Don't forget it was Khumalo who gave Masinga the pass from which he scored the goal that took us to the World Cup,' he says. 'And it was Khumalo who laid on the pass for Mark Williams to score the goal that secured victory in the African Nations Cup final in 1996.

'The current coaching staff seem to have turned their backs on Khumalo. I think they're concentrating on players who can still be sold to Europe.'

South African soccer, like South American soccer, has always revolved around individuals. Orlando Pirates had Scara Sono and later his son Jomo, who could change the tide of the game at any moment.

Kaizer Chiefs had Kaizer Motaung and later Ace Ntsoelengoe. At Moroka Swallows there was Andries 'Panyaza' Maseko, Pretoria 'Bantu' Callies had Mecro 'Masterpieces' Moripe, while at AmaZulu there was Frederick 'Sugar Ray' Xulu. They dictated the game and often decided the result of a match.

Young Chippa Lekoelea, the Orlando Pirates player who has clashed with Troussier, also believes the foreign style doesn't work for our players.

'They don't look the same,' he says. 'They're obviously playing a foreign style. Even during our training camps the coach introduced some strange training methods.

'Our style of play includes taking on defenders with the ball. But our players are now passing the ball around unnecessarily. They don't seem to have confidence in themselves. There's no playmaker controlling the midfield and dictating the pace of the game.'

And that's the problem.

Where to now? Some coaches *Drum* spoke to believe there should be a soccer indaba to discuss the way forward.

Phil 'Mr Jones' Setshedi, Barker's former assistant, says local soccer authorities have shown they have no confidence in local coaches.

'As we bid to host the World Cup in 2006 we should develop our own coaches who understand our style,' he says. 'Look at Brazil – they've always been coached by locals.

'Troussier must know South Africa have a unique style of play that isn't like that of Ivory Coast and Burkina Faso, which he's coached,' says Setshedi.

Ted Dumitru, known as 'The Professor' because of his scientific approach to the game, shares some of Setshedi's feelings. 'It would be a waste of money to take coaches overseas,' he says. 'Let Safa develop their own coaches. If they took 100 coaches through a development programme they'd come up with one exceptionally good coach who can take charge of the national team.'

Every country which has won the World Cup has done so by playing their own style of soccer, Dumitru adds. 'If we are serious about winning the World Cup one day, we need to have our own style.'

Amagluglug coach Shakes Mashaba says he's confused when people talk about style. 'To me style is something individual,' he says. Every player has his own style. All we need to do is sit down and formulate a technical method in which various individual skills and styles can be managed together.

(Drum, 2 July 1998)

To the best of our knowledge, JM Coetzee is the only published sports writer to win the Nobel Prize for Literature. Naturally his recognition by the Swedish committee didn't owe everything to his forays into the world of sport (he chose to play to his strengths, which are fiction and criticism), but certainly 15 years before that award he was dissecting the slimy sinews of sport's more twisted ideologies.

Playing total(itarian) rugby

JM Coetzee

IN July this year, Western Province played Northern Transvaal at Newlands. The match was televised live and watched, I would guess, by most rugby fans in the country. Hours after the game was over, the first newspaper reports appeared. In the olden days these reports would have been eagerly awaited and read; but today, aside from filling in the few who might have missed the game on the box, what function could they possibly have?

For the *Argus*, Deon Viljoen and Robert Houwing chose to devote the first half of their report to the Newlands crowd and to coach Dawie Snyman's comments on its behaviour, following this with a brisk summary of high points of the game and a verdict on Western Province's performance.

For the *Sunday Times* the next morning, Ted Partridge praised Johan Heunis at fly-half and described the three tries or near-tries. In a fuller account in *Rapport*, Bokkie Gerber adjudged the game ''n misoes', putting the blame on Northerns' ten-man pattern and the refereeing of Jimmy Smith-Belton. His report consisted mainly of comment on the performance of key opposing players (Nieuwoudt versus Lock, Visser and Hugo versus Malan and Geldenhuys). In a second item, Gerber expanded on the Nieuwoudt–Lock duel and suggested that Nieuwoudt be dropped.

For these sportswriters, Saturday's assignment was now completed. Were any of their readers dissatisfied? Not if one is to judge from the correspondence columns of the newspapers. While readers may now and then write in to complain about a reporter's bias, no one seems to find the entire genre of the rugby report unsatisfactory. If the vast army of rugby followers in this country are satisfied, who am I, a middle-aged academic, to demur?

Let me give my reasons.

South Africa is a country where the arts wither and the sports flourish. It is not too much of an exaggeration to say that sport has become the opium of the masses, particularly of the white masses. SATV, the sports administrators and corporate business, no doubt with some direction from above, have collectively committed themselves to keeping the minds of the white middle class off the woes of the country with a diet of boerewors and circuses. The bomb that went off outside Ellis Park stadium was no more and no less than a deadly reminder of the reality encircling that palace of dreams.

It cannot be denied that rugby in South Africa, as it is organised and run, is deeply politicised. The SA Rugby Board is complexly intertwined with the Defence Force, with big business, and with the white political establishment. Nor is this politicisation only a matter of invisible threads of influence. In what other country in the world will one see an advertisement for a gun shop at a sport stadium, as at Newlands? The players themselves tend to be conservative in their outlook. The ethic of manliness which prevails in rugby certainly has a conservative political correlate, while the nature of the game itself, and its traditions, seems, by and large, to attract the authoritarian personality type.

Yet the argument that one should respond to the use – the exploitation – of rugby for political ends with yet another boycott is almost too dreary to bear. Having become a country of factions that refuse to listen to one another, are we to go further and refuse to watch one another as well?

Is it not possible to draw a distinction between the use of the game and the game itself, and to tolerate and accept what may be the inherent political bias of the latter? For if Northern Transvaal has taught us any lesson over the years, it is that the rugby of power and discipline and forward planning, what we may call the rugby of the Right, is winning rugby (Western Province played its best rugby in the early 1980s, when it played most like Northern Transvaal). Winning rugby: not the most attractive spectacle, necessarily, but if you want the team that plays the most attractive rugby to come out on top, you are going to have to change the rules of the game. Are those who are prepared to watch only the rugby of the Left really interested in rugby?

What politically aware sportswriting can do, given the heavily politicised environment in which rugby is played *inside* South Africa, is to help the spectator, as far as possible, to distinguish the environment of the game from the game itself, and to understand that environment. It is quite likely that the sportswriters I name in this essay would have no interest in such a project, would not share my way of seeing the problem of rugby, would not even acknowledge that there is a problem. But even if they prefer to ignore the environment, or to limit themselves to the international boycott and questions of professionalism, they can at least, in writing about the game itself, help their readers to an informed appreciation of the considerable contests of skill and controlled power that occur in Currie Cup rugby, rather than allow them to sit in what amounts to darkness waiting for the odd flash of startling individual play to lighten up the field.

One of the SATV commentators – Chick Henderson – has taken it upon himself to mix in quick lessons in the laws of the game with his commentary, for which one is grateful. But live television is not a medium in which analytical insight into the game can really be taught: the viewer is too busy *reading* the image, trying to distinguish significant action in the chaos of movement, all the while aware that his vision is framed by the rectangular field-of-vision of the camera, to be able to watch reflectively. The commentator on television or radio must remain with the *now* of the action: he can do little to help the viewer or listener to an overview extending backward into what has led up to the now and forward into what the game may, by the processes of its developing logic, become.

This, it seems to me, is where the sportswriter can play a further valuable role: by re-telling the game not simply as a chronicle of penalties kicked or not kicked, tries scored or not scored, but as a story with a palpable momentum, an inner drive, and with tensions of its own: tactical paths which should or should not have been taken, heroic or foolish individual decisions, irruptions of fate in the form of unlucky bounces. The sportswriter, that is to say, can be a critic – not the kind of critic who contents himself with delivering a verdict, with damning or praising, but one who leads the reader through the experience a second time, showing him what it is like to give a knowledgeable, skilful reading of the game.

What really gets crowds worked up at rugby matches? Answer: (a) tries scored by the home team; (b) blunders, real or imagined, by the referee; (c) fighting among the players. What gets them most excited? Answer: undoubtedly the fighting.

This is a sobering thought. Team sports are rituals evolved by the collective wisdom of cultures to formalise aggression, to teach people – principally young men in the flower of life – that there are ways of expressing one's vitality other than by beating, kicking, slaughtering, raping. But in outbursts of aggression on the field, and the flare-ups of sympathetic excitement in the stands that accompany them, we catch an intimation of the fragility of this formalisation (for which another word is civilisation). Sports – physical culture – are part of the cultural life of a society. Is it absurd to think of sportswriting as fulfilling the same critical, educational role in relation to physical culture, the culture of the body, as criticism of the arts fulfils in relation to aesthetic culture, the culture of the senses?

The Monday-morning reports on the Western Province–Northern Transvaal game – by Gerhard Kirsten for *Die Burger* and Ian Smit for the *Cape Times* – were, understandably, more analytical than Sunday's reports. Nevertheless, both led off with rather sensationalistic front-page comment on crowd behaviour. 'Western Province fans blamed for defeat,' said the *Cape Times* headline, twisting Dawie Snyman's words slightly. 'Nuwelandgangers skaad Westelike Provinsie se naam,' said *Die Burger*. (Newlands fans have been booing Northern Transvaal for donkey's years. Nor has Jimmy Smith-Belton ever been given a fair deal at Newlands. Does the reputation claimed by Kirsten for Newlands, as a ground 'waar goeie spel toegejuig en skeidsregterbeslissings ... aanvaar is', have a basis in fact, or is it perhaps just a story Capetonians like to tell one another?)

It would be silly for me to quibble over details with commentators as experienced as Kirsten and Smit, except perhaps in one respect. Kirsten calls the Saturday 'in alle opsigte 'n teleurstellende dag', and claims that 'rugby het verloor'. I wonder. I found the game absorbing, a lesson in how a team with less talent at its disposal, less in the way of resources, can compel its opponents to play to its strengths. It was an object lesson in planning, preparation and execution. Rather than deploring all ten-man rugby, it seems to me that a rugby-writer would be more constructively occupied in rehearsing for his readers the repertory of counter-plays available against kicking half-backs, and exploring why Western Province could not successfully apply these counters against Heunis and Du Preez.

What more could one demand of correspondents than is given by Kirsten and (to a lesser extent) by Smit? In what follows I write not only as a spectator with 30 years' worth of memories of what the experience of watching a game of football can be, but as a writer with my own ideas of what writing can do to match and recreate lived experience.

A rugby match is an event that takes place in time, and all the feelings it gives rise to (which include tension, anticipation, anxiety, disappointment, joy) have time as their natural medium. No event on the field occurs in isolation: it occurs in the context of what has come before it, and in turn becomes part of the context of what succeeds it. When what is happening before our eyes is just a series of events belonging to no structure in time, interest flags, no matter how inherently spectacular the events themselves may be (that is why 'highlights' programmes on television leave one cold by comparison with the real thing).

Analytical accounts, because they break up chronology, because they break up the unfolding story, isolating incidents and actors no longer in time but in the new space of the text, fail to create – or recreate – the game as a dramatic experience. No one reading even as competent a report as Kirsten's can have any sense of what it was like to see the game, whether in the stadium or on television. For this reason it is up to the sportswriter with real ambitions to give the reader something of his own experience of the game *in time*, as it is up to him to help the spectator discriminate and understand the phases of emotion with which he responds to the game. (Helping to make the spectator's emotional life accessible to him has always been one of the noblest and most important educative tasks of aesthetic criticism.)

I do not want to end this essay on a dire note. I have no complaints about the standard of rugby being played in this country. What does disturb me however – if I am to judge from the people in whose company I watched the Western Province–Northern Transvaal game in the stand at Newlands – is how little of this good rugby is actually being *seen*. Similar comments might be made about the cricket public, and we all know what happened to cricket as a result: a simplified version of the game – one-day cricket – tailored to the limitations of uneducated spectators, was created, whose poor relation real cricket has now become.

When rugby in South Africa goes professional, and links with the International Rugby Board are broken, it is inevitable that there will be pressure for the rules to be rationalised. In itself this will be no bad thing. But, when it happens, what will dictate the changes: the inherent logic of the game, or the spectacle value of the result? If the decision is that the game should be rationalised to maximise its spectacle value for an unsophisticated viewership, this country's sportswriters will have to bear part of the blame.

(Die Suid-Afrikaan, August 1988)

Harmony with the hacks

Mark Keohane

There was a time when we – rugby writers – were on tour, but in fact were in the trenches fighting a war. Isolation, its legacy still prevalent every so often, had divided more than just provincial affiliations. Players were gods. Journalists were vultures, parasites, scum … the lowest common denominator. We toured together, but as opposition.

A good headline and report meant you were a 'good oke', maybe even good enough to be seen in the company of these giants. But report the facts, the disaster on the day, the lack of cohesion up front and an indifferent display from the ace in the pack, and the 'good oke' was no more. Instead the vulture had turned sensationalist – and hell, why did he have to be so negative? Why did he even have to be here?

The game has moved on. It has changed. Thankfully, so have the mindsets of players, managers and coaches. Touring now, with a professional rugby side, be it at provincial, Super 12 or international level, is made more enjoyable because of these changing mindsets.

Look, there will always be the player personality who clashes with the media personality. It's an accepted form of rugby life. You'll find your Dr Jekyll and Mr Hyde in each camp. But the 'rugby rage' between writer and player, a characteristic of those first few years back from isolation, is very much a minority occurrence.

Carel du Plessis's ill-fated tour of Australia and New Zealand as Springbok coach was the exception. It was the tour from hell and the angelic Du Plessis assumed the persona of one robbed of his halo.

In my experience as a rugby writer, it was probably the worst tour to cover. Players were barred from any form of communication with the travelling media. And when you're in a foreign country for a month it is difficult to miss one another in the hotel lifts, at the local shopping complex and at the only cinema in town.

It wasn't easy, especially when the coach has already had you removed from the hotel floor because he discovers his players are on that floor, and you're the men with the pens. Memories!

Nick Mallett, very much like John Hart did with the All Blacks, has put an end to a war that was harming rugby. Mallett understands the media and appreciates their contribution to the game. In return he asks the media to respect the role of the players. It is a simple trade-off.

So when my mates put me on the spot and quiz me about my job, I can now say, with conviction, that I have one of the greatest grafts imaginable. I get paid to watch rugby. If you're a fan of Jack Daniels and his mates, it's a bit like getting paid to sit in on an all-expenses-paid session with Uncle Jack.

Momentarily, as is common with any job, I ponder the prospects of another profession: one that gets me out of bed at 7 a.m. and into an office at 8.30. It is then that I realise the torture of such an existence and bellow out a thank-you to the career gods for what I do for a living. Hell, I could have been an accountant.

Yes, touring with the Stormers, Western Province and the Boks has its moments. When results don't favour us South Africans, these moments, some unsavoury, can be made to feel like a lifetime.

But it gives me great pleasure to report that these sports icons are human. They miss their wives and girlfriends, long for familiarity, the pressure-free existence of an afternoon on Clifton's coolest sandpit and the luxury most would call home.

Life on the road, these days, can amount to anything between four and six months for players and journalists alike. And when the results aren't going South Africa's way, player A becomes an irritation and journalist A, invariably, becomes an extenuating circumstance for any irrational player behaviour.

Fortunately, these occasions have become fewer. Mallett and Bok assistant Alan Solomons have added a new dimension at a national level and for me, locally, WP and Stormers coach Harry Viljoen had a similar impact before he stepped down.

They make touring with the national and provincial teams enjoyable and a half-decent working experience. They appreciate deadline pressures and the difficulty of having to compose a 1 000-word match report within 20 minutes of the final whistle; sometimes on final whistle. They understand and, because of this, it is only reasonable that the journalists understand them.

Touring, despite appearances, is not all glamour: hectic training sessions, early curfews because of the importance of the match and daily emotional strains are aspects of a player's life on tour the public are conveniently ignorant of.

I've seen it: where the public demand control of the player. Why? Because they've travelled 12 000 miles to support Andre Joubert, James Small and Percival Montgomery.

And there the trio are, just metres away from Billy Bronco and his pal Henk Heckle. I've seen it and smiled quietly, once again thanking the career gods that I'm not among the trio or the deadly duo about to inconvenience the three.

I've smiled, but I've also been angered at the arrogance of the deadly duo. One such occasion was at a hotel bar in Manly, Australia. The Boks had been beaten in a Tri-Nations match. The players, having returned from the ground close to the pumpkin hour – it was an 8 p.m. kick-off – wanted a quiet drink. Billy and Henk wanted a bit more.

Henk put it to Mr Joubert: 'I want a jersey, or at least a tracksuit ...'. Billy weighed in with a tongue-lashing as to the deficiencies in Joubert's make-up as a player.

When Joubert, and in this instance Henry Honiball, politely thanked Billy for sharing his wisdom and requested a gangway for escape, adulation (in a bizarre way) turned to abuse.

Players don't deserve it. Yet, they are powerless to stop it. It comes with the career, in much the same way as the good and bad headline does.

It isn't easy on the player and perhaps this is why I'll always have a soft spot for the 1993 WP squad that toured Australia and New Zealand. They got hammered on a tour that was nothing less than a suicidal mission. Officials were keen to visit Brisbane, Christchurch and Auckland within the space of 10 days. Hence the itinerary.

The reports were not favourable. The press was not good. But few of the guys took it personally. The likes of Keith Andrews, Andrew Paterson, Christian Stewart and Garry Pagel simply reminded me that if they accepted the good headline, they could not justify rebuking the bad headline. It was part of the media package in sport; a profession which allows you a second chance every Saturday.

Life on tour can be good – and it has been made even more convenient by a maturing squad of Springboks. The Boks are a good bunch of guys. But, even though one spends nearly half the year in their company, they will never be my mates. And I will never be theirs. The conflict in the respective professions does not allow for the luxury of a buddy system. But both professions do allow for moments of unrivalled ecstasy. The opening match of the World Cup, the World Cup final and any win against the Poms at Twickenham.

We all talk about those moments. I consider it a privilege to be able to express my thoughts to an audience. And whenever I have these momentary flashes questioning why I am in this wonderful world of professional rugby, I think of a career staring at a balance sheet. I think and then I thank, because I'll take touring with the Boks any day – even those dark, dark days of 1992 when the player was the god and the journalist the vulture.

(SA Sports Illustrated Fans Guide, 1995)

The will to win

Andy Capostagno

While Jake White busies himself growing back some hair, he has earned the right to carve this motto above his dressing-room mirror: 'I told you so'. The Springbok coach has earned instant celebrity status by guiding his team to the Tri-Nations trophy merely by keeping his own counsel and backing his own judgement.

When South Africa played Ireland in June, De Wet Barry was busy battling back from injury. White ignored the claims of a dozen players and called up Wayne Julies, a player so lightly regarded by the Currie Cup unions that he was allowed to languish in the Slough of Despond, a man without a contract, but not, apparently, without hope.

It's hard to recall now that Ireland were regarded as favourites for those two Tests. The selection of Julies seemed an aberration, one that the coach made in haste and would regret at leisure. But Julies did the one thing that all coaches hope for: by the quality of his play he made it damn hard to drop him.

But White knew that he wanted Barry and Marius Joubert in midfield and, when the moment came, he did not pussyfoot around. Julies was dropped with thanks, and remained a valued member of the squad. His reward is a contract with the Eagles and almost certainly a trip to Britain and Argentina at the end of the year.

Julies's story bears comparison with that of Jacques Cronje. The Bulls' eighth man was not part of White's original squad. The coach made it clear from day one that he wanted Joe van Niekerk because he added an attacking dimension unique in South Africa.

Cronje played his heart out in New Zealand and Australia and his reward was to be benched as soon as Big Joe was ready. Very few critics agreed with White's selection for the Ellis Park Test against the All Blacks. Van Niekerk could not conceivably have been match fit, but for an hour he made life a misery for Andrew Mehrtens.

When Cronje was thrown on for the last 20 minutes he played as though he'd never been away, set up the hat-trick try for Joubert and did all the things that Van Niekerk had done for the first 60 minutes. And yet there was never any doubt who would play number eight against Australia last week, and Cronje now knows that if he wants to make the starting line-up it will be in the number seven jersey, because the number eight is locked up.

Then there were White's bolters: Percy Montgomery and Jaco van der Westhuyzen, plucked from Newport and Leicester respectively, and Os du Randt, plucked from his cattle farm in the Free State. Each man has played every Test of White's reign and not one would have been seriously considered in any pre-season poll.

Du Randt was told to get himself fit and prove that he could play 80 minutes with forwards a decade younger. It seemed utter madness for the coach to show such faith in a broken down-old man, yet Du Randt came through with his mighty reputation enhanced and the ringing approbation of the crowd every time he touched the ball: '*AAAwwwwssss,*' they cried.

Yet the rehabilitation of Du Randt was nothing compared to the epiphany of Montgomery.

Only towards the end of eight trying Tests did Monty's halo slip. Under pressure, his place-kicking technique faltered and, as a result, South Africa's opponents were in the game longer than they might otherwise have been.

Van der Westhuyzen's legacy will be that with him in the side South Africans finally understood the modern truth: that the flyhalf is just another player, not the be-all and end-all of the game.

The point of the foregoing is that Du Randt, Montgomery and Van der Westhuyzen were human. They had good games and bad games, but they were allowed to grow into their roles. At no stage did White ever consider dropping them. When games are tight, and remember that three of South Africa's four Tri-Nations games were decided by four points or fewer, players perform because they know they are appreciated: just ask Victor Matfield.

Any fool can pick a Schalk Burger or a Jean de Villiers, because these are manifestly great players. But coaches with skills that extend beyond the ability to organise a *koppe-stamp* session understand that success comes from finding the extra desire in ordinary players.

That is what White has achieved this year and even if things were to go pear-shaped hence-forward, he should be able to relax for the next few weeks and remind his critics of that pithy motto: 'I told you so'.

(Mail & Guardian, 27 August 2004)

RUGBY WORLD CUP 1995

Rugby World Cup final day in June 1995 will remain forever large in the imaginations of many South Africans. It was a day that had it all – the massed icons of the new South Africa, the flyover, the pomp and ceremony – but it had that little bit extra, too. A conspicuously gifted side in the All Blacks played against a talented but nowhere near as able team in the Springboks. The All Blacks, after all, had Zinzan Brooke in their midst, a No. 8 who had already kicked a drop-goal from the halfway line in the competition. As for the Springboks, going into the final they had a head of steam. They had triumphed in the lashing rain of Durban against France and the momentum of the moment was beginning to swing their way. Bring on Nelson Mandela and the cool boot of Joel Stransky and it all boiled down to the story of grim courage and determination – and a well-timed drop-kick here and there.

– Luke Alfred

What was that about sports writers making grandiose predictions that invariably never come true? Once again, a veteran scribe was in full soothsay, and the auguries were good … But frankly it didn't matter a hill of beans whether he said the Springboks would win in style with a glut of tries, or by grinding it out as they did in the end: it was the pre-match sentiment that counted. He believed the home team could edge out the All Blacks, because the home team believed they could. And the home team believed it, because the South African public believed it. And they believed it, well, because most of them didn't know much about rugby, but they knew we had Chester and James and Francois and, most of all, Madiba. And if Madiba is with you, who can be against you?

Recipe for success

Andy Capostagno

How will South Africa win the World Cup? The short answer is, in style. South Africa are not England, thank God. Jack Rowell's claims that England are now playing total rugby were blown out of the water against Scotland when his team clinched the Grand Slam at Twickenham in March.

Against the familiar Scottish spoiling game, England looked as full of ideas as a sieve of water. They had to fall back on old faithful, Rob Andrew, to kick them to victory. Brian Moore's much publicised post-match whingeing showed how bereft of real flair this England team is.

Rowell would give his eye teeth to get his hands on a few Springboks to bolster his side. Andre Joubert, Gavin Johnson, Chester Williams, James Small, Joost van der Westhuizen, Ruben Kruger and Pieter du Randt would all walk into the England team if they were not turning out for the World Cup winners-elect.

The difference between the two teams is the difference between Africa and Europe – South Africa has style, England only has an attitude.

Why am I going on about England? Because it seems that Will Carling wishes his team to meet South Africa in the quarterfinals. Carling has gone so far as to suggest that England might contrive to lose their final Pool match against Western Samoa if it should prove to be a way of avoiding Australia at the next stage.

This is bumptious arrogance of the most English kind and Carling deserves to have his face splattered with egg if his team has the bad fortune to play South Africa in the quarterfinals.

The great Irish centre and flyhalf, Mike Gibson, is far less impressed with the English way of playing than he is with the breadth and scope of which South Africa is capable. After the Springboks had beaten Wales 20–12 at Cardiff Arms Park last November, Gibson was full of praise.

'Wales will be content,' he said, 'because they'll feel that in the World Cup they will be able to compete in a negative sense of moving the ball forward slowly until they get within range of Neil Jenkins's boot. By contrast, South Africa, with mere crumbs of possession, produced three superb tries. Those, together with the performance against Scotland, will, I hope, make British coaches start to think about their methods.'

It takes an outsider to show how highly regarded South Africa are in world terms. Don't believe the hype coming out of Australia, because it is only hype. The Wallabies are scared of the Springboks because they know what Gibson knows, that with the players at Christie's command, South Africa can score tries from the most unpromising of situations.

I have said it before and I'll say it again, South Africa will win the World Cup with tries, not penalty kicks. The Springboks will conquer by emulating William Webb Ellis – they will pick up the ball and run with it.

Against good teams, and England are a good, if limited, team, the Springboks cannot expect the glut of possession that propelled them to a nine try victory against Western Samoa. Instead they must live on their wits, an area where England seem only half prepared.

There will never come a time when the Springbok forwards fail completely. The scrum is good enough, the mauling isn't bad, and with Ruben Kruger in the side, the rucking is wonderful. The Springboks might win only 50 percent of their own line-out ball, and hardly any of their opponents'. That is what happened against Wales when Mark Andrews had his least significant game at international level. And yet they scored three tries.

It is likely that against Australia and England the Springboks can expect about the same ration of line-out ball, and against those sides they will not be able to score as freely as against the underachieving Welsh. In which case, it would be advisable to keep the ball in play.

Remember that South Africa alone will have a squad full of match-hardened players by the time the World Cup arrives. The European sides will all be out of season, Australia simply doesn't have a very competitive domestic structure and only the All Blacks are likely to last a match as well as the Springboks.

As Muhammad Ali proved 21 years ago against the fearsome George Foreman, if you can tire your opponent the battle is half won. Christie realised that simple fact early on in his appointment to the top job.

'If players are fit, they can make decisions better. They don't have to worry about how their bodies are coping and their minds can run free,' he said.

Gibson spotted it in the UK. 'What the Springboks have managed to do is to get freedom into their game and to show that it can work at international level.' Maybe our president has had something to do with that (Mandela, not Luyt).

Under Christie, even such unpromising physical specimens as Tommie Laubscher reached unprecedented levels of fitness in the UK. Christie's attitude is right, as well. He gives guidelines for play, but expects his players to think for themselves once they are on the park. It is sad to think that he is almost unique in giving that trust, but then he has some fabulous players at his disposal.

There will be accidents of course. Joost will ignore an overlap at a crucial time, Andre will drop the ball behind his own line, James will let his temper get the better of him. But all of that is irrelevant if the rest of the team is committed to the kind of total rugby which cannot help but succeed. Australia won the final against England in 1991 with a classic prop's try. Tony Daly and Ewan McKenzie flopped over the line together after Willie Ofahengaue had won the ball at the tail of the line-out. South Africa could also win this year's final with a prop's try, but Du Randt will have thrown a sidestep or two on his way over the line from 20 metres out, and he will have three teammates on his shoulder screaming for the pass!

(SA Sports Illustrated, June 1995)

Sealed with a kick

Joel Stransky

20 May – Saturday

We woke up looking forward to the World Cup launch luncheon, but the weather – rainy with blustery winds – put a damper on an otherwise great day. We headed for Groot Constantia – and if I say so myself, we were looking hell of a smart in our new kit. Being the host nation, we had to be there first to welcome the other teams. At rugby occasions like this, I realise just how fortunate I am to have been involved in this great game and to have made so many friends throughout the world. Back at the hotel we had a planning session, dinner and another quiet evening of pool. Shaky for a Saturday night! I have renamed my roommate, Mark Andrews, 'Fridge', because he freezes on the blackball.

25 May – Thursday

After a good night's sleep – believe it or not – we began the day of our opening match against Australia with a short jog and stretch. Rudolf Straeuli and I took time out to have a haircut, not vanity, just a psychological thing common amongst a lot of rugby players.

The reception we received on arrival at the stadium, and when we appeared on the field, was absolutely fabulous. And at this stage, the 15 playing were the most relaxed, and the coach was probably the most tense of all. But his job was done and done well! The crowd was amazing. To see all the flags, and hear the shouting and singing was amazing. The support we received from the whole of SA was great. The anthems were a few stirring moments and we stood hand on chest as we had decided before.

At halftime we were up by one point, yet we had not played well. Francois had some harsh words of criticism for us and we picked up our heads and turned on the gas.

The feeling after the game was one of total elation and we all knew that we had done ourselves and our country proud. We also knew that we still had a long road forward, yet with all the praise and compliments, it will be hard to keep our feet on the ground – I hope we can, I am sure we will.

4 June – Sunday

The feeling in camp today after the Canada match was quiet and worried. To lose James Dalton when he was playing great rugby was a great blow. Management will definitely be appealing and, after watching the video, he should get off as he didn't punch or kick. However, the bad news this evening was that Pieter Hendriks is to be cited for kicking. Other reasons for worry – my eye is swollen closed, but according to a specialist, the damage isn't too bad (abrasion on cornea and inflammation inside and swelling); Hannes's eye is also not good and Gavin Johnson is possibly concussed.

17 June – Saturday

Who would ever have expected a game in Durban to be delayed due to too much water on the field and to be played in those conditions?

Once we had arrived at the stadium, the frustration began. All the delays meant that we kicked off an hour and a half late, and warmed up three times. The most frustrating part was being ready to play, and then having to relax and calm oneself down.

By the time the game finally began, we were just happy to be getting on with the job. The game itself was a wet and close affair and we were pretty relieved when the final whistle sounded. The last four minutes were testing and all credit must go to the forwards for a fantastic scrumming performance. We were elated to be in the final.

22 June – Thursday

This morning's practice was dreadful. No concentration nor commitment and I left the field convinced that we could not beat the All Blacks. Maybe it is just stress and tension, and if so, we must relax and not let the moment be too big for us.

The emphasis at this stage is all on Jonah Lomu and I am sure James [Small] is feeling the pressure. But he has nothing to worry about. If anyone can handle Lomu, it's James. We have discussed our defence pattern to counteract him, but all James will do is not show him the outside gap and force him inside where we have numbers.

24 June – Saturday

To actually describe the day that has just passed is virtually impossible. It is greater than any fairy-tale and bigger than any dream come true. To sit here and think that we have won the World Cup is unbelievable. To think that I kicked the winning kick in extra time is even more of a dream.

While we were strapping and changing, we had a surprise visit by the President to wish us luck. This was inspirational enough, but for him to be wearing a Springbok jersey and cap was an amazing sight. Mr Mandela visiting us in his Springbok kit is one of the highlights of the World Cup for me.

Walking down the tunnel to go out onto the field, I walked beside Lomu – the man is a monster. I had not seen him up close before, but to see him there in the flesh gave me a bit of a shock. But the shock passed as he is, after all, only human. The bigger they are, the harder they fall, as long as they don't fall on top of you!

The whole atmosphere was brilliant with everyone singing and waving their new South Africa flags. The anthems once again touched our hearts, and to stand there in front of the whole world singing *Nkosi Sikelel' iAfrika* and *Die Stem* was one of the proudest moments of our lives. Then we faced the haka. The haka is a challenge and I believe one must always face up to a challenge, so we stepped forward and closer and threw down a challenge of our own.

The game itself was exactly what you'd expect of a World Cup Final – tight, hard and bruising. The key to our game throughout the World Cup has been our discipline and defence, and once again, both were outstanding. Lomu was restricted and not a factor, and instead the game became a gruelling forward battle, ultimately decided on kicks. We did, however, cross the line for what we believe was a perfectly good try, but Ed Morrison didn't think so. We also got blown for a forward pass when we would surely have scored, and again it seemed a tough call. But we did finish off as the winners, so these two possible mistakes are forgotten. We are a very fit side and going into extra time didn't worry us. I managed to produce the greatest moment of my life and hit the winning drop-goal. After that it was a matter of hanging on for the Cup, and that we did.

It is impossible to describe the feelings and overwhelming emotions that we experienced on our victory lap and are still experiencing now, but we are, and rightfully so, a very proud Springbok rugby squad.

Not only proud of our victory, but proud to be South Africans and proud of what we have done for South Africa. We have helped unify and unite our country, and watched as our team motto of 'One Team, One Country' became reality. To have been partly responsible and to have 'made a difference' is a wonderful feeling.

(SA Sports Illustrated, August 1995)

The final

Dan Retief

Olé! Olé! Olé! Now finally we *are* the rugby champions of the world! In an atmosphere of excruciating tension, South Africa won the Rugby World Cup for 1995 after the match had been forced into extra time with the teams deadlocked at 9–9 at the end of 80 minutes.

On an afternoon that a jam-packed Ellis Park crowd were almost too nervous to cheer, the Springboks three times fell behind a more imaginative All Blacks team and each time clawed their way back to provide a platform within range of the posts for the boot of Joel Stransky.

It was Stransky, the man inexplicably discarded for last year's tour to New Zealand, who triggered an explosion of sound and clinched the Springboks' victory with his second dropkick of the match in the 92nd minute – the 12th of the two periods of 10 minutes extra time each way. It was the Western Province pivot's second drop of the match and it gave him the distinction of having scored all his team's points in the final. Fittingly, the winning kick took Stransky's career total in Tests to 132 points – surpassing Piet Visagie to now be the second most prolific scorer, after Naas Botha, in Springbok history.

In the end, victory in the World Cup was a tribute to South Africa's committed tackling and their dauntless spirit of resolution. With the All Blacks' sinuous lock Ian Jones giving an exceptional performance in the lineouts, South Africa were always under pressure as the ball spun down the Kiwi line.

With the All Blacks playing with more rhythm, it seemed for long periods that the black panthers would have success – either in creating space for the dreadnought on the left, Jonah Lomu, or by exploiting the extra attention the Springboks were paying to New Zealand's lethal weapon.

But on the day the Springboks revealed the determination and sheer bloody-mindedness to hole the big cruiser below the water line whenever he threatened. Francois Pienaar and Mark Andrews brought off a big hit on the youngster early on and a thumping tackle by Japie Mulder had the effect of galvanising a Springbok team who seemed to be fading midway through the second half.

With the Boks applying the tactic of positioning James Small wider in the tramlines, Lomu was often forced inside or unable to get into his stride. And the moment the crowd had feared, when Lomu was finally given a run on the outside, was snuffed out by Mulder.

With the big prize of the William Webb Ellis Trophy beckoning at the end of their first World Cup, the Springboks seemed more tense than the All Blacks and seldom moved the ball on the open side, preferring to work the short side or kick the ball into the corners or into touch.

It was a tactic which could have backfired as the All Blacks had an exceptionally high number of throw-ins and Jones was always up to the task – even though the powerful punting of both Stransky and Andre Joubert was a feature of the match. In the circumstances it was puzzling that the Springboks did not give Mark Andrews the job of attaching himself to the All Blacks' danger man.

In spite of the All Blacks' greater fluency, the fact that the Springboks had the best chance of scoring a try gave them a moral edge. Pieter du Randt, Hannes Strydom and Ruben Kruger will go to their graves convinced that the loosehead prop had been driven over the line after a scrum on the All Blacks' goal line.

Moments later, referee Ed Morrison might have erred in not allowing the Boks a bit more time when they again had momentum and a pushover try was a possibility. Instead the referee awarded a penalty which Stransky goaled to make the score 6–6 after 20 minutes.

Stransky's first drop made it 9–6 after 31 minutes and in the second half, with first one side and then the other threatening, a solitary drop by the All Blacks' slick little flyhalf Mehrtens in the 54th minute deadlocked the score at 9-all.

The Springboks feared the draw, which might have made the sending off of James Dalton in Port Elizabeth a cruel decision if the team could not be separated on score or tries, but it was the All Blacks who held the territorial ascendancy.

Over 60 000 hearts stopped beating when Mehrtens was put in an ideal drop-in position, 35 m in front of the posts, but fortunately for the Boks the kicked slewed off to the right.

They gained a psychological boost when the All Blacks were given a penalty near the centre spot within seconds of the two periods of the extra time starting. Mehrtens, with an incredible kick, raised the flags to put New Zealand 12–9 up.

An up-and-under by Stransky and the spirited chase saw the Boks force a maul just before the changeover and it was Shaun Fitzpatrick who was called up for diving over the top. Stransky's nerve held, the kick from 35 m went over and it was 12–12.

With no tries and the score deadlocked, the Springboks knew they had to score. A draw would have brought the discipline clause into play and the cup would have gone back to New Zealand.

And then came the sequence which made the Springboks the world champions. Rudolf Straeuli won a 22 m drop-out after Andre Joubert had put the ball deep. The Bok pack forced a scrum, a wheel, re-set and then Joost van der Westhuizen sent the ball spinning to Stransky. Catch, drop, foot swinging through and Ellis Park erupted.

South Africans' musketeer spirit of all for one and one for all held for all of the 104 mins it took to decide a winner, and the epic journey which started against the same traditional and respected opponents at Ellis Park in August 1992 ended with the Springboks back on top of the world.

(Sunday Times, 25 June 1995)

Glorious last hurrah ends an era

Colin Bryden

Rugby, after South Africa's triumphant day, may never be the same again. The last hurrah of the old amateur game could not have been more rugged or, finally, more glorious.

When the euphoria of Rugby World Cup '95 wears off, players and agents will consider their options and study contracts, preparing for the new age of rugby that was launched by Louis Luyt and the Rupert Murdoch millions on Friday.

Whatever they earn, it is no more than the players deserve. The physical intensity and the mental pressures of a World Cup may be the stuff of manhood but, in a modern world, they must be accompanied by monetary reward.

If ever there was a kick without price it was Joel Stransky's soaring, magnificent drop goal deep into extra time in what may be the last supposedly amateur World Cup final. The roar that greeted it was deafening but it took seven more agonising minutes before the crowd could celebrate without reserve. When the final whistle blew, the roof of the stadium was in more danger than it had been when SAA's jumbo jet flew low above it in the most spectacular of yesterday's pre-match stunts.

The tension yesterday was palpable, far more so than for the opening match at Newlands. Whereas Newlands was a celebration, an outpouring of joyful emotion, with the ceremonies as much a part of the event as the game itself, yesterday the festivities seemed to take forever.

It was an age before the players appeared. Even then singers were still, futilely, on the field, their pre-recorded voices drowned by a crowd eager for real action.

The legendary impassivity of the All Blacks was tested to the limit on this all-South African day. While the New Zealand players paced about the field before going to change, there were unsuccessful efforts to coach the crowd to sing *Shosholoza* and most of the music that blared out of the Ellis Park speakers had a home flavour. During the break before extra time, the crowd waved their flags to the catchy but inconsequential 'Hier kom die Bokke'.

Flags! What a contrast to 1992 and the shameful last stand of the old South Africa when Ellis Park was tinged with orange and blue. Yesterday the bright colours of the new flag were everywhere, although some of the old fluttered defiantly.

Nelson Mandela's appearance in a Springbok jersey rubbed in to the New Zealanders the extent of the mountain they had to climb.

From the confrontation of the haka, when Jonah Lomu and Ruben Kruger were within punching distance of each other, to the anxiety of the closing minutes, there was not a moment of compromise. It might not have been one of rugby's great classics but it was a titanic battle.

According to the SABC's Robin Kempthorne, as many as two billion people may have watched yesterday's match. With the influence of the President having made rugby into a rainbow sport, many, many South Africans were among them.

Rugby in South Africa has been carried to new heights of popularity and acceptability.

The challenge, when the Murdoch money starts to flow, will be to ensure that rugby, having become a sport of all the people, strikes a balance between making money and building on the new base of support. If future television viewing should be confined to those with enough money for satellite dishes or decoders, then much of the good of this World Cup will have been undone.

Today, though, a nation can bask in the joy of celebration. The challenges are tomorrow.

(Sunday Times, 25 June 1995)

Retrospect: the World Cup of rugby

JM Coetzee

The rugby football World Cup is over and South Africa has won. The country – it is even possible to say the country as a whole – experienced a flush of pride in the achievement of a team that had become, or was on the brink of becoming, their team. Though not the most talented or inventive outfit on show, it was solid in all departments, well-drilled and determined. It beat into second place a New Zealand team that may have been better on paper but on the day of reckoning made too many jittery mistakes.

So much for the rugby itself. But the Cup of Nations is not just a sporting event. It is the occasion for a month-long orgy of chauvinism and mime-show of war among nations. In South Africa in particular it was unabashedly promoted as a nation-building exercise. So it is not unsporting to look back in a critical spirit on the events of the Cup, and specifically on the opening and closing ceremonies, where the philosophy (if one can for the moment prostitute that venerable word) behind the World Cup bared itself particularly nakedly.

These ceremonies, modified, at the behest of the roving eye of the television cameras, away from old-style brass bands and marching phalanxes in the direction of the kind of extravaganza associated with Miss Universe, betrayed how the designers of the spectacle – specialists hired by the businessmen or operators or whatever one calls the men who run the game – conceive of the new South Africa. The new South Africa they mounted at Newlands and Ellis Park seems very different from the South Africa put on exhibition by the old regime in the spectacles it organised – to begin with, it is much more feminine, without any grim-faced militaristic muscle-flexing. At a deeper level, however, it is disturbingly similar, so similar, in fact, that one might call the concept (to adopt the word I am sure its developers use) naive, at the very least.

The master-image behind the two ceremonies was clearly Archbishop

Desmond Tutu's 'Rainbow People', modified for the occasion into 'Rainbow Nation'. The rainbow metaphor does not originate with Tutu, of course: he brought it back from his travels in America, where it had most recently served Jesse Jackson (for whom a 'rainbow coalition' of interest groups was intended to secure the 1988 Democratic nomination), but where it would seem already to have had a long history as a metaphor for the ethnically diverse.

'Rainbow' thus enters South African discourse in a self-aware fashion as an ideological term, a substitute for a long series of discredited synonyms: 'plural', 'veelvolkig', and the like. It absolves itself of the taint of mere synonymy by the instrumental intention behind it: it is to be set to work to reverse the mindset of a population locked by its former masters into ethnic-political compartments. Specifically, it predicates the nation as a mental construct and nationhood as a collective state of mind. If a group of people can be encouraged to believe they are a nation and to act together as a nation, then they are a nation.

This conception of what nationhood consists in differs sharply from the conception that underlay apartheid, at least in its pristine years, and that still underlies such movements as Boere Afrikanerdom and Zulu nationalism, which set as prerequisites a common history, a common relation to a common territory, a common culture, and (most strikingly though also most vaguely) shared 'blood'.

The World Cup and the ballyhoo surrounding it were used by at least some of its South African backers as a vehicle for promoting South African nationalism. The team selected by the South African Rugby Football Union, too, was promoted as the embodiment of the nation. At a deeper level, rugby was used by the medium (television-sports or sports-television) to promote the idea that a nation and a national consciousness are to all intents and purposes the same thing, and therefore that sounds and images, if numerous and powerful enough, can create a nation.

What did these opening and closing ceremonies show us? Since history is still a contentious subject in South Africa, and the struggle for authority over the making of national history by no means over, the opening ceremony made an attempt to be history-less. It presented a de-historicised vision of Tourist South Africa: contented tribesfolk and happy mineworkers, as in the old South Africa, but purified and sanctified, somehow, by the

Rainbow. When it got to the paler end of the spectrum, however, it found that it could not proceed without becoming, intermittently, not only a pageant but an historical pageant as well. And so, to the procession of timeless Sotho in blankets and timeless Zulu in ostrich feathers it had to add what looked very much like happy eighteenth-century slaves and slaveowners in knee-breeches, bearing baskets of agricultural produce to the Rainbow feast. There were also, somewhere in the middle of the pageant, half a dozen lost-looking lads in khaki shirts and shorts whose presence seemed to be more symbolic than iconic (Were they Voortrekkers? Baden-Powell Pioneers? Mere generic whites?).

From the moment when the rainbow-procession into the Newlands stadium turned historical – a moment that was foreseeable, given the naiveté of the people who dreamed up the spectacle, to say nothing of the soteriological impulse behind Tutu's notion of a Rainbow People (a people who have passed through the fires of history and to that extent are elect or at least special) – it became difficult not to be aware of what was present in and was absent from this new history. Particularly difficult for someone like myself, who as a child had been dragooned into marching in the Van Riebeeck festivities that celebrated three hundred years of white Christian civilisation in Africa.

Who, in 1995, were the principal absentees? The list begins with Jan van Riebeeck himself, and cuts a swathe through all the colonial founding fathers, from Simon van der Stel to Piet Retief to Cecil John Rhodes. But it also includes Moshoeshoe, Gandhi, Luthuli. No Famous Men at all, in fact, no Famous Women, just People, of various tribes, Shangaan and Pedi but no Huguenots, no 1820 Settlers. Muslims and Indians but no Jews. More disturbingly, no San, no Khoi (and this on the continent, according to the theme song, 'where the world began'). Coon *kaskenades* but no *volkspele*. Gumboot-dancing but no *tiekiedraai*.

If the representation of the host country stepped a fine line between ethnic stereotyping and the service of the Rainbow concept, the rest of the opening ceremony was an uninhibited riot of clichés: gaucho Argentinians, matelot Frenchmen, gondolier Italians, shamrock-green Irish leprechauns – the parts all played by bewildered children watched over by angel-maidens in sexy, diaphanous white robes, children who had twenty seconds to shuffle about in the appropriate national dance before they were shunted off the platform to make way for the next nation.

When it came to the larger ex-colonies, rainbow nations in their own right, the image-makers faced a dilemma. What ethnic icons were appropriate to such countries as Canada and Australia? They settled, rather lamely, for a form of apartheid: in the opening ceremony the Canadians were clad in democratic blue jeans, the Australians in bushranger kit; in the closing ceremony the aboriginals had their day in the sun, beating drums, blowing didgeridoos.

Of course the moment to wait for was the relevation of how the puzzle was to be solved of setting on the platform a single image of the Rainbow People. Were we going to have a cluster of happy black, white, coloured and Indian faces as in the 'plural' South Africa of old ('One country, many nations')? And what were they going to wear? The solution that emerged from the hat had an air of desperation about it: cute black *pikkies* in mine overalls and helmets *(pikkie* from Portuguese *pequeno*, little; its English cousin has dropped out of polite usage).

For some, the opening and closing ceremonies were colourful extravaganzas, fun events that stirred the blood and brought tears to the eyes. For others, the predominating emotion was relief – relief that the ceremonies began and ended on time, that the sound system worked, that the choreography, if not exactly snappy, at least did not get into an irremediable muddle in front of the world's cameras, that only once (a bejewelled singer borne into the stadium in a litter on the shoulders of muscular old-Egyptian slaves) did we plumb the depths of Sol Kerzner-type tastelessness.

In my own case, it was the World Cup anthem that lingered in memory long after the images of the pageant itself had vanished. The tune itself has a suspicious resemblance to the middle section of Gustav Holst's 'Jupiter' (Holst's copyrights expired in 1984, so of course arrangers are free to do with his music as they please). Already ponderously sentimental in Elgarian fashion, this tune now had saccharine harmonies superadded, and words of sonorous vacuity ('As we try to reach our destiny ... to take our place in history and live with dignity'), sung by a large blonde woman doing an imitation of African American (not African) vocal timbre – a voice at the same time strident and aggressively sentimental, the voice in which the American music industry purveys its dreams of love and desire.

It is bad enough to be told via a public address system that you are part of the Rainbow Nation, but when the people who own the microphone borrow from foreigners the words and music, the images and stereotypes, in which they dress up their concept – not just from foreigners but from an industry dedicated to the manufacture and recycling of the exotic, to the construction of varieties of rainbowness – then you are in deep trouble. From the 1880s onward rugby (and, to an even greater extent, cricket) were promoted in Britain's colonies as ways of nurturing group identity within the confines of a Victorian-imperial ethos and historical agenda. When Afrikaners took over rugby they used it as a medium for their own project in identity-formation, fore-grounding an alternative ethos, alternative values (*taaiheid* and *onverskrokkenheid*, *kragdadigheid* where necessary), an alternative history. Now that rugby has fallen into the hands of an international cartel embracing a 'philosophy' of growth (a philosophy no more complex than that of a colony of bacteria), we can expect the inherent intellectual muddle of the Rainbow Project to be compounded by floods of images of South Africa as an exotic sports-tourism destination, different certainly, but only in a piquant, easily digested way.

Part of the experience of being colonised is having images of yourself made up by outsiders stuffed down your throat. Today's image-makers and image-marketers have no interest in complex realities, or indeed in anything that cannot be expounded in fifteen seconds. The truth is, their trade is not in reality at all: it is in what they call perceptions. In this respect they are continuous with the people behind the South African government of the 1980s, the ideas men and academic advisers who saw the war their patrons were engaged in as a theatre of images in which they were losing because the world audience had a perception of them as racists lording it over a subject population and a perception of their opponents as a liberation movement. Their advice to their clients was to mount campaigns to reverse these perceptions, not to change their hearts and mend their ways (such advice would have seemed to them simply inappropriate, outside their assignment). In this banal sense, they were beyond good and evil. Those concerned with the real future of South Africa, starting with the State President and the good Archbishop, would do well to keep a firm distance between themselves and these shadow-players.

(Southern African Review of Books, July/August 1995)

THE WAY IT WAS

Sport relies on cycles of renewal and decline: seasons, tours and players come and go with each year and each decade. But sometimes an event breaks free of the cycle and stands alone as an iconic moment that defines an era. Bigger than a newspaper report, more complex than an interview, it demands our attention like nothing else in sport and lingers in our memory long after the players involved have retired or the dust has settled.

In South Africa, the only thing bigger than sport is politics and, not surprisingly, most of our country's greatest sporting controversies have been political, overtly or implicitly: many of the pieces in this section contain the taste of South African history, either disguised in layers of personal recollection or else rudely displayed in the up-yours attitude of a regime aggressively denying reality. The following do not moralise: they do not need to. They simply present a view of the way it was and allow us to join the dots. What we see once those dots are joined is our own business.

– Tom Eaton

Dark trade – lost in boxing

Donald McRae

I can still remember how it started. On a cold evening in June, in the South African winter of 1967, the sun disappeared behind our high garden wall. The darkness came and covered everything. It even swallowed up the white roses and the green metal swing at the far end of the lawn. I thought we might never see the sun again. I pulled the heavy blankets over my head. It didn't help. I was scared of the dark. I was frightened of all it hid, of the sounds it suddenly made.

The giant trees scraped against an upstairs window, clawing and tapping against the glass as if calling out to me. 'Let us in,' their leaves sighed, 'let us in ...'

But, in the distance, there was another noise. It was like nothing I had ever heard before.

'*Tsa-huuuuunh! Tsa-huuuuunh!*'

It stopped; and then began again. I slid out of bed. It was worse not knowing. Holding my thumbs for luck, I slunk towards the window. I peeped through the zebra-patterned curtains.

Lines of black men trudged along either side of the road below. Under the yellow street-lights their balaclavas made me shiver. Tiny mists of breath slipped from their mouths as they walked. We called them 'natives'. I was never sure why, for it was just a name everyone used. The natives were not the same as us. They were black. They stayed in the shadows.

Some of them stopped to watch another circle of black men. They threw dice in a pool of light which fell from the corner shop opposite our new house. Whenever one of the natives picked up the small cubes he would blow on his hands. Then he would flick the dice, and groan.

'*Tsa-huuuuunh! Tsa-huuuuunh!*'

It was supposed to feel like we had reached home. Earlier that day we had moved back to the town where I had been born six years before. Germiston, 'the largest railway junction in the southern hemisphere'. Ten miles east of Johannesburg, it was meant to be a step up from the place we had just left. But we had never heard the moaning of natives in Witbank, which was Afrikaans for 'white bank'. I didn't know what 'Germiston' meant. I just knew that it was different. Its natives sounded ghostly. They sounded angry.

I closed my eyes again. I tried to listen for the trains beyond the gamblers.

The night passed and I woke to a quieter sound. Grey doves cooed in the sunshine. The shop across the street looked like any other Greek-owned store you could see in Witbank. By mid-morning even the dice-men looked ordinary. They were just natives, shuffling together for another game.

I was a slow kid. I was strictly small-town then. It took me weeks to work out that their gambling was also a cover for the business they ran from the drains adjoining our garden. Whenever someone wanted 'a nip', he would take up a spot in the band and cry: '*Tsa-huuuuunh!*' That was a sign for 'The Godfather', a fat black man called Samson, to wander over to the drain, lift up the lid, reach down and bring out the brown bottles of beer. If the lookout spotted a blue police van, the lurching groans grew louder. It was better to be caught running a dice game than a shebeen.

As the months passed, I grew used to them. I liked the natives in our neighbourhood. They made me laugh. More importantly, whenever my football flew over the brick wall one of the betting-boys would wheel away to gather it in full stride.

My favourite retriever was a wiry man the others called Cassius. It all began with Cassius. He was the one who hooked me. He juggled the ball like a black-faced clown, shifting it from a knee to a shoulder before letting it settle magically on his thigh. He pulled mad faces at me. One day, as he did his tricks with the ball, he sang a strange song: 'Ali, Ali, float like a butterfly, sting like a bee, Ali, Ali, Muhammad Ali.'

He flipped the ball back and dropped into a hunched pose. 'Put your dukes up, *basie* [little boss]!' he whispered. 'C'mon, float wit' me, sting wit' me!' Cassius flicked rangy left hands into the winter sunshine as his huge feet danced. He wore a pair of battered brown sandals which had split at the seams. They fluttered over the tar while the soles flapped up and down in a jitterbug of their own. Cassius's fists flashed in the air. Breath snagged at the back of his throat and his voice became husky with effort.

'*Jy is die baas ... jy is die baas!* [You are the master ... you are the master!]' he said as he boxed against his shadow, dipping and weaving against the wall on top of which I had scrambled. His words chugged in a way which made me think he was going away like one of our trains. But the rumble soon turned into a lullaby.

'Ali is the master ... Ali is the master!' he half-hummed, half-sang.

When he tired of hitting the thin Highveld air, he clasped his hands behind his back and swayed sweetly, sighing, 'Butterfly, butterfly,' as if serenading me.

The shebeen drinkers dissolved into fizzing laughter. 'Don't worry, *basie*,' one of them called out to me, 'Cassius's just crazy!'

'Who's Ali?' I eventually asked the insane joker.

'The *basie* don't know?' Cassius said sternly.

I must have shook my head dumbly for he spoke more gently again.

'Ali is a boxer, *basie*, the best boxer in the whole world. The heavyweight champion of the world!'

I felt a thrill rise through me. With glistening eyes he told me how he himself was nicknamed after Ali – how Ali had been born Cassius Clay. I struggled to understand how one man could have two names. Cassius stumbled before drifting on to say that the extraordinary boxer was a black American. He was a dancer and a puncher, a fighter and a poet – the man who owned those happy bee and butterfly lines. And then, with a shimmy and a wave of his fist, Cassius was on his way back to the gambling corner.

Samson ambled over to the drains while Cassius scooped up the dice. After he had blown on his hands, he echoed, 'Float ... float ... float!' He threw the numbers. Their final roll was greeted by a roar. Cassius had won. He flashed a thumbs-up. 'Sting, my *basie*, sting!' He used his teeth to lift the top from the new bottle of beer. Cassius tilted it towards the sky. The thick beer bubbled and frothed through the glass neck and down into his gulping throat.

One Saturday afternoon his sweating and bloated face swam into mind again. A dozen of us were jammed together near the front of the Rialto Cinema in downtown Germiston. All the boys, including me, were dressed in brown shoes, long socks, shorts, checked shirts and Brylcreem-greased short-back-and-sides. The girls wore sandals, party dresses and Alice-bands in their long hair. It had become the fashion to pack us off to the movies whenever another birthday arrived. While we weren't keen on the mothers' choice of *The Sound of Music* or *Annie Get Your Gun*, we loved the pre-film entertainment. I was big on *The Lone Ranger* and those zany serials which always ended with a woman tied to the track as a train raced towards her. The picture then faded into a 'To be continued next week …' promise. We howled in dismay.

Each short was accompanied by fifteen minutes of 'World News from Movietone'. We did not have television in South Africa, and so even old news at the movies meant everything to us. We loved the pictures of the Rolling Stones taking America by storm and seeing the goals from the previous year's FA Cup final. But they were nothing compared to the mixing of Cassius and Muhammad on our Saturday screen. I was stunned by what I saw.

Almost twenty-five years later I managed to track down a copy of that footage and, watching it in London again in 1992, I at last understood the enormity of what a boxer had done to me in a darkened Transvaal cinema. I could finally give words to the feelings of exhilaration and shock which gripped me that hot afternoon.

The 'Cassius' jolted me the most, hearing the name of a native booming through the Rialto. 'This is Cassius Marcellus Clay,' the Movietone broadcaster intoned grandly, 'the young negro who could have become the greatest fighter the world has ever seen …' I was surprised not to see my gambling boy but a much leaner and more beautiful face. I was even more astonished by the rush of words screaming out of his open mouth: 'I am the greatest! I shook up the world! I'm the greatest thing that ever lived! I don't have a mark on my face and I upset Sonny Liston and I just turned twenty-two years old. I must be the greatest! I showed the world, I talk to God every day. I'm the king of the world! I'm pretty! I'm a bad man! I shook up the world! I shook up the world! You must listen to me. I am the greatest! I can't be beat! I am the greatest! It was no match. I want the world to know I'm so great that Sonny Liston was not even a match. I don't have a mark on my face. In the fifth round I couldn't see a thing. My face was burning and I whupped him. He couldn't hurt me. I'm the prettiest thing that ever lived. I shook up the world. I want justice …'

I had never seen a black man on the Rialto screen before – nor anyone as charismatic or supposedly deranged. I pulled my shirt-sleeve angrily away from the clutching hand of the little girl sitting next to me. Like the rest of us, her mouth hung open as she tried to understand what was happening.

'Who's that naughty native?' she asked anxiously.

I thought of Cassius and the simple words he used. 'He's a boxer.'

'The best boxer in the whole world!' Cassius had said. A quarter of a century later, when I recognised more of what I watched, I saw what he meant. The newsreel showed Ali destroying Cleveland Williams with a speed which made the savagery look lustrous on monochrome film. He knocked down his opponent four times in the opening round as easily as if he was tipping over a skittling series of empty beer bottles. Cassius Clay, as the newscaster called him, was as slick as a seal purling through clear water. There were also more sombre moments when he planted his feet in the middle of the ring. He then appeared deadlier than a club beating down on a pup, his blows spraying blood from a cut he had already opened. But I was struck more by the ease and grace of his movements than the sheer violence. He popped off heavy punches like he was casually stripping a whirl of petals; and, all the while, he skimmed across the ring with dazzling dance steps.

'But Clay has an ugly side to his otherwise enterprising personality,' our chum with the handlebar moustache warned. The action switched to his next, and last, fight against Ernie Tyrell.

Ali brought his face right up against Tyrell's. Their noses touched. In a moment of surreal intensity, the talkative Ali said just three words: 'What's my name?'

Tyrell responded with the wrong two: 'Cassius Clay.'

'He used my slave name,' Ali wailed, 'this makes it personal … here's what I'll say: "Don't you fall, Ernie!" Wham! "What's my name, Ernie?" Wham! "What's my name?" Wham! I'll just keep doing that until he calls me Muhammad Ali. I want to torture him. A clean knockout is too good for him.'

Our birthday gang found every 'wham!' to be thigh-slappingly hilarious. But the man on the microphone called the fight 'cruel'. Ali fractured Tyrell's cheekbone and left the retina of his left eye swollen and torn. By the eighth round Tyrell was helpless as Ali taunted him. He yelled, 'What's my name, Uncle Tom, what's my name!'

I had no clue who the hell Uncle Tom was; but those fight snippets were more dramatic than anything I'd ever seen in *The Lone Ranger* or *Spiderman*. After two minutes on film, boxing became a shadowed world with its own secret codes.

It certainly appeared more exciting than pictures of the Vietnam War, Richard Nixon, banner-wielding hippies and Ali in a suit and tie facing the cameras. I think I understood that Ali was in some kind of trouble. But words like 'black nationalist', 'ban', 'prison' and 'exile' must have swirled above my head – even though they would become such deeply South African terms in later years.

But I held on to the simple fact that Ali refused to go into the army. In South Africa all white boys ended up in the army. We knew our turn was coming. My eldest cousin had already been called up. We thought he might end up fighting in South West Africa or even Angola. A cloud had formed on my otherwise blank horizon. In the end the army would always be waiting – for me and for Ali.

I sat on the garden wall the following morning, yearning to tell Cassius of Ali sparkling at the Rialto. As much as I wanted to share with him the wonder of seeing Ali move and shout, I also looked forward to Cassius relying on my report – for natives were not allowed to enter the cinema.

I saw him at last after lunch that Sunday. Samson sauntered over to a truck which carried six white men. There were four of them in the back and two up front. They wore an assortment of safari suits and string vests. Their greased hair was bristly but they stashed steel combs in their socks which they pulled up from the boots to the knees. They were 'hillbillies' to my mother and 'rockspiders' to me. The truck revved impatiently while they bartered with Samson. They wanted drink from the drains. Samson often did business with whites on the Sabbath. Except for the churches, everything else was shut on a Sunday. Our sewer was the one place in Germiston where a white man could buy a drink.

Cassius, who had just arrived, was sent to deliver the order once Samson had dragged up the booty – half-jacks of brandy and quarts of Black Label. From the top of my perch I watched Cassius float across the road like he still thought he was Ali. No one laughed. The men in the truck were not to be teased. But they had seen his shake of the hips. Cassius kept quiet for he knew he had gone too far. I watched him silently hand over the liquor with a curious bow of his head. He rubbed his hands nervously as if he was trying to wash them. I saw him squeeze his fingers together in prayer as he waited for the money.

He shook his head and said '*Aikona!* (no way!)'

'*Voetsak, kaffir!* (Fuck off, kaffir!)' the beefiest man bawled in reply.

Samson shrugged tiredly before stepping towards the truck. But it was already too late.

Cassius, leaning down into the car, was hit full face in the face by the driver's head. As blood arced out of Cassius's nose, I shook soundlessly. The beating slowed time to a dragging tick. Something terrible happened every second. The truck doors opened and the men jumped out. A knee sank into Cassius's face, splitting his top lip. He fell down. They kicked him. They punched him again. He looked crumpled and dead. I slipped from the wall and ran inside. We called the police. They were already on their way.

The hillbillies chuckled and drank as if the thought of jail could never scare them. Black people milled silently around, at a distance, watching Cassius lift his head. He had left a flat pillow of blood on the street.

When the police came, it was to Cassius they turned, dumping him into the back of their van. They chatted for a while longer with the white men before picking out Samson. He was forced into the same caged hold as Cassius.

It was weeks before Cassius returned to our corner. I found it hard to face him. While he would sometimes wave weakly to me, he never again said, 'Put your dukes up,' or tried to perfect his Muhammad Ali impersonation. Like his hero he had been forced into a kind of exile. Slowly, Cassius faded from the imaginary ring he had danced in above our drains.

(From Donald McRae, Dark Trade: Lost in Boxing, 2005)

Inside the protected citadel

Shaun Johnson

Historic as the event was, rarely can a sporting contest have been so politically charged. Never have I felt more intensely the schizophrenia of being a white South African.

South Africa was playing New Zealand at Johannesburg's Ellis Park stadium and I wanted, with all the patriotic enthusiasm that only an international sporting showdown can unleash, our 15 rugby players to win, and win gloriously. But I did not want to be party to turning that into a mean-spirited victory over fellow South Africans who are not white. I wanted the historic Test to be a symbol of the benefits for all which South Africa's turn towards justice can bring. It should have been a moment of renewal; a moment, to use the beautiful Afrikaans word, of *versoening*. There were, I know, many others who felt the same at Ellis Park on Saturday, but we had no means of stopping, or even distancing ourselves from, what was obviously going to happen.

The signs were unmistakeable early on in and around the stadium. Thousands of fans (encouraged, incidentally, by the Afrikaans press) were determined to make a political point by flying the old South Africa's flag, and for those who had not brought their own there were hundreds on sale outside. This in itself was perhaps understandable: insensitive, yes, in our time of transition, but not surprising. The defiance soon assumed a sad and ugly quality, however. A small group of liquored-up fans at one of the entrances waved their flags and held a Springbok mascot. Like some grotesque barbershop quartet they sang '*F... die ANC, f... die ANC*'. In the stands, notes were passed around urging people to sing *Die Stem*, come what may. As the South Africans and New Zealanders lined up, I waited with a sick feeling for the expected announcement of a minute's silence for the victims of Boipatong, as this would surely be the catalyst.

When the announcement came, it was not even for Boipatong, after all. The crowd was asked only to observe 'a few moments' silence for peace' in our country. But this was the signal: back immediately came *Die Stem*, and the raised finger to the devil outside, the ANC. There followed the unexpected formal playing of the anthems. Some people, still upright for the moment's silence which never happened, shifted uncomfortably, uncertainly. A lone black ice-cream seller stared down at his wares, avoiding the faces of all those around him standing ramrod straight. From that moment inside the concrete bowl, it seemed like a besieged tribe had gathered to take strength in their numbers and to send, from the protected citadel, a message of defiance to their perceived persecutors. It felt like being in a bullring, and it was uncertain whose blood was more passionately desired: that of the foe on the field or of the millions outside who knew nothing of the ancient ritual but were believed to be threatening it.

The match itself was riveting. The bad taste came back only after the final whistle. I talked and argued late into the night with friends and colleagues about the experience. Some said I was naive to have expected anything else, and I accept that. But it does not detract from the hollow feeling that comes with realising that so many whites are not changing in their hearts; not embracing the new path; not agreeing that change must at the very least involve sensitivity towards those the old system excluded and wounded. More cynically: not even realising that without the blessing of Nelson Mandela, the All Blacks would never have considered coming to South Africa.

It was pointed out to me that it was not all 70 000 people who issued the shortsighted challenge, that no one could know how many had revelled in the emotional return to the rugby world without seeing it as a victory over the ANC. I accept that too, but still the silent majority – if indeed there was one – was totally outvoted in the eyes of this country and the world. And powerful shapers of white opinion have felt no need to be coy about the political meaning of Saturday's display. Yesterday the newspaper *Rapport* published these extraordinary words on its front page:

'There are many kinds of tears. Today South Africa is probably shedding a few tears over the defeat. But yesterday before the Test, there were sobs of another kind. Softer tears. Of pride. And an iron will which said: Here is my song, here is my flag. Here I stand and I sing it today. It was the third time it was sung … A quarter of an hour before the last two verses echoed around Ellis Park. And again, just before the New Zealand anthem was played, when the man behind the microphone asked for a minute's silence. That was a political request; he received a political answer. South Africa is back … It cost blood and tears to get back, and many tears have been shed. Many kinds of tears. But next week, if we beat the Wallabies, then we laugh again. After all, there is only one truly happy laugh. And that is the last laugh.'

You can be proud without being punitive. You can have the decency to observe a moment's silence for peace – peace does not belong to any political party. Yes, ordinary whites are sick and tired of being messed around by the politicians, and having their rugby taken away from them. But what do they imagine that their black countrymen feel – they who have been denied basic rights, not just sports tours? Something good can still be retrieved from these tours by rugby, if only it will now look hard at itself, and think of others at the same time.

(From Shaun Johnson, Strange Days Indeed, 1993)

Steve Tswete entered white South Africa's consciousness from across a tearful, jubilant dressing-room in Australia in 1992, as he wept with joy and (bravely) embraced a distinctly sweaty Peter Kirsten in the afterglow of South Africa's rags-to-riches victory over Australia in our first World Cup. Two years later he would be the young democracy's first Minister of Sport, taking flak from the left for not speeding up transformation and from the right for insisting on radical revolutionary transformation implemented at breakneck speed (Three black players within the next ten years? Good God, man, are you quite mad?). But in that dressing room the tears that streamed out from under his famous inch-think spectacles were honest and sweet, unsullied by party politics and agendas, for they marked the culmination of years of tense negotiation, often endangering not only his place in the liberation movement but his personal safety. His courage and integrity couldn't but impress Ali Bacher (whose biography provides the following extract) and the outpouring of grief and respect that his untimely death elicited underlined how lucky South African cricket had been to have him in its corner.

Secret rendezvous

Rodney Hartman

Steve Tshwete was among the first group of high-ranking ANC exiles to return to South Africa early in 1990.[1] There was danger all around.

Those opposed to political change knew that important people were being filtered in from outside South Africa's borders, and from the frontline states to the north, and the ANC was anticipating what it called an 'elimination campaign' targeting its leadership. The ANC might have been unbanned, but no indemnity had yet been issued for people on its 'wanted list'. ANC formations were warned to be on the alert and Tshwete was spirited away in a safe house in the East London area.[2]

He had been the Army Commissar in Umkhonto weSizwe, the feared guerrilla forces known as 'MK' that right-wing propaganda categorised as 'terrorists'; and he was a member of the party's National Executive Committee. As a young man in the Eastern Cape he had joined the local branch of the banned MK, was involved in sabotage campaigns against minor installations, distributed a pamphlet he wrote on the coming 'bloodbath' and was finally arrested when a colleague informed on him. He was sent in leg irons to Robben Island at the age of 26 and was 41 when he was released. During those 15 years he suffered intolerable treatment that included nine months in solitary confinement and constant torture and beatings. He would say, 'You came to think of your survival not in days but in hours. You thought, if I can just survive for the next two hours, thank the Lord.'

While on the dreaded island, separated from the beautiful city of Cape Town by only a short stretch of treacherous ocean, he refused to buckle to his tormentors. He became Head of Political Education there, was described as a 'walking encyclopaedia of world revolutionary experience' and completed a BA degree in Education and Philosophy by correspondence from the University of South Africa in Pretoria. He had a great love of sport, especially rugby, and he established the Island Rugby Board (IRB), became its founding president and wrote a 19-page constitution. In his youth he had been active in the Eastern Cape in campaigns against racially segregated sport.

Upon his release from the island in 1979, he was served a two-year banning order that restricted him to his Eastern Cape village of Peelton, a former mission station on the outskirts of King William's Town. He could not believe that after 15 years' incarceration, during which he endured insufferable privation, he was now virtually in prison again without even the benefit of a trial. The restriction order claimed as its justification that he was involved in furthering the aims of communism. Its effect was to embitter him and inspire him to play a greater role in his fight against the apartheid regime.

He took up a teaching position and, once his banning order expired in 1981, he continued his political activities and suffered constant surveillance, harassment, detention, and further torture. He was a founding member of the UDF in 1983, became its first president in the Border region (Mluleki George would succeed him) and was immediately detained again for four months. His militancy and revulsion towards the apartheid system was by now intense; and it was not helped by the disappearance of fellow activists from his community and their subsequent brutal murder.

When 28 people were massacred in Duncan Village, East London, in August 1985, Tshwete was stricken with grief and hatred. He was advised by his comrades not to attend the mass funeral – which would mean him leaving the relative safety of his home in the Ciskei independent homeland, or Bantustan as such aberrations of apartheid were known – because the police would be there in numbers, but he insisted on attending. 'How can I not be with my people at this terrible time?' he told friends. When he arrived at the stadium where the funeral service was being held, the thousands of mourners acclaimed him. They knew the dangers he faced. With the police watching from a distance and unable to get near him because of the wedge that the mourners had deliberately driven between them and the podium, Tshwete broke down and wept at the sight of a child's coffin among the 28. In an atmosphere thick with tension, this great orator delivered an emotional and confrontational speech in which he whipped up passions by declaring that there had been enough burning in the township and that it was now time to burn the town. Afterwards, he sped out the back of the stadium in a waiting car to give police the slip.

Back in Peelton, the Ciskei homeland police were now on to him. They had been given instructions to arrest him and hand him over to their counterparts in the Republic. 'They arrived at our home, maybe ten police cars,' recalls his widow Pam Tshwete, 'and a neighbour who was very drunk confronted these policemen and was shouting at them and telling them to leave us alone. Some of them came into the house and told Steve that they were taking him away. I think they were distracted by the drunk neighbour who was still shouting outside so they did not surround the house as they would normally do. Steve told the policemen that he was going to get his jacket and came through to the kitchen. He told me he was going to make a run for it. He left through the back door, which was close to a railway line that was the border between Ciskei and the Republic. It was December and the mealies were tall between our house and the railway line. He ran through the mealies without being seen. Once over the railway line he was met by a friend who took him to Mzi Nguni's house in Mdantsane, where he was kept under cover.

'When the Ciskei police realised he had given them the slip, they began to threaten me. They told me that I would be killed, and my children too.'[3]

Tshwete shaved his head and disguised himself as a priest. When the time was right, he bade farewell to Nguni[4] and fled South Africa for Zambia in December 1985. He had been strongly advised by the ANC leadership to go into exile because his revolutionary pronouncements in South Africa were exposing him to grave danger from both the Ciskei police and the Republic's security forces. Pam and the children followed him three weeks later. They had two children of their own, five-year-old Yonda and her three-year-old brother Mayihlome, and two 'adopted' children, Monde Zondeki,[5] born in 1982, and his younger sister Namhla, the offspring of Pam's late sister Nokwande. She was a teacher and SA Communist Party activist who was constantly harassed by police about her brother-in-law's whereabouts. She believed it was unsafe for her children to remain with her in Peelton so she sent them to join the Tshwetes in exile. She died later in a car accident.

In Lusaka, Pam attended the university teaching hospital where she took a diploma in primary health care.[6] Steve served on a number of ANC committees, went for military training and was co-opted onto the ANC's National Executive Committee.

Now, five years later, this man who had dedicated his entire life to the liberation struggle at great sacrifice to himself and his family had finally come home …

During the 1980s, and largely with the help of Frederik van Zyl Slabbert, groups of influential South Africans had travelled north to meet with the ANC in exile. On one such occasion in 1989, Flip Potgieter, a colleague of Geoff Dakin's on the Eastern Province cricket board, travelled to Lusaka. Of those he met, he was particularly impressed with Thabo Mbeki and Steve Tshwete.

Back in Port Elizabeth, Potgieter contacted Dakin. 'Tell Ali [Bacher] that Steve Tshwete is his man …'

The message was duly passed on, and Bacher made a note of it.

Since his appointment as SA Cricket Union's one-man commission in April 1990, Ali had, as promised, been canvassing far and wide for advice and assistance. It was Van Zyl Slabbert who engineered the breakthrough. Early in 1990 he had attended a big dinner at the Carlton Hotel in Johannesburg where top businessmen met Nelson Mandela and other ANC luminaries for the first time in South Africa. Slabbert immediately telephoned Bacher. 'Here is a telephone number. Go to East London on Friday and meet with Steve Tshwete.'

The name rang a slight bell with Ali, but he knew absolutely nothing about the man he was now due to meet. In truth, at that stage, there were very few white South Africans who had ever heard of Steve Tshwete. Slabbert had been involved in facilitating so many contacts over several years that he cannot recall how that particular meeting was engineered.

Bacher flew to East London where Robbie Muzzell was at the airport to meet him. 'I've got a telephone number and a name, that's all,' Ali told him. 'Have you heard of someone called Steve Tshwete?'

'No.'

Neither of them knew that he was the head of the ANC Sports Desk, the man charged with overseeing the normalisation of South African sport.

Back at his home in the suburb of Clifton Park, Muzzell called the number. The woman on the other end of the line refused to talk to him. 'Give me your driver,' was all she would say. Muzzell handed the phone to his driver Freddy. He was given an address.

'Where is it?' asked Muzzell.

'It's in Mdantsane.'

Muzzell shuddered. Mdantsane was situated a mere five kilometres away but, for whites, it was a no-go area. It was the second largest black township, behind Soweto, in South Africa, and it was a hotbed of political activism. For a white man to go in there, particularly at night, was courting disaster. But it was there that Ali was headed, with Freddy at the wheel, in a little car belonging to Muzzell's wife Meryl. They drove off in the dead of night, and when they had not returned two hours later, Robbie glanced at Meryl and said, 'That's your car gone ...'

Bacher meanwhile had been ushered into the front room of a township house. A woman invited him to take a seat. He sank into the cushions of a large couch. There he waited alone for what seemed like an eternity. It was a very cold night.

In another room the woman, Nolundi Siwisa, was on the phone to her husband Hintsa, a human rights lawyer, activist and former detainee, who was working in his office. 'Ali Bacher is at our house and he wants to see Steve.'

Hintsa Siwisa says he then went to the safe house where Tshwete was staying and advised him of the visitor.

'What does he want?'

'I don't know.'

'Well, let's go and find out.'

Together they returned to Siwisa's house where Bacher and Tshwete shook hands for the first time. Tshwete was a huge man who peered at Bacher through very thick, horn-rimmed spectacles. He spoke softly with a distinctive gravelly voice. 'He apologised for being late,' recalls Ali, 'and said he had been to visit his sick father.'

Tshwete pulled up a wooden chair next to the couch. 'He was a big man and I was sitting so low that he towered over me,' recalls Ali. 'All the time, he was peering at me through those thick glasses and chewing on his pipe.'

Ali spoke for 45 minutes. 'He just sat there and listened while I was fighting for cricket's existence.'

Till his dying day, Bacher will never forget what Tshwete said once the monologue was over. 'He looked at me, shook my hand, and said, "I'll help you." That was it.'

It was at that very instant that two men, poles apart, formed a bond that would change their lives, and a friendship that would flourish for the next 12 years.

As Ali would say, 'From that moment he never *stopped* helping me.'

According to Hintsa Siwisa, Tshwete's first move after the meeting with Bacher was to consult with the ANC leadership, and Mandela in particular, to take the cricket process forward.

At the same time, SA Cricket Board officials were mulling over the article from the *Sunday Star* that outlined Bacher's brief to seek a new non-racial order for cricket. Mluleki George suggested the full SACB executive should meet in KwaZulu-Natal to discuss the way forward, but Krish Mackerdhuj seemed reluctant to do so. George asked him to list his objections. He replied, 'Distrust, history … and money.' The real problem, it seemed, was that SACB did not have the funds for all its executive committee members to attend the meeting. Financially, it was a cricket body that was forced by circumstances to fly by the seat of its pants; and the story goes that certain board members in Cape Town once staked the sparse money in the committee's account on a race horse that a contact on the course had tipped as a 'certainty'. The horse duly won and the winnings allowed delegates to fly to the next meeting.

On this occasion, however, there was no suggestion of any crazy gamble.

[An Eastern Cape colleague of Steve Tshwete's] Mthobi Tyamzashe telephoned Bacher to advise him of the situation. 'Don't worry, I'll fix it!' said Ali. 'Provided, of course, you find this acceptable?'

'Okay, but you dare not tell anyone that you're getting involved. I'll tell Mluleki George, but no one else.'

Bacher went to two of his sponsors, SA Breweries and Bakers Biscuits, and each of them chipped in R5 000. He put the R10 000 in cash in a bag and sent it to East London where an arrangement was made for Tyamzashe to collect it. 'I passed it on to George,' says Mthobi, 'and we didn't even count it!'

At their next meeting, George held out the bag to Mackerdhuj, 'Here's your money,' but did not say where it had come from. Tyamzashe had, in fact, contacted Sam Ramsamy in London – the only other person in the know – to suggest they say the money came from SANROC. Ramsamy says he did not know how much money was involved but was prepared to go along with the ruse because he did not want the question of cash to put a spanner in the works of the exciting new developments.

Less than eight months after the Mdantsane meeting, the first session of unity talks between SACU and SACB took place in Durban. It was Tshwete who facilitated them and it was unanimously agreed that he be asked to chair them. All it took was three meetings under his exceptional guidance to achieve unification.

'Steve was brilliant,' says Ali. 'When things looked like they were going off the track, it was he who pulled everyone back into line.'

He was, indeed, a man among men; and he would play an extraordinary role in hastening a new life for all in the democratic South Africa that he had helped create through his blood, sweat and tears.

Notes

1 Steve Tshwete was a member of the ANC's delegation at the first round of talks with De Klerk's government in May 1990. These were held at the president's official Cape Town residence of Groote Schuur. The three-day summit drafted the famous Groote Schuur Minute which was the first joint document charting South Africa's course towards democracy.

2 Hintsa Siwisa interview, August 2003.

3 Pam Tshwete interview, November 2003.

4 Mzi Nguni is one of South Africa's most successful professional boxing managers who has trained several world champions.

5 Monde Zondeki, a fast bowler, made his one-day international debut for South Africa

against Sri Lanka in December 2002 when he took a wicket with his first ball. He was in South Africa's 2003 World Cup squad and made his Test debut against England at Leeds in August 2003.

6 Pam Tshwete became an ANC MP in October 2002 and is a member of the parliamentary portfolio committee on health.

(From Rodney Hartman, Ali: The Life of Ali Bacher, 2004)

'The way it was' wasn't always simply political. Sometimes it was downright mystical. This report, attributed by us to the generic 'Mr Drum' (because there was no other name on it, and the versatile Mr Drum used to crop up all around his magazine), reads like something out of an exotic and politically incorrect adventure novel of the 1920s. Until, that is, one considers that South African teams still use juju to sway sporting results, whether by burying muti and body parts under the pitch, or by putting the Springbok squad in a dark hole for hours at a camp called Staaldraad ...

Take the juju out of sport

'Mr Drum'

I intended to go out of the club alone and wash my hands of soccer, but the majority of players followed me and walked out. Thus the Wanderers United, a new club under my presidency, has been born in Durban.'

The practice of muti in sport may stem from the belief that many African clubs see a league match as something of a fight. In tribal fights, the mutiman played a very important part, and no faction went into battle without having 'the necessary medicines' applied.

There are several mutimen who have been making a nice income as permanent witchdoctors of certain clubs.

Real nice work, if you can get it. Five-hour week, travelling expenses paid. And, what's more, the other guy does all the puffing, snorting and jumping. The main thing you have to worry about is not losing your horn and having a box of matches handy to light the herbs.

The normal practice is for the muti to be administered for the first time on the day before an important match or on the big day itself. Often, the players go to 'camp', where they sleep in one room under the watchful eye of the witchdoctor. It is said that he then makes magic passes over them and creates a strong team spirit.

In the morning, the ceremonies begin in earnest. Almost every witchdoctor has his own method of making his team invincible. A common practice, however, is to give each player a concoction which makes him retch. This is supposed to take out all the impurities from his system.

The players then strip to their waists, sit around a clump of burning roots and inhale the smoke. They are made to jump over the smoke while the witchdoctor instils into them immunity from preparations made by opposing witchdoctors. Then a small incision is made in the body of each player, and some powder is rubbed into the wound.

This can present a gruesome sight, particularly if the witchdoctor becomes a bit too merry in wielding his knife. Mr Khambule said that he once came across a ceremony by chance, and was shocked by what he saw. The players were lying on the floor; with blood all about the place. 'I thought there must have been a fight.'

The grand finale takes place before the team leaves 'camp'. The men of the front line have a doctored horn placed on their foreheads, and the witchdoctor mutters the magical words, 'Goal, goal'.

The witchdoctor always goes to the field if the match is an important one and if the opposing team is strong. Each player must walk slowly in formation into the ground – as in a funeral procession.

And if things don't go too well, there's another fortifying ceremony at half-time.

Players take an oath

All this mumbo-jumbo is carried out in the strictest secrecy, and you are unlikely to notice much unless you watch for it.

Every player has to take an oath that he will not disclose what happens during the muti ceremonies. He is also asked never to disclose the name of the team's witchdoctor. The manager of one club told me that he was not prepared to tell me anything – not because he was scared – but because the information might get into the hands of other teams who could offer a higher price for the services of the jujuman. 'We have a pretty good man, and we want to keep him with us.'

An idea of the lengths to which soccer teams have gone 'to make sure of winning' was given by the manager of an Indian side on the North Coast which has since abandoned juju practices. In fact, all Indian teams in Natal have decided to rely on their own sporting talents, rather than on the dubious ones of witchdoctors, to score the goals.

'I am too ashamed to have my name mentioned,' he said, 'but I am quite prepared to tell you about the rituals we underwent.'

His story is: the team travelled about 30 miles in a closed van before each match to see their man, who lived in a little shanty in a sugar plantation. The medicineman charged them £1 15s for a visit, gave each player some fat to rub on his body before the match, and presented the manager with a concoction, plus instructions that it should be buried at each of the goalmouths on the stroke of midnight on the night before the match.

The burying of the 'medicine' was supposed to make it impossible for a goal to penetrate the goalmouth – but only if it was used in conjunction with another preparation, which was given only to the goalie of the favoured team.

'And funnily enough, during the years we used the muti, we never lost a match. But at the same time, our team received constant coaching, and I suppose the visits to the witchdoctor gave our players some psychological courage.'

Several unscrupulous managers of African soccer clubs in South Africa are said to have cashed in on the muti craze. The manager of one Natal club is alleged to have pocketed large sums over a period of years under the pretext that he was paying it to a witchdoctor who did not want to be known. The manager, it is said, used to give the players a weird concoction, in a small bottle, to rub on their boots. He is believed to have devised the 'medicine' himself. Its powers were never proved.

Chicken, cane spirit and rice

Some witchdoctors regard soccer players as among the easiest of victims. Like the jujuman on the Natal North Coast who used to demand all sorts of saleable material to perform his rituals.

He'd ask the team for a black chicken, seven different kinds of cotton, seven yards of coloured material, a bottle of cane spirit and seven pounds of rice.

Then, at the dead of night, he'd take the team to a certain spot and kill the chicken. All the 'ingredients' would be placed at the spot and a ritual would be performed. Then the players would be told to go home.

As soon as they had left, the jujuman would make off with his booty. What he couldn't eat or drink, he'd sell.

But somewhere along the line there was a fly in the concoction, and the jujuman was stabbed in the side just as he was carrying off his loot.

One Natal soccer team used to visit the tomb of a prophet with a package of sweetmeats before their games. The priest in charge of the tomb blessed the sweetmeats, kept half for himself – or perhaps for the spirits – and returned the other half to the players. The blessed food was considered a sure aid to victory.

But what is to be done about the muti racket in sport, the belief by some people that 'medicine' is better than training?

Mr Khambule suggests that schools should take a bigger interest in sport, and that children should be educated to believe that muti is nonsense, and that practice is the only muti that can produce results.

He also thinks it important to keep hammering away at players that they can't win all the time – not even with muti.

(Drum, March 1959)

The great leap backward

Mark Keohane

The year is 2004 and the Springbok coach is black. His name is Chester Williams. The manager is white and a global rugby icon. His name is Morné du Plessis. The assistant coach is young, vibrant and has done wonders at under-21 level. His name is Jake White.

It's 23h05 on a Wednesday evening in early December. I should be working, but I am dreaming. My phone rings. It is a reality check. Rudolf Straeuli is the Bok coach, Gideon Sam is the manager, and as images of naked Boks leopard-crawling across the veld are beamed into my study courtesy of SkySports, the world is staring at Bok rugby in horror.

Kamp Staaldraad, the four-day hell camp in the first week of September 2003, has stripped Bok rugby of its dignity. South African rugby is an embarrassment. The Boks have been shamed. In between writing this and you reading it, things may have changed. The world may be smiling again, its faith restored in the leadership of Springbok rugby. South Africans may be wearing green again. Who knows, perhaps Chester and Jake are actually coaching the Boks. Now I'm reminiscing: Paul Delport, diminutive but dynamic around the base of the scrum, urges his youngsters on. Earl Rose, not as small, but not particularly brawny either, puts his boot into the New Zealanders with another three points. The young Boks are champions of the world. Yes, there was a month in 2003 when South Africa's under-19s and under-21s simultaneously were world champions. It was the easiest month to get people to talk about the virtues of South African rugby. The game in South Africa was a winner, trusted and identified with by many. Seven black players in the under-19 side. Six black players in the under-21 side. And world champions.

Yet Bok rugby is rotten. The World Cup was a disaster and the Springboks are closer to eighth than fifth in the game's pecking order. It is close on Christmas and not the easiest month to get tongues wagging. SA rugby administrators are on the run, ducking responsibility, hiding and praying for a distracting crisis in cricket. The Boks, whether the game's administration acknowledges it or not, determine the world's view of South African rugby. The innocence and successes of the youth teams are sideshows. It is a bit like the schools' rugby day: every other team may win, but if the first XV gets smashed the day is best forgotten.

Springbok coach Rudolf Straeuli has proved technically inept in his 18 months with two wins in 12 starts against the game's top four teams. He has trodden an equally destructive public relations path with allegations of prejudice, racism and provincialism within the Bok squad preceding the quarterfinal World Cup exit and the now infamous Staaldraad.

Transformation, as important as winning in the corridors of SA rugby, has been spat at in 2003. Bok rugby, like the professional game in South

Africa, is white. There is a sprinkling of colour in strategically-placed positions. There is a black president, a black chief executive, a black deputy managing director, a black team manager … and the obligatory black wing. Whites call this change, but farce is more accurate a description of the South African game.

Whites, since 1992, have dominated unified South African rugby. It sickens black players and black administrators, but their nausea is counterbalanced by status and healthy-looking bank balances. Few take ownership of the fight at the highest level. Sarfu president Silas Nkanunu rubber-stamped a Bok team including only one black player – after publicly declaring his desire to have nine black players at the 2003 World Cup as part of his transformation pledge. Mveleli Ncula, Sarfu chief executive, publicly condemned the lack of transformation in the Bok team. But what is the consequence of this bold statement? Nothing. I put it to Ncula that he is a puppet, seated in an impressive chair, made to look good, but with no influence and absolutely no authority. He disputed this.

'I am not a puppet … what I am is deeply embarrassed about what has gone on at this World Cup. I have to answer to a black community. It simply is not good enough.'

It makes for a great headline. Then what? Nothing. No consequence.

It is the story of South Africa's transformation programme in professional rugby. In 2003, the Cats were the only Super 12 team to consistently exceed the unofficial quota. An Australian coached them. In the Currie Cup's Premier Division, South Western Districts was the only team to use black players frequently. Free State showed a desire to break the quota restriction, but injuries meant they also slipped into the minimum requirement category. South African rugby's leadership talked a massive game behind closed doors.

There was no consequence to the boardroom bravado. There never is. Nkanunu, at the time of writing, was not sure he would be the president. He was being challenged by Brian van Rooyen, a coloured man who once audaciously tried to oust Louis Luyt as Golden Lions president. Nkanunu has failed with the Boks. For all his other perceived successes at youth level, his first team has stuffed it up on every score. As principal, he stands co-accused with the coach, manager and captain.

Van Rooyen could be the new president by now. If so, you will have heard of his promise to clean the game up and of his desire to take decisions. But he talks of Andre Markgraaff, Dawie Snyman and Luyt as assets and saviours to the South African game and Bok rugby. Van Rooyen has some very good ideas and a determination to make decisions. Suggesting Markgraaff and Snyman are the answers is pretty scary.

Professional rugby in South Africa is split along racial and cultural lines in the boardroom and on the playing field. There is white Afrikaans, white English, African, coloured, and conservative coloured Afrikaans. There is a belief among black administrators that the 'conservative Afrikaans coloured' is in cahoots with the 'conservative Afrikaans white' and that both want the black leadership defeated. Influential black board director and Bok team manager Gideon Sam charged as much when he crassly announced to me in a rage that the African leadership was going to 'f*ck up the coloureds' who believed Africans could not run the game in South Africa. Van Rooyen, when I spoke to him in November, said he was aware of the complex interracial politics of coloured and black. 'It will always be there in our rugby. We have to deal with it and move on.' Sarfu CEO Ncula took the party line and said he did not like to differentiate between African and coloured. 'We are black.'

If only it was that simple, but South African rugby is not about black and white. The professional game is white and the amateur game impressively cosmopolitan. Then you do an analysis of 'what is SA Rugby Pty Ltd?' and 'what is Sarfu?' and you realise the company is the old white South African rugby and the amateur body is effectively the disadvantaged social sector. South African rugby, through the professional and amateur bodies, is as split in its appearance as the game was prior to unity in 1991. SA Rugby, the company, offers the success of the under-19s and under-21s as its excuse when dismissing the failures of the Boks. Sarfu, the amateur body, turns to the under-19s as a pointer that it is doing something right. Accountability from company employees and elected board members has been zero in 2003. Before that it may have been one or two on a scale of 10.

Rian Oberholzer, as managing director, has survived (at the time of writing!) in South African rugby because he understands the dynamic of the game's underworld. Oberholzer is a very good administrator, an equally effective politician and a shrewd business operator. But even he staggered through the 2003 World Cup half-dazed and seemingly paralysed at the mediocrity. The general leadership silence in South African rugby following the Boks' RWC defeat against New Zealand was damning. The absence of leadership when the sordid details of Kamp Staaldraad were revealed exposed the pit South African rugby – and not just the Boks – is holed up in.

The hapless Bok supporter has the right to know what a cock-up 2003 was. Straeuli's grand plan of scientific selections, scientific World Cup preparation, merit transformation and all-out attack in Australia was the only dummy thrown by a Bok all year. Vision 2003 – to grow the game, transform, make money and win – was the cop-out to every failing since 1999. Now that the Boks have crashed at the ultimate test of acceptable black representation and satisfactory results, Vision 2003 has become Vision 2007.

Which brings us back to our under-19 and under-21 world champions. These players don't know rugby politics, money and the group classification within South African rugby. A prominent provincial black player once told me the first time he realised he was a black rugby player was the day he attended his first provincial senior training session. The coach let it be known he was a quota player and that he should not get into a comfort zone because of it. Provincial coaches in South Africa are white, all 14 of them. All four regional coaches are white. The under-21, SA 'A' and Bok coaches are white and 85 percent of the player base is white when you break down the run-on XVs every weekend.

And then to add to the confusion, SA Rugby's marketing campaigns are aimed at blacks. People working at SA Rugby and Sarfu do a lot of good work. Many of them genuinely believe in a game that flirts with all South Africans and can be attractive to all South Africans. There are green and gold squads and development programmes comparable with those in any country in the world. In the senior professional game, the only consistent application is the theory that 'white is right'. Depressingly, the black leadership of SA Rugby has accommodated this attitude and spoken of the tolerance required to change the inherently racist mindsets. But patience is an excuse for weakness in decision making. Sam, in his capacity as Bok manager in 2000, defended Nick Mallett's selection of only one black wing to play Australia in Sydney. Three years later, Sam is still defending the selection of a near-lilywhite Bok team.

In the corridors of SA Rugby it is the lack of African players that infuriates the black leadership. Privately the talk is a lot more heated than anything said publicly. African administrators don't see coloured players as black. Coloured administrators don't see their players as black either. Ashwin Willemse is not the symbol of hope to township folk, just as Chester Williams never was in 1995 or Errol Tobias in 1981 or Avril Williams in 1984. Gcobani Bobo and Lawrence Sephaka are the rugby tangibles in black support. And the game of transformation cannot survive on two names in the next decade. Already Sephaka is sounding like an administrator in defending everything that is white about the game. Bobo has not allowed himself to be used as a political pawn, not by black or white. Other black players have been guilty of shutting up when it has been convenient and opening up when it has been convenient.

Dale Santon's recent attack on black administration is a classic example. Santon, his 15 minutes of fame exactly that because it is all the game-time he got at the World Cup, branded the black administrators sellouts because they allowed a situation where only one black player made the World Cup quarterfinal match 22. Santon told newspapers he was mad at the lack of game time and said it was indicative that black players were still regarded as inferior. He confirmed a 'clear the air' meeting with Straeuli about the tokenism in his selection. These are 'brave' words from a man who has just announced his international retirement. Where was Santon a few months ago when the black community demanded black players fronted up against prejudice and racism in the Bok set-up? I'll tell you where Santon was: addressing the media in Pretoria and telling them there has never been any prejudice or racism in the Bok squad. Who is the Uncle Tom? Santon or the administrators Santon now labels sellouts?

While this fight goes on, the white conservatives sit back and play the role of puppeteer. Rudolf Straeuli, when discussing black representation in the Springbok team, concluded that we (as a Bok management) put the pressure on ourselves. He felt we were more obsessed with transformation than anyone else. I argued the point vehemently that for rugby to be accepted as a national sport in South Africa, it needed to consistently produce black Test Boks. Straeuli might have felt he was right, because, at the World Cup, no influential rugby or political VIP seemed to care. Or if they did, they didn't show it. The Boks fielded just one black player in 22 against Samoa and the All Blacks and the only political offering came via former president Nelson Mandela, who called Straeuli and captain Corné Krige to offer his support of the team and to remind them that the entire nation was backing them. Sports minister Ngconde Balfour, previously bullish on transformation, was missing. Balfour, who told the world he would root out racism in all sports, pledged his commitment to increasing black representation in all traditional white sports. He said this a few years ago. Two years ago he castigated Bok coach Harry Viljoen in a meeting at the Cullinan Hotel for having only three black players in 22. In 2003, when only one black player ran out to face the All Blacks, there was not even a whisper from Balfour.

The black leadership of South African rugby and the political leadership assigned to safeguard equality and opportunity in sport are as accountable as their white rugby counterparts for the total disregard shown to greater black representation at this World Cup. Balfour was bullish about SA Rugby Pty Ltd's decision to independently investigate allegations of prejudice and racism in the Bok squad. I met with him personally and he expressed deep concern about the lack of genuine goodwill towards black players at the highest level. He assured me he would not tolerate prejudice. A few days later he was meeting with the Bok management behind closed doors and a few hours thereafter he was urging the nation to back the Boks in the World Cup. Prejudice and racism issues, he said, would be addressed after the World Cup. To South Africa's rugby leadership and Balfour, the winning of the World Cup was deemed sufficient motivation not to resist the lack of transformation. It simply reinforced the view that black rugby players were not good enough.

Speaking up now is more a political statement than a principled conviction. The black leadership is silent. These are individuals who previously fought hard against the white dominance of the sport. Once within, the delights have seemingly proved overpowering.

There is hope for rugby. There simply has to be. But there is also much fear that in 2004 Bok rugby symbolises everything we despaired of or hated about apartheid South Africa.

(SA Sports Illustrated, January 2004)

Rugby and politics

Chris van Wyk

IT'S a warm Friday evening in April 1976. A Kombi and a car pull up outside Bill's Farm and the driver gives three excited hoots. Bill waves to the Kombi from behind the counter. From every window of the vehicle come screams and laughter, wolf-whistles at passing girls, snatches of pop songs.

Between the Kombi and the car in front stand about 20 boys. If their coach stops selling fruit and vegetables and gets his arse into the Kombi, they will have their full complement and be on their way. The Saru [South African Rugby Union] Easter tournament starts tomorrow afternoon in Port Elizabeth, and if they leave now they can be in PE by the early hours of the morning.

But they can't leave just yet; they don't have enough petrol or money in their pockets. They need about R60.

They wait.

Here come three women, who spend a total of R6 on onions, tomatoes, potatoes and apples. Two teenage girls arrive and spend R4. A little boy comes in with his mother. They buy mostly fruit – R3.

Bill counts the money.

'How much?' Mark Alexander, a small plucky forward wants to know.

'Thirty-five.'

More customers come straggling in, unaware of the urgency. They seem to be gazing at the navels on the oranges and counting each lettuce leaf.

'Come, come, come,' Bill hurries them on.

'Sixty rand.'

Six more customers arrive.

'Ninety rand!'

Bill locks up the shop and climbs into the back with the boys. 'Okay, boys, let's go and beat up the Cape!' There is a loud cheer, a peep, peep, peep! And they're off.

The annual Saru tournament, when Eastern Province, Western Cape, Tygerberg, Border, Kimberley and Transvaal all came together at Easter to play rugby, had its moments both on and off the field. Bill had made this trip dozens of times since the sixties, first as a teenage player in Mannie Musson's Newtonians, and, after Musson retired and Bill himself grew too old to play, as coach. What made the tournament particularly exciting for the boys was that there was a cup and a shield to play for. All weekend it would be rugby, rugby, rugby.

Every thrilling match lasted 80 minutes, but the challenge of keeping the tournament happening every year called for total commitment and sacrifice from Harold Wilson and Dan Qeqe in Port Elizabeth, Ebrahim Patel and Bill Jardine in the Transvaal, Jim Summers in Kimberley, and the Reverend Makhenkesi 'Arnold' Stofile in the Ciskei.

In the mid-seventies the Easter tournament was held in the Transvaal, home of Tirfu [Raiders Rugby Club] and Bill's Newtonians. After a week of battle, the final was to be played between the tough Tygerberg team from the Western Cape and the dark horses, Transvaal. Derek [Jardine] had been selected to play in the final and Bill watched from the touchline as he took to the field.

But mere minutes into the game, Derek's crotch crashed into a Tygerberg knee – or boot. He doubled up with pain, tried bravely to get up, but fell down again and remained motionless. Bill ran onto the field with a little kitbag to where his son was lying. He reached into this bag and removed a tube, whose contents he squeezed onto his hand.

'Where's the pain?' Bill asked.

Derek pointed, grimacing, to his private parts.

Bill reached under his shorts and smeared the horse liniment on his son's testicles.

'Now get back to the game,' Bill instructed. But there was no need for orders: the horse liniment stung with such a ferocious intensity that Derek was up like a rocket. Throughout the game the flanker never stopped moving, even during half-time.

Transvaal went on to win the match. But this did not ease the excruciating pain its flanker suffered long after the trophy was help aloft and the applause had died down.

'For months I was peeling scabs off my balls,' Derek says.

In 1971 Saru welcomed another rugby union into its fold – a defector from Craven's race-based Federation. The KwaZakhele Rugby Union (Kwaru), headed by Qeqe and Silas Nkanunu, was based in Port Elizabeth's African township, New Brighton. Prompting the move was Kwaru's disillusionment with the multi-national sports policy.

'We were fed up with the apartheid rugby,' says Qeqe, 'that we must be playing alone, coloureds alone.'

Sacos [South African Council on Sport] was aware that the admission of a union that was not 'coloured' would inevitably invite censure and harassment from the government. But they welcomed Kwaru into their ranks without hesitation.

'Here we found true friends such as Bill [Jardine], Ebrahim Patel and Dullah Abass,' says Qeqe.

Of course, the government did disapprove of Kwaru's move. And in case it hadn't yet noticed, Kwaru went on to flout another apartheid law: it admitted two white players, Cheeky and Valence Watson. The talented Watson brothers turned their broad backs on the chance of representing their country as Springboks, choosing instead to play non-racial rugby.

The government reacted: Kwaru was barred from playing at Port Elizabeth's Adcock Stadium a month before it was due to host a Saru tournament. Qeqe despaired. But only momentarily. As he gazed on a neglected, bare patch of veld on the outskirts of the city, a mad idea lit up in his head.

There were two kinds of people Bill was specially attracted to: those who never despaired about their hopeless situation, and those who had inspired, even madcap, ideas about how to overcome their plight. Qeqe had both these attributes. The Kwaru president had been an impressive hooker in his day, and played both provincial rugby and cricket. A retired teacher and primary school principal, he was a businessman well known in New Brighton for getting things done. And so, when Bill heard what Dan had in mind, he was down in Port Elizabeth like a shot.

The patch of veld was cleared and levelled, the rugby field was measured and marked out, grass was planted and instructed to grow, moveable terraces were hired and placed around the stadium. Goalposts were cemented into place. Wire fencing was bought, rolled out and planted in a rectangle around what was now a stadium.

For a week before the tournament was scheduled to take place, the organisers worked into the night, guided by the headlights of five or six cars. And the night before, Qeqe, Jardine and dozens of other men were adding the finishing touches.

On the day of the tournament, rugby fans converged in their thousands on the instant stadium, eager to be entertained. And there was drama on the field too. Most memorable was the final between Eastern Province and Kwaru. Cheeky Watson had seen a corridor in the EP defence, held onto the ball and bolted for the tryline. With virtually seconds to spare, a try would win Kwaru the game and the trophy. With the ball in his right hand, he looked up at the cheering crowd and waved. A fatal mistake. Des Booysen, the EP wonderboy, flew at Watson from his blind side and smashed the ball out of his hand.

The final whistle blew and the crowd erupted.

It was a memorable moment, not least for Bill Jardine.

A man who had an equal passion for rugby and politics was Reverend Makhenkesi Stofile, a stocky, broad-shouldered man with a pleasant, warm disposition who is now the premier of the Eastern Cape. The two men first met on a rugby field in the province, and after a dubious introduction, became lifelong friends.

In 1978 Saru decided to reintroduce the Rhodes Cup, donated to the South African Coloured Rugby Board by Cecil John Rhodes at the turn of the previous century. When the English came to plunder and colonise Africa, Rhodes did more colonising and plundering than most. He founded the De Beers Mining Company in 1880 and Gold Fields in 1887. He was prime minister of the Cape Colony from 1890 to 1896.

Saru teams from all over the country converged on a rugby field in Uitenhage to see who would take it.

Transvaal was playing Victoria East, and their respective coaches, Bill Jardine and the Reverend Stofile, were tightrope-walking the touchline, goading their teams on.

'*Moer hulle!*' Bill shouted. 'Fuck them up!'

The good reverend, finding this conduct unbecoming of a coach, marched up to Bill and told him as much.

'And what are you gonna do about it?' Bill demanded, and continued to urge on his team with all the four-letter words he could fling at them. They seemed to work, because Transvaal went on to win in grand style, scoring three tries in the second half.

That evening the teams sat down to supper in the hotel where they were all staying during the tournament. Stofile was sitting with his boys, and across the dining hall Bill was having supper with the triumphant Transvaal. Stofile's side had an important match the next day, so when he saw the five-litre vat of Autumn Harvest being deftly passed from hand to hand among members of his team, he stood up and told the waiter to give them no more than a glass each. The waiter gave the good reverend the necessary assurance. But 15 minutes later, the box of wine was still being passed backwards and forwards. Stofile rose from his chair, stormed up to the waiter and punched the poor fellow across a dining table. Another punch landed on the waiter's jaw – this time from the fist of Bill Jardine. 'Hey, this is my fight,' Stofile objected. 'Not any more,' Bill told him. Hotel security intervened and pulled the two coaches away from the unfortunate waiter.

Later the two coaches were summoned to appear before a disciplinary committee.

'Explain yourselves!' the committee demanded.

Stofile explained his actions.

'And you, Bill Jardine?'

'Me?' Bill pointed at his own chest in righteous indignation. 'I had nothing to do with it. This is the man' – pointing to Stofile – 'who did all the fighting.' Bill's forsaking of the reverend was just another of his crazy pranks, and Stofile quickly forgave him for it.

A year later Bill and the Transvaal team found themselves back in Port Elizabeth, to celebrate the first anniversary of Kwaru's affiliation to Saru. Uncle Dan had built the makeshift stadium again, with the help of a confectioner. There were flour, eggs, yeast, marzipan, vanilla essence, green cake colouring for the turf, and white icing for the touchlines and trylines. The huge rectangular cake had pride of place in the New Brighton community hall, where Saru administrators, rugby players and guests of honour had gathered.

There were speeches and anecdotes and, of course, because Bill was down from the Transvaal, ribbing and joking. Wonderful moments were recalled and great plans announced. Handshaking, backslapping and photos.

Then somehow the rugby field cake disappeared. How? With hundreds of guests milling around and chatting? The KwaZakhele birthday boys searched everywhere, but the night ended without the big cake being tracked down. Oh well, it was a good party anyway.

The next morning it was time to go to Port Elizabeth station to see Bill and the boys off. After more backslapping and handshakes, the train slowly pulled away. And the Transvaal boys, safe behind the SAR plate glass, produced the cake as they waved goodbye to their angry Kwaru friends.

Over the years of rugby tournaments in the Transvaal and the Cape, and Saru meetings and Sacos meetings, the friendship between Bill and Stofile deepened, and the more they talked the more they both realised that they shared more than just an interest in rugby.

Bill told Stofile about his Portuguese grandfather and African grandmother and their smallholding in Craighall where he spent so many childhood weekends and holidays. 'They had to sell the place for a song,' Bill said. 'Because of Group Areas.'

'There's nothing I don't know about oranges,' Stofile said. 'Growing oranges in Addo [in the Eastern Cape] for white farmers on our land, for marmalade for the toast of white people all over the world. And we were poor.'

'I left school in standard six,' Bill said.

'In standard six I also stopped schooling to go back to work on the farm,' Stofile said. 'My father, who's over 60, still works on an orange farm.'

'I made handbags for less than two pounds a week,' Bill said.

'After matric I went to work on a machine at Industex in Port Elizabeth,' Stofile countered.

In one of their many discussions during the seventies, Bill mentioned that he needed to get in touch with Yusuf Dadoo in London.

Stofile raised his eyebrows, as Dadoo, an Edinburgh-trained medical doctor, was none other than the leader of the banned South African Communist Party. 'Is he a comrade of yours?' Stofile asked, gingerly.

'Yes,' Bill said, equally cautiously.

'He's a comrade of mine, too,' Stofile said.

Thus they revealed themselves to each other, announcing that their other work was clandestine, that they both worked for the ANC underground. Stofile, it turned out, was in charge of the entire ANC underground network in Ciskei and Transkei. Over the next decade the two men began working together on one of the more dangerous ANC projects: smuggling youths out of the country to train as Mkhonto weSizwe soldiers in Tanzania, Angola and Zambia. Stofile would send the young men and women from the Eastern Cape up to Johannesburg. From there, Bill would smuggle them across the border into Botswana.

In 1985 a range of political organisations met at the offices of the South African Council of Churches in Johannesburg. The All Blacks were preparing to send a team to tour South Africa later that year, and Stofile was chosen to visit New Zealand as part of the campaign to stop this racist tour. Because of his invaluable connections, Bill was given the job of helping his friend plan the campaign and introducing him to potential allies such as Precious McKenzie, a professional weightlifter from Port Elizabeth who had emigrated to New Zealand …

(From Chris van Wyk, Now Listen Here: The Life and Times of Bill Jardine, 2003)

Dancing Shoes is dead

Gavin Evans

When the *Rand Daily Mail* closed in 1985, I began writing for its 'alternative' successor, the *Weekly Mail*, dividing my attentions between politics and, for the first time, boxing. From the start [Arthur] Mayisela and [Brian] Baronet featured prominently. I can't pretend I approached this dispute with anything resembling journalistic neutrality. I was a Mayisela praise-singer and a Baronet detractor. In mitigation, my prejudices were probably influenced by my political experiences over the previous three years. For one thing I received regular hints of the enemy's designs – ranging from threatening midnight phone calls to having my motorbike brake cables cut or the petrol tank spiked. I'd also had three spells of detention and interrogation, including my spell in Sun City. More significantly, I had seen what the 'regime' was doing to others.

In early July that year I drove my aged Honda 550:4 down to the small

Eastern Cape town of Cradock to join a 50 000-strong crowd of mourners at the funeral of a school teacher, Matthew Goniwe, and three other murdered Eastern Cape community leaders. It later turned out they'd been hacked to death by a team of military intelligence and security police goons, on the direct orders of a key cabinet committee called the State Security Council. After 'eliminating' these irritants, PW Botha's government used the presence of Communist Party flags at their funeral as an excuse to declare a state of emergency in half of the country in a vain bid to reverse the climate of 'ungovernability' engulfing the townships and to break the consumer boycotts that were crippling white businesses. The official final straw was a huge colour picture on the front page of the *Sunday Times* featuring the mourners walking in front of a Communist Party flag (with my father in full bishop's regalia in the foreground of the picture). Matthew was a man I'd met and admired and I was moved by his funeral and enraged by the government's cynical attempt to blame his murder on a rival opposition group and then use it as an excuse for further atrocities.

A few days after I returned from the funeral I interviewed Baronet for the first time and, perhaps inevitably, we didn't take to each other. He seemed irritated with the direction of my inquiries and I was exasperated with his curt answers. 'When are you going to fight Mayisela?' I asked. From his reply I could see the taunts were getting to him. 'I'm near the top of the world ratings. I'm rated fourth in the WBA and soon I'll be number one. Who's he beaten? No-one, that's who. The only fight that interests me now is one for the world title.'

'But don't you think you should beat him first – he's South African champion after all?'

'He's nothing, man. He doesn't belong in the ring with me.' He walked away, annoyed.

For a man with thirty professional fights, Brian was still astonishingly handsome, the scar tissue around his fragile brows adding a bit of rough to his boyish charm but nothing to frighten the aunties. He wore neither the droopy moustache nor the long at the back, short at the sides 'mullet' hairstyle that were *de rigueur* among white boxers, and had a more defined sense of style than the rest. Boxing people loved to describe him as a 'male model' (not a female one, to be sure) and he seemed to relish this. The way he walked, talked, carried himself, gave the impression of a young man well pleased with himself. We didn't click.

Arthur, on the other hand, knew I was on his side and would put his arm around my shoulder, joking with an air of amused resignation when discussing the nepotism of the Boxing Board. He would turn up in his shorts or his loose, khaki chinos, sometimes with his two children in tow – and that was another thing I liked about him: despite the estrangement of divorce from his wife, Mpho, he gave the impression of being a devoted father, warm and relaxed with his children. He was an intelligent man, not just 'for a boxer' – Zulu- and Sotho-speaking but fluent in six languages, quick-witted and capable of pontificating on topics way beyond the scope of his profession. He was also a proud man with a strong sense of himself and plenty of attitude without much hint of swagger. Whenever we spoke he was engaging and charming, but when the subject of Baronet came up, he would spit out his feelings. He had once liked the lad, but now he hated him, or at least despised what he represented.

I was so inspired by Arthur's defiant demeanour that I came to view his cause as symbolic of the wider conflict, and soon the connections between boxing and politics became irresistible. The two worlds employed a common lexicography – struggle, fighters, bombs, explosive – sometimes borrowing clichés from each other. 'Comrade, we've got the government on the ropes,' or 'Hey, *bra*, this youngster's ungovernable – he won't train.' The black versus white rivalries, judged by a majority of white officials appointed by a white board, watched by a racially divided crowd, completed the picture. After Goniwe's assassination and my own detention, the compelling conceit that boxing was not only a metaphor for the struggle but an integral part of it was swallowed without the requisite scepticism, and so, not for the first time in my life, this game wormed its way back into the forefront of my obsessions, albeit under a conveniently political umbrella.

On my release from detention I began using my journalistic pulpit to push for a 'showdown' between the Fighting Prince and the Golden Boy – Mayisela and Baronet. Two years before, Mayisela's Soweto manager, Marcus Nkosi, had approached the garrulous, open-minded young promoter Mike Segal. Segal, like his better-connected rival Berman, had been concentrating on the white end of the market, but he took a chance on a tentative venture with Mayisela – first as his sponsor, then as his business manager and finally as his promoter. When it came to marketing, black boxers were still invisible in the first half of the 1980s. 'But I was lucky with Arthur,' Segal recalled. 'I've been in boxing over twenty years and I've promoted extremely popular world champions, but none of them matched Mayisela when it came to grassroots black support. Even before he fought Baronet, he was really big in Soweto. When he was in my shop, people would crowd around. They wanted to be with him and he responded as one of them. There were no airs and graces – never – even after he'd made it big, he would still travel third class on the train, and the people loved him.'

Rodney Berman, however, was reluctant to allow this popular rival to get in the way of his little earner. As he explained it: 'I've never taken seriously challenges that this guy is better than our guy, because to me boxing's never been a sport – it's purely business – and I didn't think Arthur was good for business.' But there were other pressures to be taken into account – bottom-line obligations to fulfil. Berman ceded control to Sun City, which had a date to fill and was prepared to take a risk, but Baronet and his manager-trainer Doug Dolan required persuasion. 'I approached Brian myself,' said Segal. 'He'd always told me he knew from their sparring sessions that he had the beating of Arthur, so I said to him, look, take it. The money's good, Sacco's not happening and Sun City have this vacancy, and so, eventually, he agreed, and Dolan came over too.'

Sun City's idea was to make the best of the world title disappointment by attracting large numbers of black boxing fans to the gambling resort for the first time. They built the moment to a local crescendo, making sure they filled the bill with three other black–white rivalries. Ringside seats were sold at a cut-rate price of R60 (instead of the usual R200) and the punters received R36-worth of free gambling vouchers. Despite all this, no more than 1 500 blacks turned up, with most of the seats taken by 4 000 white Baronet fans.

In the days before their encounter, Mayisela told me over and over that Baronet's world ranking, his favoured-son status with the Boxing Board and his marketing contracts were all a product of his white skin. The rivalry became infected with racial trappings, which he would mix with personal barbs. 'Baronet's a chicken,' he would taunt. 'He's scared, *bra*. He's been avoiding me.' Standard boxing fare – ever since the early Ali days – but in South Africa it was a novelty from the black boxing fraternity, whose expected role was to drop eyes to the white man's shoes and mumble platitudes of gratitude with soft deference. Arthur's contempt for such conventions riled the establishment, and his rivalry with Baronet took on overtly political overtones of a kind seldom heard in South Africa. As Segal recalls it: 'You have to remember that those were still apartheid days, and Arthur viewed Baronet in that light. Here was a guy he knew he could beat, who was getting all this glory, whereas he was struggling. He carried a lot of anger on his sleeve, and much of it was directed at Baronet.' This anger spilled over to his supporters, who viewed his campaign as a national vendetta. The mission to defeat Baronet became a political cause.

I made the trip with my social worker-cum-activist friend and flatmate Maxine (her first-ever boxing event), and my new girlfriend Pat (we'd finally got it together a week earlier, after three months of doe-eyed persistence on my part). We each remarked on the highly charged atmosphere. You could taste the tension, the sense of scores to be settled. '*Skop die bobbejaan*' – kick the baboon – I heard one white drunk shouting during a preliminary fight, followed by, 'Hit him in the guts, Sakkie – there's no point hitting a *houtkop*' – woodhead – 'in the head,' which drew the instant retort from the cheap seats: '*Shaya umlungu*' – beat the white man. As I returned to my seat after a toilet break, a white ringsider remarked to me: 'Jesus, it feels just like Dingaan and Piet Retief' – only this time the bystanders were vicariously involved. The inherent logic of the game kicked in: their war was to be fought by their champions. It was David and Goliath with the Israelites and the Philistines on standby.

Everyone was attentive by the third fight, featuring the national super featherweight champion Brian Mitchell against his old rival Jacob Morake. Mitchell, a tough kid from a deprived white Johannesburg background, was one of the rising talents of South African boxing. The son of a South African champion who had fallen to alcohol, he was man who had reacted to his deprived childhood with great drive and a fierce determination. He always learnt from his mistakes and therefore showed consistent improvement until he became a double 'world' champion and one of the finest boxers ever produced in South Africa. Entering his third year as national champion at the age of 24, he was then still three years from his peak but already a formidable fighter who deserved his world ranking with the WBA. Unlike most white South African boxers, he had never shied away from fighting in the black townships, and it was there that he developed his early reputation as hard man to beat. In fact, throughout Mitchell's 49-fight career, there was only one man who managed it: Jacob 'Dancing Shoes' Morake, but that was three and a half years before this fateful November Sun City night, and in the intervening years Mitchell had twice avenged that early points loss.

Morake was a thin man whose body looked even more vulnerable because it was terribly disfigured through the kind of childhood burning accident so common in houses reliant on open stoves and without constant childcare. 'He was 11 years old and making the fire on the stove was one of his chores,' his sister Mercy told me. 'It exploded and he got horribly burnt and scarred.' Boxing was his way of winning respect, and he was good at it – a sharp, quick-footed boxer good enough to turn professional, good enough to win a provincial title, but not quite good enough for the very best. By the time of this, his fourth fight with Mitchell, he was on the slide, but his father was dead and his mother ill, which made him the family's sole breadwinner. The money he earned in his day job as a junior clerk with the Legal and General insurance company just wasn't enough to go around, so he said yes to the Sun City gig. 'You see, his boxing was helping to see us through,' said Mercy.

He took the fight at short notice, knowing he probably couldn't win – that Mitchell had his number – but hoping he would give a good enough account to be asked back sometime. And he certainly did his best, but this time his best was too much to ask. Jacob's courage, his trainer's desperate hope and the callous inaction of a police colonel who doubled as a referee secured his brutal demise. Fifteen years later, when I e-mailed Maxine in her home in Mexico City to ask what she remembered about that evening, she said she could still 'feel' the fraught atmosphere after Morake's demise. 'It had a profound emotional effect on me, especially being my first boxing match. I remember wanting that fight to be stopped because Dancing Shoes seemed badly injured, even in the round before he was knocked out, and I remember white men in the audience standing very still as his unconscious body was carried out of the ring. It was very obvious to everyone that he wouldn't make it.'

Tragedies usually defy categories of taste, and boxing is a sport where notions of taste seldom apply, but the Sun City response showed a crassness that enraged me. It was horribly apparent that Morake was in a deep coma and that what remained of his life was precarious. What the crowd needed, what I wanted, was some acknowledgement – a sign of grace, of compassion, of contrition even: a delay in proceedings, a moment's silence, a prayer. But no, instead we got ring announcer Naidoo and his 'big hand for Charles the Challenger', his 'be upstanding' for the boycott-busting Aussie cricket 'rebels', his big welcome for the 'galaxy of stars', and finally the Sun

City competition to win the Isuzu *bakkie*. This did the job for most of the whites. 'Oh well, I'm sure he'll be OK,' they seemed to say and got caught up with the real reason for their attendance. What Naidoo knew only too well was that Morake and Mitchell were not what this event was all about. They were just so much garnish before the main course. The point was Brian Baronet, the Golden Boy of South African boxing, the milk cow for Sun City, the man to pull in the gambling crowd. Brian Baronet and, yes, OK, his opponent Arthur Mayisela, but mainly Baronet.

I had staked a small dose of professional credibility on a Mayisela win – being the only white boxing writer to incline that way. I reasoned that Baronet was open to a right cross, that Mayisela had a thumping right, and that Arthur was stronger with a more reliable chin, and I knew he'd trained harder than ever before, building his stamina by running up and down the mine dumps while living in Segal's home under the supervision of a dietician. But the real reason for my prediction was simply that I wished it so. The formbook indicated a different conclusion. Mayisela's sparse record showed eighteen wins, a draw and three losses, and even if that was deceptive, it hardly indicated a world-beater, especially considering he was 32 years old. Baronet, at 25, had racked up twenty-nine wins out of thirty. He possessed quick hands, nifty footwork, impressive power in his right uppercut and left hook, a snappy jab, superb conditioning and loads of courage. And you just knew who'd get the decision if it were anywhere near to close.

But after the Morake tragedy, I *needed* Arthur to pull it off and I certainly wasn't alone. My friend Maxine still recalls the atmosphere. 'The blacks were very charged after that. Some were chanting, "*Slaan die baas; moer die Boer*" [hit the boss; fuck up the Boer]. It felt like Mayisela had the destiny of South Africa in his hands, and if he lost after Dancing Shoes was killed, the future of South Africa could never be won.' There was a measure of desperation in this hope because from what I'd seen, the white establishment always found a way of securing its will, and no doubt about it, Brian Baronet was the establishment man.

Baronet's dancing entrance, to the inevitable sounds of Queen's 'We will, we will rock you', drew sustained white applause while Mayisela's more muted entrance drew a guttural roar of defiant hope from the bleachers. Then, as if to reassure themselves, the whites sang their national anthem with more than the mandatory gusto: '*Ons sal lewe, ons sal sterwe, ons vir jou, Suid-Afrika*' – We shall live, we shall die, we're for you, South Africa. The blacks were more than usually silent. They had come in the hope of vindication through their champion, Arthur Mayisela, and the callous disregard for the fate of Dancing Shoes had sharpened that hope and added to it their urge for revenge. I was caught up with the emotion of the occasion and had abandoned all semblance of fairness and decency, let alone journalistic objectivity. 'Fuck him up, Arthur, *fuck* him up,' I muttered as he entered the ring.

I can still picture the contrast in their fighting styles revealed in those early moments. The stalking Mayisela, tautly muscled, round shouldered, shaven headed, smooth brown skin, moving forward with languid purposefulness, picking his punches carefully, his guard high, his unblinking eyes on his quarry; the elegant, athletic Baronet, square shoulders, neat build, white skin, hairy chest, straight brown hair, big brown eyes, moving quickly around the ring, firing off cocky combinations. For two minutes it looked an even contest and then Mayisela registered his first right cross and drove Baronet back, and it suddenly became starkly apparent that the Golden Boy had no defence against this kind of accuracy. He must have found it equally unnerving to discover that his own showy flurries had no effect on his opponent. Mayisela was a boxer who never knew what it was like to be dropped.

Arthur added to the pressure, driving Baronet back with his greater strength, hooking to the body and then slamming home his right over Brian's jab. Arthur was a heavy puncher, but not usually devastating, and the damage was accumulative. Every so often he would jolt the white man's head back, and the gaps between these moments shrank as the rounds progressed. In the seventh round, with Brian severely cut over the eye, the hope of the 1 500 finally began to turn to faith. They rose and began singing the inspirational mining song *Tshotshaloza* but this time like a battle hymn. Many were crying at the sight of their hope being vindicated.

The body punches took away Baronet's legs, the head blows dulled his senses, and he was reduced to a hesitant haze. Mayisela picked him off at will, buckling him with every right, but referee Stan Christodoulou seemed reluctant to intervene. I wondered whether he was hoping against hope that Baronet would find the punch to reverse the tide, as he had done before. Whatever the reason, the final rites in the ninth round were brutal and unnecessary and Baronet collapsed to the canvas, unconscious for well over a minute. 'Oh shit, here we go again,' I said to Pat. I feared we were about to see a second tragedy, and in a sense we did.

Finally, Baronet, bleeding heavily and still thoroughly dazed and confused, was helped to his feet, his dreams, and those of his family and thousands of followers, obliterated. Many years later, when I spoke to his mother, Phyllis, about the fight, she still could not quite believe what happened that night. 'He should never have lost,' she said. 'I don't know how it happened. He saw the Morake fight, and that definitely affected him, because he wasn't himself in the ring, and then he was severely cut, but he should never have lost.'

The crowd at the back couldn't quite believe it either, and there was a momentary pause before they released a long-suppressed roar. I too felt a surge of unrestrained, undignified, unkind relief. But then I remembered Dancing Shoes and the three of us rushed off to the press conference for information on Morake's condition. After the drinks and snacks were dispensed, a Sun City jobsworth rose, thanked the boxers for a 'truly enjoyable evening', announced the date of the next show, and, oh, 'Just in case you wondered, Morake is recovering in hospital. He's doing very well and we expect a full recovery.' I turned to my friends. 'He's lying. He just made that up,' I spat. We drove through the night, elated with Mayisela, fearful for Morake, talking incessantly, trying to make sense of it all, knowing that the morning would confirm our fears. Five hours later, Dancing Shoes was dead.

(From Gavin Evans, Dancing Shoes is Dead:
A Tale of Fighting Men in South Africa, 2002)

The impact of the crude segregationist policies of the apartheid regime on South Africa sport was invisible only to those who were wilfully blind, but for many fans the spectacle of the game and the camaraderie of team loyalties were a temporary escape from the realities of the country. But when a golfer classified as black because of his Indian ancestry beat the white establishment at its own game, and strolled to victory across the 18th green of one of that establishment's most exclusive citadels, heads comfortably buried in the sand had to confront political and social realities.

The prize-giving that shook the world

Chris Nicholson

Throughout his golfing career Papwa's powers of concentration continued to mystify the white South Africans who watched him. Some speculated that his state of absorption could be a translation of *yoga* to the sporting terrain. The sacred sixth-century BC Hindu text, the *Bhagavad Gita,* would not have been familiar to many of Papwa's critical observers. It describes the goal of liberation in terms probably more relevant for Papwa's situation than yogic transcendence, proclaiming that 'inner peace is beyond victory or defeat'. This inner peace, or *moksha,* is the spiritual ideal of all Hindus – a state of existence in which all doubts and disbeliefs are dispelled, and emotional tension and strife overcome for all time. In January 1963 Papwa needed to come close to this state for a week and he would face many obstacles.

The Natal Open had the usual format for a prestigious tournament. There were 72 holes: 18 were played on each of the first and second days, a Friday and Saturday, and on the last day 36 holes were played with a break at lunchtime. On each day of the tournament, Louis Nelson picked Papwa up from his humble shanty. It was a short distance from the Durban Country Club – along Riverside Road, to the Connaught Bridge over the Umgeni River – but a world apart from the club's magnificent buildings built in the Cape Dutch style. The wooden windows opened out to the north on the first and 18th holes, while to the right, bowling greens and tennis courts had been built.

A large swimming pool beckoned in the tropical sultry heat of late January. Around the pool the white members lay and soaked up the sun. From time to time they would beckon or snap their fingers at white-uniformed Indian waiters who hurried off to bring them tall drinks, garnished with little umbrellas. Inside, a magnificent dining room tantalised the most fastidious tastes, with curries and breyanis a firm favourite with the members and their white guests.

The meals were served by Indian waiters who stood silently in the corner while the members decided on their choice of meal. In the kitchens, Indian chefs mopped their brows as they prepared the spicy delights that tradition had taught them. From time to time a manager would move through, maintaining the white tradition of checking everything.

Apart from the eating and drinking facilities, there were luxurious change rooms with showers. Where air-conditioning did not reach to refresh the tired golfers, large fans circulated the humid air and brought relief from the heat.

Away from the main buildings of the club, the Indian staff had their rudimentary quarters. Even less comfortable were the rooms provided for the Indian and African caddies who vied to carry the golfers' bags – basic wooden benches and a single washbasin completed those premises.

Although the club had decided as a matter of its own domestic policy not to admit as a member anyone who was not white – and Jews, Afrikaners and other groups were also excluded at certain stages in its chequered social history – the organisers were quick to point out that it was the government and the law that prevented Papwa from entering the buildings and enjoying the meals and other facilities. Consequently, they felt no guilt that Papwa ate his meals with the caddies and that he changed in Nelson's car. Many of the caddies were old friends of his and they encouraged him when he stepped in to eat his lunch or drink his tea from a thermos flask.

At least Papwa was reasonably familiar with the course as he had caddied for a number of tournaments there. Much was expected of him and the pressure that he was playing under made him nervous. His first round was a disappointing 73, but on the Saturday he carded 70 and was tied in second place with Barry Franklin with only one stroke separating them from the tournament leader, Cobie le Grange. While large numbers of whites came out to watch the tournament, Papwa had the biggest gallery, composed, quite naturally, mainly of Indian supporters. His game was solid and he was wonderful on and close to the greens. His best shot in the second round was at the long eighth, where he slammed a wood off the fairway to only eight feet from the pin, and then sank the putt.

On the last day of the tournament winds and rain were interspersed with fine weather. The conditions were extremely difficult and even Papwa's most ardent fans reckoned that he lacked the experience to meet the challenge. His performance in the afternoon seemed to confirm this view – in the final 18 holes he dropped shots at the second and fourth, both short holes. His friends and the other members of the gallery were gripped by sadness …

In the afternoon Papwa moved into the trance-like state that reminded spectators of cross-legged meditating Hindu swamis, which had won him the Dutch Open. When his partners spoke to him their voices sounded a 1 000 miles away. His forehead was cold and his legs worked mechanically, but he drove and chipped like a champion, picking up shots with birdies at the fifth and sixth holes. His clubs appeared to be a natural extension of his body – every cell and fibre seemed under control and the ball obeyed his instructions. His only errors came at the ninth where he dropped two shots after hooking his tee shot, and the long 14th where he putted three. On the homeward stretch he adapted himself brilliantly to the windy, rainy conditions – he did not drop a shot to par and scored a birdie at the tenth.

Hinduism maintains that all wealth is contained in the 'wisdom of the hand'. Hindus so prize the ability to create that they say that the 'hands that create' are divinely guided and that creativity and religion are inseparable. There was something akin to divine guidance in Papwa's hands that day – who will forget his chip from the bunker at the short 15th? That shot was judged by the sports journalist Derek du Plessis to be the most spectacular one of the tournament. Papwa played a flat sand wedge and hit backspin for 18 inches to finish up within four feet of the pin. Had he dropped a shot at that hole he would have needed a birdie for victory. His closest rivals in the final round were Gary Player's brother-in-law Bobby Verwey, and the gravel-voiced Denis Hutchinson. They had already completed their rounds and were waiting anxiously in the clubhouse.

Papwa needed level par on the last three holes to win the tournament. He duly parred the 16th and the 17th, then strode confidently to the last hole where a par four would give him victory over Verwey and Hutchinson. The 18th hole at Durban Country Club has the green in front of the north face of the clubhouse – to the left is the Indian Ocean and to the right a murderously steep bank leading down to the practice tees.

The gallery thronged round and the marshals battled to hold Papwa's supporters behind the ropes. Although there were complaints from some competitors that the gallery was unruly, Cobie le Grange was more objective and said that he thought the crowd was particularly well behaved. Many sought to touch Papwa to inspire him – not that he needed assistance at that stage; the press, racial typecasting firmly in evidence, described that he had 'played like an Eastern fakir with mystic gifts and had charmed the ball from the tee to the hole'.

Papwa stood quietly for a moment at the elevated tee box of the final hole of the Natal Open Championship. With some deliberation he placed his ball on a peg and looked towards the clubhouse. Then he took a deep breath and let rip with a huge drive. It seemed to be destined for the green but caught the south-easterly breeze, veered to the right, hit the top of the bank, and started tumbling down. Disaster had struck as he was poised to become the first 'non-white' to take a South African title against all comers.

The crowd parted ranks and the marshals shouted at stragglers to give the golfers a chance. Down the steep slope Papwa stumbled and spotted his ball at the bottom – from its position he could not see the flag. Back up the bank he strode and took a line on the eastern buttress of the clubhouse. He looked into his bag and spoke softly to his caddy. What club was needed for a miracle such as this? His gaze swept the lower ranks of the bag and, with a smile, his eyes fell on that old comrade-at-arms – the pitching wedge. It had saved his bacon in the Netherlands, but would it rise to the occasion again? He opened the face and addressed the ball for what seemed like an eternity. Then the club descended, bit into the sandy bank and the ball flew high and true – falling as ordered on the edge of the green.

It was the shot of a true champion and all that he needed now was two putts for victory. The first putt narrowly missed the hole and he tapped in the winner. Pandemonium erupted as the cheers of his followers knew no bounds. They swarmed across the green and picked up the blue-jerseyed Papwa, holding him shoulder-high while photographers battled to take pictures of the historic moment. He had won the tournament with a purse of R800 by one stroke from Verwey and Hutchinson.

For what seemed like an eternity he was head and shoulders taller than all the other golfers. Then they slowly brought him back to earth and reality. He checked his score card and handed it in to the markers. Then, mobbed by his supporters, he walked slowly to the car to change. Boys crept closer, holding out their hands to touch him; old eyes filled with tears of joy; and young women gathered around. Louis Nelson asked them all to turn away as Papwa changed.

At this point, the weather conditions conspired with the convoluted state of South African law on the occupation of land to provide a denouement that was to have long-lasting consequences – it began to rain. As Papwa pulled off his golf shoes and stretched awkwardly to tie up his black ones he was wondering if an exception would be made to allow him into the clubhouse. He turned the mirror sideways and asked Nelson for a comb. 'Three cheers for Papwa!' yelled a young man. As the crowd roared its response a white official came through and asked them to hurry – the white golfers and their wives were getting wet. By this time the rain was pelting down. Papwa pulled on his suit jacket and walked fast to the caravan erected on the terrace. Shielding his face against the rain, he searched out the sponsors and the tournament officials. Huddled under umbrellas they beckoned him impatiently to come forward and receive the trophy: 'There is no time for a formal speech, but I would like on behalf of all of us to congratulate the 1963 Natal Open Champion: Papwa Sewsunker Sewgolum.'

As the heavens opened and rain lashed his smiling face, Papwa stepped forward, shook hands with the sponsor, and was hurriedly given the cup for winning the Natal Open Championship. He was at once champion and pariah – under the Group Areas Act denied entrance to the clubhouse on whose very grounds he had made history by winning the tournament. Encircled by his thronging supporters in the pouring rain, he held the trophy aloft in triumph as friends lifted him shoulder-high again. The flashes of the photographers lit the darkness as often as the lightning split the sky, and the heavy clouds growled in response. Then the golf officials and the rest of the players filed into the clubhouse to present the white golfers with their prizes, while Papwa and his admirers walked away through the downpour.

(From Chris Nicholson, Papwa Sewgolum: From Pariah to Legend, 2005)

Eats, shouts and leaves*

Andy Colquhoun

David Barends was a talented Cape rugby player with pace and a swerve and desire to make a name in the handling code. He was born in Bredasdorp and was such a good schoolboy rugby player at Genadendal High that he was soon playing for his local Rock Roses club.

He was stocky but naturally quick, holding the Boland schools' 100 metres record, and in 1966 he joined Progress RFC in Cape Town, instantly becoming a first-team fixture. He rose quickly through the ranks of local rugby, winning selection for the old SA Coloured Rugby Union for whom he was so impressive in a test match against the SA African Springboks that he was signed by English rugby league club Wakefield Trinity. If Trinity noticed that Barends was black they didn't mention it; they just saw a player good enough to fill a jersey.

A week after arriving on those damp northern shores, Barends scored two tries on his debut, and before his career was out he represented Great Britain against the Kangaroos and Kiwis.

Or there was Green Vigo, another Cape Town man who is still mentioned with affection whenever two or more RL men of a certain age reminisce. I have a BBC videotape entitled '101 Great Rugby League Tries' and there – right in the middle of it – is a Green Vigo hat-trick.

There were others as well, names unknown and mostly forgotten such as Enslin Dlambulo of the Western Province Bantu rugby team or the richly gifted Goolam Abed, who made the same trek to the professional rugby fields of the north of England in the 1950s. And what about Winty Pandla

*Newspapers reported that Springbok Percy Montgomery's decision to sign for Newport in Wales was motivated by the fact that quotas in rugby meant he could no longer figure in South Africa's plans.

who 'went north' or John Newman who ended up playing in Australia?

They were all black rugby players to whom the denial of access to South Africa's best and biggest playing fields was probably incidental to their exclusion from most other places as well.

So, forgive me if I am absent at the impending wake for the disappearance of a gilded Springbok generation. And I beg your indulgence for spilling not a tear at the recent delivery of incontestable proof that this country has finally gone to the dogs; what other conclusion is there to draw when we are told that Percy Montgomery was simply too blond?

My excuse for not joining the national outpouring of grief at the blatantly forced evictions of so many Springboks is that I'm so nauseated by the sanctimonious bullshit that the apologists have tried to foist on us that I'd be in danger of retching over the coffins of our dearly departed if I were to join the crowds at the graveside.

Monty as victim? It's an insult to even think it. It's an insult to the memory of the Vigos and Barendses who managed to escape this country to find expression for their game and it's an insult to the countless thousands who didn't – and that includes white players such as Carel du Plessis who were denied the international stage to give full expression to their talent.

Quotas haven't forced one player overseas and, even if they had, it's the fact that this country is run by a government that believes in transformation that has allowed Monty to earn one cap, never mind his 50.

It's also the fact that South Africa's government is now welcomed among the comity of nations that allows our players to go overseas and earn contracts that are worth as much as R6m or R7m over three years. If that's victimisation, then please, someone victimise me.

This may read like anti-Monty rant but it's far from that. All he is doing is exercising a sensible option and everyone needs to wake up to the fact that when a Springbok hits 27 or 28, he is going to begin to think about timing a trip north for a pension top-up. And there's not much SA Rugby can do about that until Trevor Manuel works a miracle and reverses 20 years of exchange-rate history.

But it would be nice if those who go, take a leaf out of the Braam van Straaten book and simply say they are going for the money or to spend more time with their family rather than insinuate that they have been let down by SA Rugby or by South Africa 2002.

Springboks on the point of departure should note that claiming there is no security in a provincial contract worth somewhere between R500 000 and R1 million a year goes down like a bucket of cold sick with men who normally occupy the beds at the Pretoria Police College where the Boks will take up residence next week. A trainee constable grosses R32 400 a year, which soars to R42 000 for the privilege of going out onto our streets to stop his neighbours stealing his gun.

At the end of his rugby league career David Barends stayed on in England and got himself a job because in those days there was the quaint notion that a career in professional sport was not an automatic entitlement to a life of ease.

For the past 20 years or so he has worked for the National Probation Service in Doncaster, Yorkshire, a field in which I imagine great fortitude and generosity of spirit are required. If we all had a little more of those qualities we might have been spared the grubby finger-pointing of the past week.

(Saturday Argus, 18 May 2002)

Once upon a short time ago, football was *fun*

John Perlman

'Anxious Errol' sounded sceptical. Should white football fans really come back into the stands?

The richly-toned voice of National Soccer League (NSL) secretary Cyril Kobus, coming across the airwaves on a radio phone-in, quietly assured him that they should.

Not so fast, 'Errol'. It depends quite a bit on what you want.

I always wanted to see the black team win.

But when the whites of Wits beat Kaizer Chiefs to win the John Player Special knockout a few weeks ago, I thought 'Good!'

It is a perfect night for football; the air is gently chilled. With two legs of the final already played, Kaizer Chiefs and Wits are locked together at 2–2.

This game is the decider, 'The Soccer Series of the Century', our sponsors confidently proclaim, with 15 years still to go.

But as the game is about to start, there is an intrusion: 'Please welcome James "Quick" Tillis to Ellis Park,' booms the sound system.

The huge video screen behind the north goal tells us that Tillis, a black American boxer, will fight Gerrie Coetzee at Ellis Park on August 31.

Tillis has been quick to tell the newspapers what he thinks of apartheid. Stories about the way blacks are treated here are just propaganda, he says. He has had no problems.

And tonight Tillis has been well briefed. He appears on screen in a yellow hat and raises two fingers in a Kaizer Chiefs salute.

The crowd cheers and whistles, and our host for the evening yells out: 'James promises to whip Gerrie's arse for you.'

The game gets under way and starts to boil. After a nervy start, 'Teenage' Dladla (actual name Tutu, and in his late twenties) finds his feet and begins to carve up the Wits defence. Other gifted Chiefs swarm forward into the acres of space he opens up.

This is football's version of a Sipho 'Hotstix' Mabusa tune. Three years ago it was as reliably available as a jukebox hit, but last year Chiefs sounded more like Duran Duran, soulless but successful.

This is the old song, and it's easy to see why thousands love this game.

For all the sparkle, goals are hard to come by – brilliant music is no guarantee of a hit.

Then just after half-time, Tutu makes it 3–2 and limps off injured. With him off the field, Wits claw back. They snatch an equaliser seconds before the end, and then the deft left foot of Wits' lone black player, Mike Nthombela, wins it in extra time.

There is definitely something wrong here. After two hours of wonderful football, Wits are holding up their trophy to sullen stands, while Chiefs start to slink away.

They don't get very far because bottles are raining down.

They've been flying since 'Teenage' left the field – some for the ref, a couple for the linesman and even one for Chiefs' Zeb Nhlapo for shooting high with the goal gaping in front of him.

I've seen supporters restrain bottle-throwers in the past, but that doesn't happen now. After winning all five trophies on offer last year, Chiefs' love-and-peace fans are in the strange land of defeat, and they don't like it.

Whistles and cheers for James 'Fast-One' Tillis, jeers and flying glass for gutsy Wits and magical Chiefs – that's one reason why I was glad to see Wits win.

I didn't always feel that way. When Chiefs, Swallows and others came in from the townships eight years ago and blew some of the cobwebs off South African football, it was love at first sight.

White fans like myself and 'Anxious Errol' were having our brains turned to soup, watching teams of local good ol' boys and rejects from Scuthorpe and Hereford in the English fourth division labouring through goalless draws.

Once in a while we'd spend afternoons waiting for 'visiting stars' like Rodney Marsh and George Best to light up. They seldom did. Then off to the Colosseum to see if Liberace, Janis Ian or Chubby Checker could do any better.

Then in 1978, along came a choice – stay as you are for the rest of your life, or change to the Mainstay Cup.

Football the game passed the ball to 'Teenage' Dladla, 'Computer' Lamola and Jomo Sono, to Kaizer Chiefs, Witbank Black Aces and Bloemfontein Celtic. Football the business placed its bets on thousands of African people and the hard-earned money they would pay to watch them.

White fans could take it or leave it. Not everyone liked afternoons shoulder-to-shoulder with boisterous, one-eyed crowds, aggressively ignorant of the rules of the game.

In Johannesburg's northern and southern suburbs, die-hard fans of Rangers, Highlands and Wits were soon huddling together in small groups, close to the press box. No such thing as a home game now.

But for a certified soccer junkie, the new game was a heady drug. Forwards dribbled dizzy patterns, then laid off strings of one-touch passes, all at high speed. Defenders protected their goals with flying headers and bicycle kicks.

All this happened to the tune of thousands of whistles – much more exciting than the televised singing of Liverpool fans, and readily available in 3-D.

And this wasn't just football.

It was wanting things to be shared by all South Africans. It was believing that townships were lit up a little by memories of sprawling white defenders and goalkeepers stooping to pick the ball out of the net.

And whites were welcome to join in. It was like the first Juluka songs, ringing with hope and renewal. New music for new South Africans, and great to dance to.

Football wasn't going to set people free, but maybe it could inspire them to want that, and do something about it.

All of that is still there, but that isn't enough anymore.

That may seem like a sudden change of tune, but football's sour notes have been getting louder and more frequent for some time.

People paid twice the normal price to get into last year's Mainstay Cup Final.

NSL PRO Abdul Bhamjee said this was because they were paying to see Juluka as well. He didn't say they would be miming to a badly amplified tape.

At the opening game this season, security guards stood by while Orlando Pirates official China Hlongwane was knifed by six men in the middle of Ellis Park.

With 35 000 witnesses, there was one arrest. There have been as yet no prosecutions. Some of the assailants quietly melted back into the crowd to watch the game.

I've seen badly injured players carried off the field on benches because there are no stretchers.

I've seen NSL security do nothing while thugs beat people up, and later lash out with sjamboks at fans who get too close to the dignitaries presenting the cup to the winning team.

And while officials appear to be doing nothing about problems like these, one of them comes on the air to tell the fans that for another R20, they can come back to Ellis Park and see a black dude flatten the white man's hero.

That's offensive because Gerrie is a likeable fellow. He keeps breaking the hard-guy mould some would like him to fit – he doesn't like racists, and he always says he expects to lose. He is much nicer than James Tillis.

But more important, politics has moved far beyond that kind of facile equation. And football politics needs to move as well. Does a winning Kaizer Chiefs team mean that their supporters have any control over the National Soccer League?

Politics and football are about much more fundamental issues than winners and losers, issues like abuse of power and unequal sharing of the riches.

A few black people get rich on football, but most players don't earn much at all. One serious injury can finish a career, and there is no pension waiting when the final whistle blows.

The mass of people whose money keeps the game alive get entertainment and maybe a winning team. All they can really do if they don't get that is throw bottles.

It's sad that football fans only act when their team loses or when the referee rules against them.

I would be happy to watch Chiefs or Pirates lose if I thought players and supporters were taking football seriously for the political business that it is, and demanding that the talent and money they put into it is properly rewarded.

Faint hopes at the moment, unfortunately.

The Federation Soccer League is much clearer about politics, but the mass of people watch and follow the exploits of Bush Bucks, Orlando Pirates and Chiefs. This is the major battleground of sports politics, and it will not be won simply by offering people an alternative.

But meanwhile, don't swap a seat in the stands for a private box or Match of the Day videos from England.

Come back, 'Errol', and enjoy. There is plenty of nerve-jangling excitement for you, even if your addiction is a minor one.

But if you want something more, beware, because underneath the fun lies a large undertoad.

(Weekly Mail, 23–29 August 1985)

What happens when a Baa-Baa comes home

Dan Retief

The runny-nosed pickaninnies loitering the main street of Hanover use the side entrance of the local café.

The main entrance, leading to the self-serve area and tables and chairs of the tearoom, is reserved for whites and black policemen.

A few urchins in this cluster of buildings in the heart of the Karoo, on receipt of a silver handout from the city-slick and camera-hung Johannesburg newsmen, go into the shop via the second entrance.

They have only a counter and sparsely stocked display shelves facing them. On this side of the apartheid line you don't browse. You ask for your '5c Wilson toffees' and they are fetched from within the store.

Solomon Mhlaba, tall, handsome and hero of these children, used to buy sweets at this counter.

He grew up in this little village which consists almost entirely of the standard steepled church, a hotel, a café, a few houses and two garages tacked on to the Johannesburg–Cape Town highway.

Solomon Mhlaba used to work at one of these garages as, to use his description, a petrol boy.

On your way to the Cape for the annual Christmas holidays he probably filled your TJ limousine. Possibly you tipped him with whatever small coins were left in your change.

Recently things have changed for 25-year-old Mhlaba. He went to Britain as a member of the controversial and subsequently highly successful South African Barbarians rugby side.

He played fullback and surprised his teammates and South African pressmen with his skill.

Mhlaba handled a wet ball with aplomb and put in many dangerous runs on the slippery surfaces of British rugby fields.

He stayed in some of the best hotels in Edinburgh, Leicester and Torquay and like his seven black and eight coloured teammates spent four weeks in a completely integrated society.

At Llanelli's Stradey Park, he rubbed shoulders with the likes of Gareth Edwards and Phil Bennett and he found what it is like to be judged purely on one's ability as a rugby player.

When you visit Mhlaba in Hanover, literally in the middle of nowhere as it is equally far from Johannesburg as from Cape Town, you wonder how he ever coped with the culture shock of being taken up in the Barbarians' side.

Mhlaba stays with his wife and baby daughter in a semi-detached house he shares with his brother in Hanover's 'location'.

His part of the home consists of three rooms. The lavatory is outside and there is no running water. Mhlaba, however, considers himself fortunate that the communal tap is right outside his house.

In the living room are displayed the many trophies Mhlaba's team, the Home Sweepers, have won in the segregated Karoo league in which they play.

Mhlaba is more fortunate than most rugby players in that his home overlooks the Home Sweepers' rugby field, if it can be called that.

Across the rutted track which is the street leading to Ikhaya Lethu (Xhosa for 'our home'), there is a mean-looking barbed-wire fence which forms one boundary of the field.

The 'field' is no more than a sun-baked strip of hardpan, littered with stones, broken bottles and beer cans. As you watch, a whirlwind sweeps the surface before depositing its dust on the nearby houses.

The rusty posts are everything but square, but, says Mhlaba, it is not so bad for they get a gardener before the start of the season to level off the surface.

They play their rugby against teams from Middelburg, Noupoort, Richmond, Beaufort West and Colesberg. Hanover does not have a white team, but Mhlaba's success for the Barbarians may have done some good, for a local lad (white) named Pienaar has told Mhlaba he would like to play for the Sweepers.

Mhlaba's brothers Heinz and Emmanuel play with him in the side he captains. They learnt the game from their father, William, who works at the garage where Solomon used to be a petrol attendant.

The construction of the new four-lane highway to Cape Town has brought unexpected affluence to the Mhlaba household, for Solomon has landed a job as a clerk on a construction site.

He is happy there. Two of his supervisors bought him clothes when he went on the tour and he was made a gift of R100.

Unlike most rugby players, Mhlaba considers it an unexpected bonus that the company does not subtract any of his wages when he is away on rugby trips.

He plays for the South African Rugby Association (Sara) XV, having to catch the overnight train to Port Elizabeth to make it to matches.

You would expect him to be displeased with his squalid surroundings now that he has seen the other side of apartheid, and it comes as a shock when you find he refuses to question the system.

'I don't talk of those things,' he said when I asked him whether he minded not being able to go to the local hotel to have a beer with me, as we often did in Britain.

But surely he must have been depressed by Hanover when he returned? Again the answer is negative. 'This is what I'm used to,' he said.

Hennie Shields, the coloured centre from the Strand who is considered to have a good chance of making a Springbok side, made a similar reply when when pressed on the problems of returning to a segregated society.

Asked if he objected to having to catch a third-class train to work, he said: 'I would get one of the third-class coaches anyway. The second-class tickets are too expensive. It's not worth it just to be special.'

It seems rugby players are essentially a-political – either that or they have been conditioned not to speak out on the issues.

Free-Stater Martiens le Roux, who emerged as the leader in the Barbarians side even though traditionally a captain is not selected, will also have no truck with the politics of the tour.

His reply to the obvious questions about whether the Barbarians' success will bring about mixed club rugby is that he would 'rather not talk about these things'.

There seems to be a general tendency to ignore the implications of the tour. It is as though the Barbarians are being praised for having had the better of Peter Hain, rather than for what they accomplished in the field of race relations.

The real issue, the fact that they only made it through Britain because they were multiracial, seems to have been missed.

It is a problem which concerns manager Chick Henderson.

When he addressed guests at the South African Rugby Player of the Year Banquet in Cape Town recently, attended by representatives from every union in the country, he included a veiled warning to rugby men to appreciate the basic reason for the Barbarians tour having been a success.

'The message I carried to Britain was from the SARB,' Henderson said. 'It said that we had taken apartheid out of rugby. But this must be an ongoing message or we shall lose our credibility.'

Most rugby officials believe it would be a great gesture towards non-racialism for a Hennie Shields or an Errol Tobias to turn out for a 'white' club.

Dougie Dyers, the Barbarians' coach, however, does not subscribe to this form of instant integration.

His platform for reform is based on 'geographic and not ethnic rugby'. Dyers says all coloured, black and white clubs should be allowed into the same league.

'Why should Errol Tobias leave his club in Caledon to play in the best of surroundings and leave his compatriots in the bush?' Dyers asks.

Granted, mixed club rugby has started happening – Western Province's Defence XV is mixed, including four Barbarians in De Villiers Visser, Henry Meyer, Louis Paulse and Nicky Davids, and two black sides took part in the Transvaal junior league last season.

There are other instances of mixing, but what of Solomon Mhlaba and other like him? Was he just a window dresser's dummy or are the men who control rugby sincere about including him in their game?

Next year will show just how much good the Barbarians did. Certainly the new decade holds plenty of promise, unlike the '70s, which broke with the Springboks staggering through the demo tour.

Considering the changes which have been made in the last 10 years Solomon Mhlaba's contribution may not turn out to have been in vain.

Perhaps he blazed a trail for one of those ragged little boys in Hanover who watched in such awe as he drank a cooldrink with us white folk.

(Rand Daily Mail, 15 December 1979)

HUMOUR

In Heel against the Head, *the comic virtuosity of Paul Slabolepszy and Bill Flynn combine to sum up South African sport's relationship with humour in one* plat *sentence. Dressed as a spectacularly unpleasant-looking woman, Flynn is not in the mood for Slab's ribaldry: 'Laugh,' he says, 'and I'll* moer *you.'*

That the play and the subsequent film focus on the obsessions of Springbok supporters is entirely fitting – the 'Laugh and I'll moer *you' ethos is perhaps most deeply entrenched in rugby, amongst supporters for whom the game is no laughing matter. Of course, they're not entirely alone: Pirates and AmaKhosi faithfuls aren't exactly giggling when they start throwing or setting fire to things.*

And yet we can laugh at our sports stars. Hell, we do laugh at them. Every time we watch the Cats.

– Tom Eaton

Before there was Ben Trovato and David Bullard and Darrell Bristow-Bovey and Tom Eaton, there was a dodgy Catholic monk with an unholy penchant for blowing the collection money down at the track on the gee-gees. Thomas Equinus – rogue theologian, possible supplier of narcotics to Brother Luiz, constant and athletic lover of The Catholic Girlfriend – purported to write about horse-racing in the Weekly Mail *during the late 1980s, but really just made us laugh.*

If one nag looks like the next, must I tip the duds?

Thomas Equinus

When you go to the races as often as I do, all the events and the horses eventually blur into a monistic whole. The horses all look the same, the races all seem like re-runs of previous races (except that one never seems to remember what happened in those races) and the pre-race parade reminds one of the Eastern cyclical view of history – the same old sagas are played out again and again and again.

When one reaches this point, it's best to take a few weeks off from punting. Or so I thought until I heard Brother Luiz's interesting theory on the matter. (Luiz is an acid-head masquerading as a Catholic priest by virtue of a phoney curriculum vitae in which he claims to have studied Canon Law with the Pope.)

During an amphetamine nightmare, Luiz perceived the whole universe to be one; indivisible, a harmonious and integrated system held together by an all-pervading substance, whom some call God, others cosmic gel. Since all material objects represent extensions of the divine substance, all the racehorses are in fact the same horse.

What you bet on, then, according to Luiz, is which bit of God is going to outpace which other bit, choosing from the bits of God which have been entered to run in the same direction at the same time.

When Cardinal Frankie was out here, Luiz went into one of his trances and started expounding his diabolical theories. This resulted in a long telephone call between Frankie and John Paul concerning whether a certain Luiz Martinez had indeed graduated *cum laude* in incense fragrances in the Vatican class of '72.

Naturally Luiz had done his homework, so the name checked. It's unlikely that when the real Martinez's skeleton is dredged from the piranha-infested waters of the Amazon, our local junkie's ruse will be discovered.

Finances have been tight of late, but I purchased some of Luiz's wares this week in a last gasp attempt to effect precognition with respect to the saddle-cloth numbers on the bits of God which have been running a storm in the imaginations of Luiz's paying customers.

My Catholic girlfriend kept shouting out 'eight' as she alternated between the lotus and foetal positions. All I could see was the number five as I mused kabbalistically on the aesthetic merit of Luiz's candelabra. The first seven winners on the card, then, will bear the numbers five and eight. The last two will bear the numbers seven and two, to correspond with the year of Luiz's fraudulent graduation. Well, I've got to try something, haven't I?

Those brothers who know of Luiz's little secret have begun working on their own curricula vitae, fleshing out drab fact with colourful fiction.

Brother Mike has just hugely increased his chances for sanctification by penning in a six-month suicide mission to a leper colony. Brother Paul has now officially parleyed with the Blessed Virgin on a hillside in Spain, while I am now once again celibate. I invited my Catholic girlfriend to align herself with the pure status of the mother of the church, but she felt that at her age virginity was far more of a stigma than a status symbol.

The only person who hasn't wanted to spice up his CV is Brother Richard. His life story is so horrendously pious that he has little need to bolster it with a few well-chosen lies. Anyway, he doesn't have to substantiate stories about how he walked on hot coals to prove the Lord's power to a group of snarling head-hunters in Borneo. Every time we oil his wheelchair, we are reminded of the veracity of the tale.

I feel sorry for the Bishop. Brothers George and Horace have started research in the quest to discredit our beloved leader's credentials. George, in typically sensationalistic fashion, is claiming that the Bishop was once a munitions smuggler in Peru. Horace, more realistically, is paging through the records of diocese choir boys who have left town in a hurry.

But on to the horses, those fragments of divinity ranged against each on primordial predetermined circuits of contention. The main clash of the extensions of the divine is sponsored by Barclays Bank. This auspicious institution has put up R200 000 in the interests of finding out which pampered equine expression of infinity can hoof it faster than the others. Mankind, clearly, is well served in this endeavour. I will be at Turffontein on Saturday to take advantage of the universal insights this horsey battle will afford me.

The Barclays National is a three-horse race with 12 others included for ceremonial decoration. Jungle Rock, Model Man and Enchanted Garden are true superstars and are clearly superior to their rivals. Of these, Jungle Rock is best suited to the course and distance and he should win this race if he can overcome a bad draw.

The presence of Jungle Rock in the parade ring generates the sort of excitement that makes racing the greatest sport on earth. They don't come better made than this Jungle Cove colt, and his performances on the track lately have more than matched his very good looks. Bartie Leisher has managed to get the best out of Jungle Rock since he's been engaged to ride him, and this Catholic jockey will know what to do tomorrow. No jockey, incidentally, overcomes a weak barrier position better than does Leisher. I'm all for calling JR a winner, dearest brethren.

Next best will almost certainly be Model Man. Patrick Lunn's Elliodor colt has won eight of his 12 races, including the Mainstay and the Spring Handicap. This exceptional customer also has a second place in the SA 2000 and a fourth place in the Durban July to his credit. With an inside draw Model Man looks to have a great chance. But the Turffontein straight gives the field plenty of time to look for galloping room and Model Man has to hold off one of the finest gallopers I've ever seen. I don't see the Durban horse beating Jungle Rock, but then, in turn, no other horse in the field is likely to beat Model Man.

That includes the horse of the year, Terrance Millard's Enchanted Garden. This filly's win in the John Skeaping really could not have been more impressive, but she needs more than a mile to show her true calibre, and she doesn't have that extra ground tomorrow. Whether she goes to the front or runs off the pace, it's unlikely that she'll be able to spend long enough in top gear to wear down her opponents. Jungle Rock does his best work between the 600 and 200 m marks and his speed at this crucial stage should see him home against a filly who does her best work just a little later.

Of the rest, late chargers like Count Du Barry, Match Winner and Rule By The Sword make the most appeal. But the big three stand in a class of their own and should fill the first three places comfortably. The other 12 can fight for the R10 000 fourth place.

The second feature on the card is the SA Airways 1200. This is not the easiest race in the world to find a winner for, although Herman Brown's Enforce has the credentials, I suppose.

My racing friends, though, are bandying about a maxim: 'Don't touch the Natal horses'. Artillery proved an exception to this principle last week, but it is true the Natal raiders haven't been impressing recently (remember Jungle Class?), and I'm sticking my neck out for a horse wearing the number five, Warm 'n Woolly.

Jean Heming's chestnut filly flew at Germiston two weeks ago to dead-heat Your Affair. Another furlong will be ideal for this horse, and on-form Cecil van As will have time to bring this horse on the scene with a dramatic finishing burst.

(Weekly Mail, 28 November – 4 December 1986)

The cute goodies I found in Equinus' socks drawer

*The Catholic Girlfriend**

**Equinus is on enforced leave for the week. His Catholic girlfriend has kindly taken his place.*

Thomas had to go to Rome on urgent business this week 'though I still can't figure out why he needed his tennis racket for a workshop at the

Vatican: but just as God moves in strange ways sometimes, so does Thomas ... I don't know, maybe the Pope gets time to play a bit between giving benedictions and blessing airports.

So he left me with a bag of dirty laundry and a list of things to do while he's away:

1. *Get my Canadian Air Force Exercises tape back from Brother Mike.*
2. *Don't open the door to anyone who says he's come to collect – he doesn't mean a Christmas Box.*
3. *See PG Glass about installing those mirrors we talked about on the bedroom ceiling.*
4. *Tell the editors you'll write my column and don't let the thin one intimidate you.*

The pleasant tingle I got from number 3 was totally spoilt by number 4; I mean the only thing I know about horse racing is how to spot a loser – it's usually Thomas. But the editors said that didn't matter because his column rarely has much to do with horses anyway and only a few religious fanatics rely on his tips.

I told them I couldn't write about religion either because although I am Catholic I have been lapsed since I was 17 and set my hair alight at midnight mass. Now I can't go near more than two candles at a time. Believe me, I know what Michael Jackson went through: I sent him a get-well card and got back the sweetest reply which I sold to the *Sunday Times*.

So then the editors said it *still* didn't matter and that a column was a column and it had to be done and I could go ahead and write about anything I liked and the thin one started to look a bit threatening so I decided not to tell them about any more of the things I couldn't do.

Umm, I've got this very nice baklava recipe I would give you which is Thomas's favourite although he doesn't really have the stomach for it, despite his catholic tastes in other departments – that was a joke, hey. I remember Thomas saying you had to have three really good jokes per column and at least two more that will pass at a push.

Talking about other departments, Thomas has got this truly amazing collection of riding crops at home, which is how I first discovered his interest in horse racing. I keep telling him he should put them in a display cabinet in the lounge instead of padlocking them into his socks drawer, but then, as he says, it's more convenient to have them at hand so we don't need to go rummaging for them in the middle of the night.

Actually I discovered something very peculiar in Thomas's drawers while I was putting away his clean clerical stock yesterday. It was a bundle of letters tied together with a leather thong, each one signed 'Yours in the struggle, Freddie'.

Now Thomas gets plenty of fan mail and I've resigned myself to his receiving dirty letters from one particular woman who calls herself the Flying Nun from Newcastle – hey, it's the price you pay for falling in love with a celebrity. But this Freddie person really has me puzzled.

I know that reading them wasn't a very nice thing to do, but I felt I had to get to the bottom of it. At first I thought he was some old racing buddy because he kept using phrases like 'whip him on' and 'faster, faster!' but the way he put these phrases together with other phrases made me eventually think not. And then in the last letter … oh look, I don't want to upset you too, but I'll have to demand an explanation for all this when Thomas gets home this weekend.

On a cheerier note, let me say it was really fun to meet you all and leave you with my baklava recipe: 1 kg flaky pastry (you can buy it ready-made at Woolies); 5 kgs pistachio nuts (salted); 19 eggs (beaten) and two glacé cherries (for decoration). Enjoy!

Meanwhile, Thomas insists I tell you something about this week's races, giving me a chance to show you where he learns his trade, as well as his theology and his passion for riding whips.

Tomorrow, racing returns to Gosforth Park for the last time this year. The field in the main race, the R50 000 Allen Snijman Stakes over 2 000 m, appears to be a fairly moderate one and all but two of the 14 contenders will do battle under a monumental weight of 58,5 kg. The four-year-olds Chestnut Grove and Il Capo carry 57 kg.

Early favourite is likely to be Roy Magner's charge, Match Winner. This colt has proved to be a genuine and consistent sort.

In October this year he finished a creditable second to Enchanted Garden in the John Skeaping and went on to run third behind Bleriot in the Bookmakers Handicap at Newmarket. This week he finished fourth in the Barclays 200 000 and crossed the line 8,5 lengths behind Model Man.

What punters must gamble on is how the colt will have taken the run and whether he has the stamina and ability to give of his best for the second time in five days.

Fair Value and Uncle Percy both have some appeal. Fair Value finished more than a length in front of Match Winner in the Bookmakers Handicap and, having rested from racing for three weeks since, might have the edge on the ex-Zimbabwe horse.

Over the past week, Natal horses have gone a long way towards dispelling as heretic my misguided friend's notion that trekking horses and jocks 600 km from Durban to the Transvaal is a waste of time and punters' money. Uncle Percy has not disgraced himself in the past in top-class company and there is no logical or other reason why he should not be in the firing line on Saturday.

Natal is also represented by Versailles and Gondolier and the latter, in particular, seems to be the proverbial dark horse when least expected and most cursed.

Of the balance, Royal Play and Il Capo merit some consideration. The former was running on when finishing 6,5 lengths behind Sea Horse at this course last month. The 1 300 m journey was clearly too short for him and he could surprise over more ground.

The reasons why I would include Il Capo as an outsider are as complex as they are profound. If you're brave or of unwavering faith, follow me and ask no questions. The Divine may even consider bestowing upon you an abundance of spiritual and material benefits as just reward.

(Weekly Mail, 5–11 December 1986)

To the dedicated betting man, it shouldn't matter whether the runner has four legs or two ... And to the larcenous and wildly unprofessional journalist it doesn't matter whether the interview is legit or entirely made up ...

Nose to nose: Flash Fordyce meets the palsied padre

Thomas Equinus

Equinus: Bruce, I'm ready to pour a fortune onto you. Give me the go ahead.

Fordyce: The odds are useless. Rather back a 50–1 shot and pray for divine intervention.

Equinus: Can you lose?

Fordyce: I never start off thinking, 'I'm going to win.' There are 11 000 runners out there; one tactical mistake from me and an inspired effort from any one of them, and that's it.

Equinus: You really see that happening?

Fordyce: Give us a break, Equinus, I'm trying to sound modest.

Equinus: Bruce, you keep running your 'last Comrades'. Is this truly the last one?

Fordyce: Would I lie to a priest? Everyone expects me to win year after year. I'm tired of that. There *is* life after Comrades. I'm looking for other distances, other things.

Equinus: Which opponent do you fear most?

Fordyce: Bobby de la Motte. There's no way he's only running for gold.

Equinus: But he's yet to prove himself on the up run.

Fordyce: The man has run second twice in the Comrades Marathon, Equinus. Does that mean anything to you?

Equinus: I see your point, Bruce. And Hosea Tjale? Has he blown his chances by racing the Korkie and the Two Oceans?

Fordyce: I would reckon so, but sometimes runners break the rules and get away with it. Thomson Magawana broke every rule and won the Two Oceans. Still, I keep thinking, 'What might he have done if he'd built up to the race correctly?' Tjale's raced hard, but he can't be counted out.

Equinus: How long before the Comrades can one make love?

Fordyce: Two minutes. They don't call me the top seed for nothing.

Equinus: Bruce, you said recently that you really pity those guys who have to spend more than six hours on the road. Are things really tougher at the back?

Fordyce: I'll come clean. It has to be tougher up front. I'm committed to racing hard until the end. Imagine the drama if I stopped and walked?

Equinus: Have you ever wanted to?

Fordyce: Back in '82 it seemed like a good idea.

Equinus: You mean you guys are human after all?

Fordyce: I'll think about it and call you back.

Equinus: Don't the wheels have to come off sometime?

Fordyce: People have been telling me that for a long time. I don't agree. If you prepare properly, you need never have a bad Comrades. That doesn't mean that some years aren't worse than others. I didn't drink enough in '85 and in '82 I was tactically naive. Still, those were okay for 'bad' runs.

Equinus: Are you primed for '87?

Fordyce: Right on target.

Equinus: What advice can you give to first timers like me?

Fordyce: You're running? I can just imagine the odds. Why not dope yourself to the eyeballs and go for broke?

Equinus: Come on, Bruce. I need that bronze.

Fordyce: Go out and enjoy it. You won't do your best time in your first Comrades, so go and find out what it's all about.

Equinus: When you look back to when you started running, are you surprised at what it's all turned into?

Fordyce: Sure. Who envisages making a living from running a strange distance once a year? It's also strange being instantly recognisable. Only PW, Pik and Gary Player are better known.

Equinus: I suppose there must be groupies?

Fordyce: Groupies chasing road runners? Where have you been, Equinus? I've never had to fend off a horde of screaming devotees. That doesn't mean I go short. How about you?

Equinus: A sad story, Bruce. A couple of phone calls with deep breathing, the odd proposition in the mail.

Fordyce: Too bad, Equinus.

Equinus: Bruce, do the Transvaal runners have the edge on the Natal boys?

Fordyce: Absolutely. Training at altitude's an important factor, but there are others too. The competition here is much stiffer. Transvaal racing puts you in your place. Then their training puts them at a disadvantage. They're geared for long distances, for long, exhausting training runs. I go around the country a lot to talk about training methods, but I'm seldom invited to Natal. They don't want to hear – it scares them. They tend to glorify their own runners down there; there's little demand for Transvaal wisdom.

Equinus: Has success changed you?

Fordyce: My friends don't think so. I asked both of them just last week. If anything, my success has made me less shy and introverted. I've got a lot more confidence now.

Equinus: When you retire from running, will you go back to archaeology?

Fordyce: Archi-what? I'm into business now. A million doors are open to me. I can move into that world whenever I like.

Equinus: With the Comrades only days away, how do you feel?

Fordyce: I've tended to be neurotic in the past, but right now I'm surprised at how un-neurotic I am. A couple of times recently I've had to say to myself, 'Hey, you've got to run this race.' Equinus, I've been grooving along, man.

Equinus: And the angry young man who wore a black armband to victory in '81?

Fordyce: My political beliefs are well known. I'm the same boy I used to be.

Equinus: Bruce, I want to wish you luck. What's the right jargon? Burst a Nike?

Fordyce: Don't be ridiculous! You say 'Good luck on the day'.

Equinus: Good luck on the day, Bruce.

Fordyce: And to you, Equinus.

(Weekly Mail, 29 May – 4 June 1987)

Tyson 2000

Darrell Bristow-Bovey

How strong is Mike Tyson? Why, he is so strong he does not even need to hit you. The wind speed of his gloves windmilling above your head is enough to knock you down.

The more I watch Tyson's recent fights, the more convinced I am that I have chosen the wrong career. I am sure with a little training I could last two rounds of not being hit by Mike Tyson. Just last week I was not hit by Larry Holmes, and I cannot begin to count the number of times I have not been hit by George Foreman. And let me tell you, George Foreman does not hit you a whole lot harder than Tyson does not hit you.

Last Saturday Iron Mike dropped Julius 'Dead-weight' Francis five times in five minutes with a series of cuffs and waves and an unprovoked cuddle, leading me to suspect that the chief objection to his fighting in Britain had been raised not by women's rights activists but by Equity, the British actors' union.

Tyson at least knew his lines and had rehearsed his moves; it was such a shamefully ham-fisted performance from Francis that both Tyson and his current overlord Shelley Finkel were scrambling after the fight to insist that Tyson had knocked him out with a body blow. It was a necessary subterfuge. Even Stevie Wonder, seated at ringside behind David 'I wear the pants in this house' Beckham, could see that Tyson had missed with the punches to Francis's head. The fight was the least convincing piece of sporting theatre since the Pakistani cricket team played Kenya, yet there is no denying that when Tyson fights he generates a primal excitement.

Tyson's aura was built 15 years ago, based equally on his ferocious fighting ability, and his hype as the baddest man on the planet. In a curious irony, today it is the talent that is over-hyped, whereas my fear is that Tyson may be badder than we realise.

Tyson has been beaten by every quality boxer he has fought. Even our own Francois Botha, as fearsome as a tub of yoghurt, nearly put him away. Like Graham Hick on a flat pitch, Tyson can bully the weak and mediocre, but he folds against quality. He remains a drawcard purely because of his reputation for unpredictability and uncommon violence.

Tyson, truthfully, is not right in the head. He was not healthy when he went into prison, and if anything he is worse now. It is questionable whether he should be allowed to walk the streets. Listen carefully to one of his interviews – this is not a man feigning badness, but someone in tenuous and decidedly sporadic contact with what you and I call reality.

It has become a cliché to say that our interest in Tyson is similar to the urge to rubberneck when passing a car crash, but the tragedy of it is that on some level, we do not believe it is real. On some level we believe the blood and the piece of ear and the swearing and baby-talk are all hype and make-believe. We no longer blink when Julius Francis comes over all swagger and strut at the press conference, only to dive like Jacques Cousteau on the night, because we have come to accept that boxing is showbiz. Shows like WWF wrestling and even those poxy Gladiators have blurred the line between sport and play-acting to such an extent that we expect melodrama and plot twists; we almost expect real-life sport to appear scripted.

The more pantomimish Tyson appears, the more likely we are to accept it. It is a telling fact that Tyson was invited to join the WWF wrestling circus, but was ultimately regarded as not sufficiently stable to be a regular. When it comes to being a psycho, Tyson is too real to pretend, and yet he is too cartoonish for us to truly recognise what we are looking at. Tyson is a symptom of the devaluing of the real, and he may yet be its biggest victim.

When we finally get bored with Tyson we will switch channels, but Tyson confused, uncontrolled and becoming rapidly more so is stuck with himself. I hope I am wrong, but I have a feeling, with Mike Tyson, the worst is yet to come.

(From Darrell Bristow-Bovey, Business Day, 3 February 2000)

Martina Navratilova

Darrell Bristow-Bovey

I am not ordinarily someone who admires lesbians. Lesbians and I, historically, do not get along. We struggle, you see, to find common ground. We are often trying to meet the same woman, we squabble over the same pool tables and I am always afraid to take off my denim jacket in case a lesbian tries it on. Have you ever tried retrieving a denim jacket from a lesbian? You could lose an arm that way.

So no – by and large, lesbians and I are like icebergs and cruise liners. We may occasionally share the same waters, but it is usually better for all concerned if we do not bump into each other. And yet there are some notable exceptions. It would be my very great honour to bump into Martina Navratilova. Of course, if I did, I know who would come off second best. She may be 46 years old, but that is one tough old broad.

Back in the 1980s I was never a Navratilova fan. Chris Evert-Lloyd was my gal. I used to sigh for her little frilly skirts and her slender wrists and I used to lie awake at night gasping with pleasure at the thought of her two-fisted backhand. She was slight and feminine and I could imagine one day when I was older taking her to the matric dance. If Chrissie was the good princess in the morality play of women's tennis, Martina was the ogre, the beast that kept cropping up to deny virtue its rewards. She stalked the courts like a panther stalking Bambi. 'It is not fair!' we used to cry. 'Martina's too muscular and fast! She must be cheating. Real women are just not built that way!'

Martina today is as strong and muscular as she has ever been, but when she steps on court in the presence of today's lady tennis players – Davenport, the Williams, the other Williams – she looks as Chrissie once did. She looks like a girl playing men. And who would have predicted, 20 years ago, that it would be Martina who staked the lasting claim in the affections of those who follow, however peripherally, the world of tennis?

Yet it was Martina who turned out to have the personality, the charm, the intelligence. And it is Martina who is still winning tournaments.

Last weekend, at the age of 46 years and three months, Martina Navratilova won the Australian Open mixed doubles title, playing with Leander Paes. That is 29 years – 29 years! – after her first Grand Slam mixed doubles crown, and provided her with the final title in her collection. She has now won the singles, doubles and mixed doubles titles at every single Grand Slam tournament. It is scarcely credible. And despite having returned to competitive doubles tennis 'for the fun of it', and despite having found a full and active life outside the game, she is as fiery, focused and competitive as ever in her long career. It is inspiring to watch.

Martina is one of those rare, life-affirming stories that the soulless world of professional sport still manages to produce, despite itself. Like George Foreman in the 1990s, or Steve Redgrave's heroics for the English rowing team, or Roger Milla playing for Cameroon, or Courtney Walsh almost single-handedly carrying the West Indies through their lowest ebb, Martina is a parable of commitment and intensity that defies the youthist propaganda of a commercial world that all too easily forgets its real heroes. Martina reminds us of the days when the money meant less than the winning.

(From Darrell Bristow-Bovey, Business Day, 30 January 2003)

Bulls have support from a man wearing a lampshade

Darrell Bristow-Bovey

Every so often I have occasion to find myself in the small hamlet of Parys. The small hamlet of Parys, while being neither as large nor as cosmopolitan as its namesake in France, and lacking such other typically French features as swanky restaurants and the Eiffel Tower, has many things going for it that the real Paris does not.

For instance, there are almost no Frenchmen in Parys, and that is an advantage not to be sniffed at. Or indeed, to use a more typically Parisian response, sneered at and spat at.

Whenever I am in Parys I visit a local watering hole rejoicing in the name of Heinie's, which is a good place to absorb local colour and also to absorb beer.

This weekend I was there, watching the Bulls play the Reds. Ordinarily I avoid watching the Bulls play. I am not one of those fairweather SA sports fans who only support a winning team, but watching the Bulls goes beyond the call of duty.

Even Bulls fans do not watch Bulls games any more. It is too depressing. In medieval times, the equivalent would have been watching the village idiot beat himself repeatedly over the head with a stick.

But there I was, and I am glad I was. It was worth watching if only for Joost van der Westhuizen, who is still in my book the best scrumhalf in SA and possibly the universe. He is as hard, predatory and downright miraculous as ever he was. Without him, the Bulls would have lost by 370 points.

It was also worth watching the game in order to be gifted a glimpse into the inner life of a hidden SA. A man sat himself next to me. He wore large glasses and a wig he must have found in a Parys second-hand store. I think it had once been a lampshade, but the gent had trimmed it to resemble those limp, lank hairstyles favoured by European soccer players in the 1970s.

The game began. It seemed clear to me, and I would have assumed to every sentient creature watching, that the Bulls were once more busily going about the business of beating themselves. As passes were split and players fell the wrong way in tackles, I groaned and hurled my face in my hands.

So did the gent with the wig, but gradually I realised that his lamentations were directed not at the quality of play, but the referee.

The worse the Bulls played, the more forceful he became. 'We can't play against 16 men,' he spluttered in Afrikaans. 'The referee hates us,' he added. 'This is what they do,' he told me after the Bulls had missed three tackles and let in an easy try, 'they sit in Australia and they say to their referees: "Whatever you do, don't let those *boereseuns* win."'

I have always considered myself as enthusiastic a ref-basher as the next man, but now I realise that is only true if the next man is not sitting next to me in Heinie's bar. I do not know what psychic debt it would have cost that man and his pals to admit that an SA rugby team might simply not be good enough, but it was more than they were equipped to pay.

It must be exhausting to have the unflagging conviction that every foreigner out there, every other person in the entire world, is engaged in a ceaseless conspiracy to make your life an individual misery. It is a burden that must make the shoulders sag.

Still, there are up-sides. We watched the Stormers game, and while my heart sang with the joy of it, my happiness had nothing on the man with the wig. He turned to me at the final whistle, a strange light glowing in his eyes.

'They all try to beat us,' he yelled, 'but they can't. We are kings. There is nothing we can't do.'

Then he adjusted the lampshade on his head and went to the bar with shoulders held square.

(From Darrell Bristow-Bovey, Business Day, 19 April 2001)

Gordon Forbes's A Handful of Summers *is one of the best – if not the best – book ever written about sport in South Africa. Telling the story of Forbes's wonderful life growing up on an idyllic African farm, the book goes on to detail the adventures (and misadventures) of a young amateur tennis player set loose on the world tour. With a gallery of lovable sidekicks and bit players such as Abe Segal and others, Forbes tells a story that is humane, risqué and frequently very funny – a book about sport when sport was still closely associated with fun rather than money.*

Diary notes: Paris 1955

Gordon Forbes

Roland Garros is tucked into the woods in the Bois de Boulogne. The Renaults and Citroëns arrive at our little hotel near l'Etoile to take us to the courts. The drivers wear berets and smoke Gauloises and grunt at our questions. You wind through the little streets and finally cross the river and plunge into the trees. Soft European woods, with moss and dead leaves under-foot. Sometimes we pass Longchamps and the Racing Club, but there are so many different roads that the tennis courts always take me by surprise when we come upon them. You can go for quiet training runs through the woods and hardly hear your own footfalls.

The Roland Garros Stadium in Paris was disappointing after the splendour of the city; a gaunt, concrete amphitheatre which held thirteen thousand people, inflicting each with a raw behind and softening only when it was filled up. Paris was memorable for me that year because:

a) It was the first time I had been there.
b) Because I won the mixed doubles with a young American girl called Darlene Hard, who was playing her first tournament in Europe and whom, by chance, I met and entered with on the morning they closed the draw.
c) Because Russell Seymour and I beat Mervyn Rose and George Worthington in a doubles match at 15–13 in the fifth set, having saved eleven match points, and:
d) Because a lunatic Australian player dragged me into a brothel and made me watch an 'Exhibition' pronounced (and performed) the French way, and thus introduced me to my first taste of the tricky side of love.
e) And because I came within a hair's breadth of defeating Ham Richardson, one of the best players in the world and an *expert* on clay!

The doubles match was one of the most remarkable in which I have ever played. Russell Seymour was considered more of a singles than a doubles player, and as Abe Segal and Ian Vermaak were our recognised doubles pair, Russell and I had to make do with one another's methods.

We ploughed through several rounds of young Frenchmen, then found ourselves facing Rose and Worthington, who were Australian, seeded, and considered to be very tough to beat.

We got into the match from the very start and sneaked the first set before they had woken up. Angrily they retaliated and took the second, and then amazingly, we found ourselves locked into a tight third set with neither side giving an inch. We began playing points which defy description. Rallies developed which balanced themselves on the very edge of impossibility – cascades of volleys which sometimes left all four of us open-mouthed. French spectators packed themselves tightly around the court to watch us win a long third set, then lose a short sharp fourth.

The fifth set made all that had preceded it look tame. All told, we had eleven match points in our favour and Rose and Worthington had thirteen. Twice Worthington served for match, and in one of these games they led forty-love. Three consecutive match points. Somehow we fought back to 40–30. Worthington gathered the balls to serve to me on the left court, and as he was about to serve, Rose, who was up at net, called out to Worthington over his shoulder:

'Watch the line, Wortho, I'm going across!' 'No, don't,' Worthington called back. 'I'm going across!' cried Rose again.

'No. Don't,' said Worthington firmly.

'OK, I'm going,' cried Rose.

I listened wide-eyed. I had never heard doubles partners shout tactics to one another across the court. They usually made secret signs. More puzzling still was the fact that they didn't seem to understand each other. I decided to consult Seymour. 'What the devil is Rose going to do?' I asked him urgently.

Russell gave the short bray of a laugh he used when he was really desperate. 'You tell me!' he said. 'He's either going across or else he isn't!' 'Well,' I said, 'what should I do?'

'You must either go crosscourt or down the line,' said Russell.

Nobody was being very helpful, so I got ready to receive. Worthington served a high kicker to my backhand and moved in behind Rose to 'cover the line'. Rose, meanwhile, true to his word, set off across the net to cut off my return. One of the cardinal rules of men's doubles is that you *watch the ball* and *not* the net-player. Really good doubles players eventually develop a method of being aware of what opponents are doing while still watching the ball, but it is a tricky business and never foolproof. I was vaguely aware of a tremendous scissors movement taking place on the far side, but I'd committed myself to the crosscourt return, and so made the best of it. I gave the ball a low slice and knew at once that it was either going to be a very good shot, or else just too low. It was not quite either. It hit the tape of the net with a whack, ran along the top for about two feet, parallel to the moving Rose, then toppled over onto his side of the court. Rose lunged, but couldn't possibly dig it out. The crowd went crazy, and Russell, who was given to understatement, told me that I had hit a 'useful return'.

We won the set at 15–13, and the match, and in the next round beat the French team of Robert Haillel and Pierre Pelizza before losing to Pietrangeli and Sirola in the quarters.

The brothel incident was less athletic, but almost as remarkable and was, as I have said, all the work and ingenuity of a lunatic Australian.

Why he chose me, I never understood – we had met only briefly and were not well acquainted. Perhaps like my friends the pilot and the game ranger, he sensed in me a yearning to do some dangerous deeds with women. As it was, I would never have conceived or undertaken the venture single-handed. The painted ladies who lined the little streets at Place Pigalle fascinated me, but I passed them at a near jogtrot, for fear of being 'got in the night'.

The lunatic Australian was big and raucous, and having finished his meal of vegetable soup and steak with *petits pois*, he pushed back his wooden chair, drained his beer and said, 'Come with me,' in a way which I couldn't disobey. Off we went (in a taxi, no less. No Metro for him) and were set down at the famous little square.

Of all the seamy places in the cities of the world, Pigalle, I think, has the softest touch. It did then, at any rate. It is sly and seductive, unhygienic and sometimes vulgar, but seldom vicious. In those days, it was almost gentle. The girls in the bars would chat and nibble and smell of sinful scents, and good-naturedly agree to almost anything. My Australian, having answered 'Wait and see, mate, you'll be all right' to all my questions, finally stationed himself in the middle of a little cobbled street and brazenly confronted the line of girls on the sidewalk.

'All right, ladies!' he cried. 'It's your lucky night. Let's have a look at you!' He turned to me. 'You choose one, and I'll choose one,' he said, 'and then we'll make negotiations.'

He was a swift chooser.

'Got mine,' he said. 'You got yours?'

Hastily I selected a tall one who seemed to have soft eyes. I pointed.

'Right-ho,' he said. 'Good choice. Bit of length can't do any harm.' He beckoned them over with two forefingers, and they approached giggling.

'How much?' he said firmly. '*Com bien? For une exhibition? Un três bien exhibition extra-ordinaire!*'

There is no sound more remarkable than an Australian tennis player delving into French. 'Aaah!' they said, laughing and nudging one another. '*Une exhibition! Aaah! Monsieur est três romantique! Pour faire une exhibition formidable, six mille francs.* Seex thousand francs!'

'Bloody hell,' said the Australian. 'Seex thousand! Have to be one hell of an exhibition for seex thousand! We'll pay you five. *Tu comprends? Cinq. Cinq* bloody *mille*, and not a dollar more!'

'Aaah, monsieur! *Cinq mille?*' Their mouths turned down at the corners.

'That's right, *cinq mille*. And we'll throw in another five hundred if you are *três, três formidable!*'

The bargain was struck, and they set off, beckoning us to follow.

By now I was in the customary state of nervous tension which beset me whenever I felt that something uncontrollable was about to happen. It was true, certainly, that I had successfully cracked it. But the possibility of performing in a group was another matter altogether, producing disturbing visions of calamity in the presence of three people. In a display of what I judged to be nonchalance, I paused at a fruit barrow and bought a bunch of bananas.

'Bananas!' said the lunatic Australian. 'Hell-of-a-time for bananas. Could come in handy though.' He broke one off the bunch and ate it thoughtfully while we turned into a little doorway. 'Mind the skins. Don't want to slip on our asses on the way down, do we?'

The room into which the girls led us had a large bed and a smell of Paris and old perfume and other things essentially French. Coyly they began to undress, gradually revealing all the lacy things that fit onto ladies of that kind, collapsing against each other in a gale of giggles at the sight of the bananas and continuing until I began to wish I'd selected some other kind of fruit. They were naked at last, and began caressing one another with soft little mewing sounds, and touching their tongues together – their fingers, thighs, tummies, arms, bridling coyly, with sly words and breathy laughter.

I sat watching, transfixed, while the lunatic Australian muttered 'Bloody hell' to himself occasionally and sometimes also, 'Would you bloody credit it?' 'Would you ever bloody well have believed that?'

'All right,' he said at last. 'That's enough of that; now show us the exhibition.' And they gravely began a demonstration of the various lovemaking positions.

I was filled with unease and curiosity and stood in a corner, eating bananas like one possessed. At last it was over.

'Only nineteen,' said the lunatic Australian. 'I thought there were supposed to be fifty-seven …' He looked across at me.

'You finished your bananas yet, Forbsey?' More laughter.

With a little skip and a sly smile, the girl I had chosen, whose name I remember was Françoise (inevitably!), took me by the hand and led me off to another room.

Later, when I found the lunatic Australian in the street below, we walked off to take the Metro.

'Make bloody good wives, those kind of French girls,' he said laconically. 'A man could do worse than take one of them home to tea.'

In those championships I played one of my best-ever matches on slow clay. In the third round I found myself drawn against Hamilton Richardson, who was ranked about second or third in the United States and who was one of the players whom, during our farm practice sessions, we used to 'become'.

We played for hours, I remember, and for me the match was fine, and filled with deft, thrilling shots that I had never believed I could make.

Finally, it was the fifth set, 5–4 for me, 15–40, his serve, match point on the centre court, the Roland Garros Stadium, Paris, France, and the kind of hush that falls upon crowded tennis stadiums when seeded players are about to be beaten by unknown juniors. To add to the already tense situation, Richardson missed with his first service and was left with one ball between himself and disaster. There was no doubt about it. If ever I was to play a remarkable shot, this was an opportune time.

Twenty-five separate pieces of other people's advice flashed through my mind … and these in addition to the random bits that I was giving myself at the time. Eventually out of the confusion emerged a cryptic instruction that Abe Segal had once given me:

'If ever, Forbsey, you get to a real big point, just forget everything, look at the ball carefully and hit the shit out of it. That way, even if you hit it over the fence, you feel a hell of a lot better than if you just stand there crappin' yourself and bein' careful …'

In those days I had a sliced backhand and was unable to 'hit the shit out of the ball' if it came on that side, so I decided to 'run around my backhand' at all costs and bring my forehand to bear. My decision coincided with one by Richardson to serve to my forehand his second service – a brave move, and one which left me waiting tensely with a forehand grip held ready, about four yards from the passing ball. The failure of my strategy appalled me and I could hear in my mind Abie (who was watching from the stand) saying under his breath: 'Jesus, Forbsey, where the hell are you goin'? You got to be in the right area, buddy. Don't leave before the action starts!'

Unnerved and preoccupied by those gloomy thoughts, I did not give the forty–thirty point much thought, deciding at the last minute to 'play it safe'. The result was a tame backhand into the middle of the net, and the end of a marvellous opportunity, offered and retracted by the sly gods which control such situations. Bloody tennis gods! They could easily have had Richardson miss that second serve!

My performance evoked some dressing-room advice from Tony Trabert (another one of our farm heroes), who said to me: 'Listen, kid. When you get to very important points, forget about everything except watching the ball. Then hit it firmly and make your opponent play the shot.' His advice was sound and carried me through quite a number of tennis crises. But I still believe that I might have won that match point and a lot more had I gone to the trouble of having one of my rackets painted black.

(From Gordon Forbes, A Handful of Summers, 1995)

Diary notes: summer 1955

Gordon Forbes

ABIE has taken up poker. He arranges his face into a slanted smile, narrows his eyes, and sardonically produces a pack of cards to practise his shuffling with. I think he thinks that if he can manage to shuffle extravagantly, the rest is easy. He's mad, of course. The poker school consists of a very tricky bunch of players. Mervyn Rose, Don Candy, Sven Davidson, Herbie Flam, Malcolm Fox, Hugh Stewart and Warren Woodcock. Others occasionally sit in. They're very good, and know every trick and percentage backwards. Malcolm Fox is supposed to have virtually cleaned out an entire troop ship on his way back from Korea. Warren Woodcock has an angelic face, and Mervyn Rose is evil, through and through. Abie, meanwhile, believes that there is nothing to it but shuffling and dealing. He absolutely relishes the way they look across at each other, eye to eye, adjust the stakes and say: 'Your hundred, and another hundred.' He'd like it even better if they could play in lire and he could say: 'Your million, and another million!' He also likes the way they arrange themselves at a corner table surrounded by awe-stricken onlookers, who are riveted by the piles of money. Woodcock and Rose, apparently, have encouraged Abie to play. It's his own fault, of course, because he loves to act the big spender, and have everyone believe that if he is not already a millionaire, he's about to become one at any moment. He's been losing steadily for the last week. Twice I've caught him in the corner of the dressingroom, doling out money.

But this afternoon, catastrophe struck. As usual, they were playing in the players' restaurant at Roland Garros, a dungeon of a place. The table was littered with 'sandwich jambon', Cokes and ashtrays, with the air decidedly thick.

'Seven card stud', Abie says the game was called. A tremendous round developed and the pot grew and grew. By the time the stragglers had fallen out, at least three hundred dollars in French francs lay on the table, in carelessly crumpled notes, and only Abie and Mervyn Rose remained. A fortune was at stake.

By the time they had finished betting, the pile had grown to a thousand dollars, and then Abie's full house of aces and kings was pipped by Rose's four miserable nines. Gloom and tragedy, and frantic telephone calls to Abie's 'shippers'. Whatever they are. Whenever Abie runs out of money he phones up these mysterious 'shippers'. I asked him how one went about getting 'shippers', and he told me that 'good shippers are one hell-of-a-hard thing to find'.

Just at that time tennis was weighed down with literally dozens of the most extraordinary characters. Colourful lunatics, one could almost say. To the extent, almost, that anyone young and unsuspecting coming on the scene might be excused if he thought that in order to reach the top in the game, one needed to be slightly touched.

Of course, Trabert and Seixas were reasonably sane, and so were Harry Hopman's squad of young Australians, Hoad, Rosewall, Hartwig *et al.* But as for the rest, virtually the whole lot were, to a greater or lesser extent, off their heads. Looking back at those tennis years, I find a whole list of names marching through my head. Art Larsen, Warren Woodcock, Herbie Flam, Torben Ulrich, Hugh Stewart, Gardner Mulloy, Mervyn Rose, Andre Hammersley, Fausto Gardini, Beppe Merlo, Pietrangeli and Sirola, George Worthington, Gil Shea, Don Candy, Freddie Huber. Abie Segal, of course. Even Drobny and Patty had their moments. As a newcomer I used to look on, amazed. Don Candy, for example. Now *he* had the charm of a truly funny man. His matches would always develop into critical situations and invariably, at such times, bad calls would occur, usually involving Continental umpires who spoke just enough English to intensify confusion. In any case, umpiring in Italy, Spain and almost all Latin countries was notoriously partisan, and chaos prevailed almost at the drop of a hat. Candy soon became keenly aware of the absurdity of such situations, and adopted a policy of countering chaos with chaos. Often we would watch his matches, eagerly awaiting incidents. Some of his better inventions bordered on lunacy.

During one particular match, for instance, linesmen's chairs were in position, but no linesmen. Drama was in the offing. Inevitably, at a critical deuce point, the bad call turned up and Candy pounced.

He began gesticulating and arguing in furious Spanish gibberish for a full two minutes with the empty chair on the offending line which he felt should contain a linesman. Then he suddenly stopped, walked to the umpire (who had made the call in the first place), pointed to the chair and said:

'I want that man removed!'

'There is-a no one there,' said the umpire. 'Well, I want you to get someone,' said Candy, 'so that I can have him removed.'

'But-a if-a you get-a someone, and then you remove-a him, then-a you would have no linesman,' said the umpire, mopping his forehead.

'But we already have no linesman,' said Candy.

'Then-a why-a you-a want to remove him if-a he comes?' asked the umpire.

'Because he made a bad call,' said Candy.

'But-a he wasn't there,' said the umpire.

'But if he had been, he would have,' said Candy.

'Ah, then, if he had,' said the umpire, 'then-a you could remove him.'

'But I couldn't,' said Candy, 'because there's no one there!'

'THAT-A-WHAT I SAY!' shouted the umpire. 'There's no-a one there!'

'Instead,' said Candy, 'we play a let. If you play a let, I will not insist on removing that man,' and he pointed again to the empty chair.

'All-a right!' said the umpire wearily. 'We play a let. *Mama mia*, a let, a let-a.'

On another occasion, faced with an appalling decision by an Italian umpire who could speak no English at all, Candy approached the man, pulling faces, moving his lips, shaking his racket, tearing at his hair and generally going through all the motions of a furious diatribe, but silently, without uttering a sound. The umpire watched him with growing alarm. He put his finger in his ear and shook it, then clapped both hands to his ears and released them. This he repeated several times. Suddenly he descended from the chair and with a worried look on his face, he hurried off the court, probably to see a specialist. Candy watched him go, then climbed into his chair and in a loud voice reversed the decision, immediately causing his Italian opponent, who had been watching the proceedings in a smug sort of way, to go into apoplexy.

Candy's methods were never vicious. Sometimes he would approach errant linesmen and whisper something to them in a very confidential way. This caused volatile opponents to rave about it being unfair to influence linesmen, to which Candy would reply:

'Relax. I was agreeing with him. There is no rule which says you can't agree with a linesman!'

He was what could be called an industrious player. No fabulous flights for him. He gave workmanlike performances, running round the backhands and hitting conservative topspin forehands from close to his ribs. His service was utilitarian, his backhand safely steered and his volleys sound. But he had a huge heart and a great deal of Australian cunning and resource and, although he didn't win many big tournaments, he badly scared nearly all the top players a number of times.

Then there was always the possibility of overhearing snippets of conversations between Candy and Torben Ulrich, who at the time was busy inventing his remarkable world of meditation, profundity and dreams. Whenever Candy came upon Torben Ulrich in one of his profound moods, it seemed to trigger off within him an opposite reaction and he used to put on an air of excessive heartiness and good fellowship.

'Good morning, Torben!' he might say lustily, to which Torben would often reply, slowly and deliberately:

'Explain to me, Donald. What exactly is a "good morning"?'

'Sunny!' Candy would say. 'No rain!'

'Aha, then,' Torben would reply, 'perhaps it would be more accurate to say, "sunny morning, Torben," because you see, for me, a sunny morning need not necessarily be a good morning.'

'All right then. Sunny morning, Torben!' 'Yes, Donald. You are right. The sun is certainly shining.'

Such exchanges took place in dozens of variations, always with a bland display of off-handedness, each treating the other with suitable indulgence of the kind with which fathers treat small children. Once in the midday heat of July in Athens, Candy came upon Torben sitting reflectively on a bench at the tennis club, with a wet towel on his head. Don sank down beside him.

'Hot,' he said in a precise, firm voice.

'Yes,' said Torben. 'You could say that it is hot.'

'Too hot to practise tennis,' pursued Candy.

'I am not going to practise tennis,' said Torben.

'I thought you were about to say to me, "Let's practise tennis,"' said Candy.

'Even if it were cool,' said Torben, 'I would practically never say that to you. It would be much more likely that I would say to you: Donald, I think that it would be better for both of us if we *did not* practise tennis!'

'Then that's settled,' said Candy firmly. 'We are not going to practise tennis today.'

'Yes,' said Torben. 'That's settled.' Then he added: 'In a way, you know, it was never really *not* settled.'

On still another occasion (one of the rare ones when Candy and Ulrich *did* get to practise) they had been playing for some time when some eager club members approached the court. As usual during tournaments, practice courts were at a premium, and the members waited impatiently. At last one of them spoke to Ulrich.

'Have you been playing long?' he said.

'As long as I can remember,' said Torben.

'How much longer will you play?' asked the member.

'We may go on for many years,' said Torben. The member looked disgruntled. 'You see,' said Torben in a soothing way, 'we hardly ever feel like ending our game exactly at the same time.' Candy, who had been listening, now approached.

'He's mad,' he said to the now puzzled member. He tapped his temple. 'He believes that he is born blessed, but in actual fact, he's mad!'

'That', said Torben, 'is a matter for discussion. Because, you see, it is hard to define who is mad and who is not.' He fixed the club member with a penetrating stare and said: 'What exactly is madness? Perhaps you can tell me!'

Torben was, and is, an extraordinary human being. With him in view one would automatically consider such phenomena as intellectualism, the power of the mind, mysticism, things deep, gurudom even. He had, for a start, long hair and a beard, which in those days were unheard of (we were busy imitating the crew-cuts of Trabert and Seixas) and which lent him the somewhat scary appearance of the son of some grave god. He moved in an aura of private contemplation which I, for one, was reluctant to interrupt. He explored thoroughly the fields of nearly all sensitivities, always distant and thoughtful behind his youthful, hirsute disguise. Pleasantries generally escaped him. All remarks addressed to him would make their way into his head for consideration. I once said to him as he left a court after a match:

'Torben, did you win?'

'No,' he said.

'Then what happened?' I asked.

'I simply played in the usual way. It was my opponent who lost,' he said.

His delivery was slow and deliberate, each word weighted with consideration. He played the clarinet and tenor sax (very well, when the time was right), immersed himself in the angular harmonies and oblique progressions of new jazz and carried, at all times, a record player and records – Miles Davis, Art Farmer, Mulligan, Terry, Bill Evans, Parker, Powell, John Coltrane. Complicated cadences always drifted out of Torben's quarters, sounds which greatly puzzled Don Candy. His music was more straightforward – a simple set of guitar chords and songs, about John Henry being a 'Steel-Driving' man, 'Muscles and Blood', 'Whisky Bill' and 'Home on the Range', which he did with a stetson and a Roy Rogers delivery, sometimes startling everyone with a yodel or two. After putting up with Torben's music for some time, he decided to remedy his taste and bought a record of marches. Armed with this, he broke in on Torben's contemplation of

Thelonius Monk's 'Round Midnight', turned off the player and presented Torben with the record.

'What', he asked, 'do you think about this?' Torben examined the record carefully, then handed it back.

'I would avoid thinking about it,' he said.

'Try it,' said Candy, unabashed. 'Put it on.'

'My machine', said Torben, 'would not be able to reproduce it.'

'Why not?' asked Candy in a challenging voice.

'Because,' said Torben, 'this is a machine which plays music. It cannot perform other functions.'

'And this', said Candy haughtily, 'is a musical recording. It cannot, for instance, be played through a washing machine.'

'It would not surprise me', said Torben, 'if it was not perhaps better to play that record through a washing machine.'

'In any case,' said Candy, 'I did not come here with the intention of discussing the possibility of having laundry done. I came here to introduce to you a new kind of musical experience.'

'I think, Donald,' said Torben, 'that I would find it more valuable if you told me how to get my laundry done.'

A long wrangle ensued, involving the unlikely combination of laundry and music. At last, Candy's persistence won the day. Monk was removed, the marches installed. Suddenly the player began to emit stirring martial sounds. Candy marched up and down the room several times, delighted, saluting and giving Torben an exaggerated 'eyes right'! Torben regarded the player with a puzzled expression, as though it had betrayed him. Abruptly the march ended and Candy came to a halt, gave a final salute and stood easy. Then he picked up his record and strode from the room, like someone who had done a trick. Torben was silent for some time, before he raised his eyes to me and said:

'It would be much better if people had never discovered the way to make war!'

Torben's tennis game, too, was heady and profound. He would sometimes become so engrossed in the science of the game that the winning of it became incidental. At such time he might embark on a series of acutely-angled volleys, each more fine than the last; or lob volleys or topspin lobs; or a roundarm sliced service which bit into the breeze, drifting across the net in a curve, light as thistledown, not bouncing but settling onto the grass with a soft sizzling sound. It was one of these services which had ended up in the water jug under the umpire's chair and left Teddy Tinling waiting with a forehand grip.

(From Gordon Forbes, A Handful of Summers, 1995)

Brushing up their short game

Tom Eaton

'There's action, and then some. But when it's drizzly springtime in Delft, with that familiar aroma of cheese, mildewed sheets and raw sewage festering under a leaden sky, you know it's time for world-class golfing action. Yes folks, welcome to the 400th Dutch Masters, live from crappy Holland! And a warm welcome to my co-anchor, Bob Weinberger.'

'Thanks, Chuck, great to be back. Boy, there's nothing like it, is there? The polders, the cows, the clogs. Just this morning I was cutting the complimentary cheese in my hotel bathroom, and thinking how much we love this tournament.'

'We sure do, Bob. Of course this year's Dutch Masters is, as always, brought to you by Peter Stuyvesant: just one draw and you're hooked. I sure do like them golf puns. So, take us through the lineup.'

'Well this year we've got a couple of new faces. Gerrit Dou has been making waves on the Leiden tour, and he's shooting up the money list thanks to big wins at the Queen Christina Open in Stockholm and the Medici Classic in Florence. Some controversy about that last win, though, Chuck: it turned out his "Lady at her Toilet" didn't feature an actual toilet scene.'

'That must have come as quite a disappointment to "Kinky" Cosimo de' Medici, Bob. Well, moving on we've got young Anthony van Dyck and veteran Peter Rubens. What's the word on these two?'

'Gee, Chuck, I don't know. I guess they've just never kind of kicked on. Both brilliant golfers, no question, and there was a time they looked set to take the green jacket off Rembrandt, but in recent seasons they've maybe just been a little too focused on their driving and concepts of divinity. Huge shots, often with biblical themes, and I reckon they just forgot about the short game. Rubens especially. He tore up the European tour for years, looked totally unstoppable after "The Apotheosis of Henry IV and the Proclamation of the Regency of Marie de' Medici on May 14, 1610", but then I guess he kind of got the yips.'

'Sorry to interrupt, Bob, but we've got a disturbance down at the first tee, a huge crowd of kids, maybe fifty or sixty … oh, it's the Vermeer family. And there's Jan himself, stud golfer of Delft and mullet pioneer. Gee, they sure love him here.'

'And he loves them right back, Chuck. Those fifty kids are just the ones we know about. But we were talking about short games, and this guy has the best short game in the world. Sure, he's pedantic and slow, but holy crap, what a winner.'

'Is it true that "Girl with a Pearl Earring" was originally called "Girl with a Perlemoen Nose-stud?"'

'Sure is, Chuck, and let me tell you it was a mess, that big old green sack of slime hanging off that pretty little face. Luckily he changed caddies, and the rest is history.'

'We've just had a viewer e-mail us a question about the big white ruffs that everyone's wearing today, both the golfers and their models. Is this some sort of 17th century Flemish fashion item, Bob?'

'Great question, but no. Those are just to keep people from licking their stitches.'

'Such vibrant customs and sanitary habits here in the Low Countries. And now to the guy that everyone's been talking about all week. Okay, Bob, tell me this. He's got the longest drive in the game, a putter that's always on fire, unrivalled brush technique, he's won about half of the last 400 Dutch Masters, he's second in the money list behind Pablo Picasso, and yet those who know him say he's a deeply unhappy man. Why is Rembrandt van Rijn looking so glum?'

'Well, Chuck, it's hard to speculate, but I'd say it has something to do with his wife and three of his four kids dying. He's also just declared bankruptcy. And you must remember that life can't be easy for someone whose middle name is Harmenszoon. I mean, think about it. It rhymes with "poon" and "loon".'

'And "spoon", Bob. And "June".'

'Yes, but those aren't really ...'

'And "noon" and "croon".'

'Never mind. The point is, I think his performance at the Masters last year, where he carded a self-portrait and "St Paul at his writing desk", showed someone deeply aware of his own failings, and unflinchingly documenting his misery. He still putted like a son of a bitch, though. Let's join the action on the first tee ...'

(From Tom Eaton, Twelve Rows Back, 2005)

THE BEAUTIFUL GAME

The frequency of high-quality international sport available to your regular fan nowadays paradoxically makes life more difficult for journalists and writers. There is so much good sport on offer, either to be watched live or on television, that it is supremely difficult to tease out the significance and beauty of any particular game. Only a handful of journalists are able to do this consistently: to take from a Test or a Currie Cup final that which really matters and expand it to the point where as spectators of the event we are able to exclaim: 'Yes, that's right, why didn't I think of that?'

The flip side of there being so much high-quality sport readily available nowadays is that competition at the top of the soccer, rugby and cricket pyramid is intense. Teams and their coaches change their approach, their game plan, their strategy on literally a weekly basis. Nowhere is this more noticeable than in a Tri-Nations season, say, or in the fact that competition at the top of Test cricket has forced the Australian cricket team under coach John Buchanan to re-invent Test cricket, examining its myths and shibboleths – that scoring 250 runs in a day's play is adequate, for instance – and so turning the game on its head.

With such vitality in international sport there are many opportunities for fine writing, for evocations of not only the beautiful game but the brutal game, the passionate game, the cynical game.

– Luke Alfred

The romance of sport

Chris Greyvenstein

IT may sound naive but after 18 years in the sportswriting business, I still find sport thrilling and romantic. Over those years I have been close enough to sport and sportsmen to see the commercialisation and I have known many 'idols' with clay feet. And yet I refuse to be disillusioned completely because in sport we have one of the last remaining strongholds of adventure, individualism and romance. Sport, in its finest sense, may be fighting a losing battle against a mechanised world but it is still, as Bertrand Russell put it, man's last opportunity to compete for superiority in contests which yield utterly useless results.

The romance of sport, and I prefer to call it such, is not only to be found in the glory of victory or the graciousness of well-taken defeat, but even more so in the fears and foibles, the successes and failures, of the winners and the losers.

What will I remember, years from now, of the fourth rugby Test between South Africa and France at Newlands last August? Will it be the dullness of the match or the drawn result? Neither. It will be the sight of HO de Villiers giving his friend and teammate Eben Olivier an encouraging last-second pat on the shoulder as the Springboks ran on to the field. And I will remember how Olivier sprinted 25 yards into the French half to fetch the ball so that he could give HO a high 'sight setter' before the kick-off. This is a regular ritual between the two friends and showed me that loyalty can exist even in the white-hot tension of international sport. I felt better for seeing it. There is also an old-world courtesy in sport which is a throwback to the days when even war had rules. The tournaments of King Arthur and his knights could hardly have produced a more gallant loser than Gert Celliers proved himself to be one afternoon during a national trials match at Wellington.

Jannie Engelbrecht had just shattered former Springbok wing Celliers's hopes with a devastating dash to the corner flag but as he walked back from his try, there was Celliers to congratulate his rival. Surely there is hope even in this embattled world while there are still men who can conquer their disappointments as Gert Celliers did. I cannot remember much else of that otherwise undistinguished game but, being a sports romantic, that one incident made everything else worthwhile.

But, the cynics will say, humans can prove themselves to be decent and loyal in other spheres of life, not only on the sports fields. Of course they can – but where else, except perhaps in the slaughter of war, can they prove it as dramatically as in sport?

Sport is a harmless simulation of war in many ways and, as such, supplies the compatible outlet that the savage in each of us must find, whether as a spectator or as a competitor.

Where can you get a better example of courage than the man who enters that loneliest place on earth, the boxing ring? Boxers are often maligned as being too insensitive to know fear, but anyone who has ever heard Willie Toweel recite the 'Memorare', that most beautiful of all confessions of Faith, in his dressing-room will know that even a prizefighter recognises and must conquer fear every time he climbs through the ropes. But there is humour, too, in sport. There was that day in Ireland in 1961 when a very famous Springbok forward, straightening up after kissing the Blarney Stone, blurted out: 'Ah, now I've also got the gift of elegance!'

Loyalty, courtesy, courage and humour. All part of sport. Yes, perhaps I am a sports romantic because in its finest exponents I find the qualities which can make my world a saner place.

(From Chris Greyvenstein, The 1967 Sport Annual, 1967)

A weird game at Woollongabba

Louis Duffus

'How would you like to go to Australia?' It was the manager. He came into the sports office one winter afternoon when I was alone and asked the question casually, little knowing that he was lifting me above the first six heavens with a pounding heart.

The sending of a correspondent for a group of predominantly evening papers had this distinct advantage. Australian time is six to eight hours ahead of the Union so that close of play cables arrive in South Africa in the morning.

I packed for my third tour within two years.

Cameron was elected captain and embarked on the *Anchises* with the youngest cricket side ever to go abroad from his country. The average age was twenty-five. Taylor, at forty-two, was the only member of the party over thirty.

It was twenty-one years since the previous South African team had played in Australia, an interval so long that it was like going back to a strange land. Its cricket was to prove so different from anything we knew that it might have been played on another planet.

There were few other passengers on board. The team had a net in the well deck and, except when the Roaring Forties persuaded them to remain horizontal, the free run of the ship. Taylor was the life and soul of the party, and a few days out from Fremantle gathered the players in the lounge while he good-humouredly read out items of interest about the new country, 'so that they could talk intelligently with their hosts at dinners'. His lesson, however, was no substitute for human contact, and when one clear Sunday afternoon the ship edged into the quayside, sixteen faces peered over the rail eager to form impressions of the neighbours with whom South Africa has few contacts except through sport.

A dockyard on a Sunday afternoon probably does not provide a fair cross-section of a nation. Silent, hard-faced men with blue suits and black felt hats, and a sprinkling of women in brightly coloured dresses, watched the ship berth. The travellers and the sightseers stared at each other with rather embarrassing frankness. Then Australia spoke.

It spoke with a confidence, cockiness and humour that were to be encountered time and again throughout the next four months until they became key-notes of national character.

He was a tough-looking gentleman with no collar or tie, but he wore a friendly gleam in his eyes. Certainly no civic authority come to utter kindly commonplaces.

'Where's your great wicket-keeper, Cameron? Where's your Don Bradman?' he bellowed.

Having, like a suit at bridge, no Bradman, someone showed him Cameron. As the barracker sized him up, the South African captain accidentally dropped his hat. He grabbed at the falling headgear, but it fell into the water between wharf and ship.

'Fine bloody wicket-keeper he is!' roared the onlooker, and we knew we had, in truth, come to Australia.

It is as natural for the average Australian to be outspoken as it is for most South Africans to be shy. Psychologists can no doubt account for the difference. But if the cricket authorities had organised a network of intimidating propaganda it could scarcely have been more thorough than the spontaneous comments which, for the next few weeks, were gratuitously offered to the side to convince them that they were not likely to do much good against Australian cricketers. What made it worse was the sneaking feeling we had that the disconcerting prophecies might, as they did, prove painfully true.

The barefooted youngsters who watched the first practice in the delightful city of Perth began the theme song of the season.

'Clarrie Grimmett will get you all out,' said one small urchin as he watched Bruce Mitchell strap on his pads. Then he referred to his autograph book. 'Oh,' he went on, with complete assurance, 'but you're an opening batsman. Of course, you won't *see* Clarrie.'

Three of them stood behind the net where Van der Merwe was batting.

'Hit one over the fence, mister,' said one. 'Go on, mister, hit one over the fence!'

'Why?' asked Van der Merwe.

'We want a ball, see?' the youngster replied.

One group took particular interest in the bowling. Yes, they decided among themselves, Vincent was good. McMillan was also good, turned them a bit. Bell would be 'bonza' on a faster wicket. Their praise was comparatively lavish. But inevitably came the rejoinder, with a nodding of assenting heads, 'Yes, but that'll never get Braddy out!'

Everywhere was born evidence of Australia's two salient traits, independence and friendliness. Some of us played golf on the beautiful Lake Karrinyup course, twelve miles from Perth where a kookaburra laughed appropriately just as Taylor had missed his putt, and where the flies came out in squadrons from the neighbouring bush.

'We have been given a wonderful welcome,' said Taylor that evening over the wireless. 'People have greeted us everywhere. Even the flies are following us around.'

They played a comfortable draw against Western Australia and set off on the three-day train journey, including its 300 miles of dead straight line, past the romantically deserted mining towns of Kalgoorlie and Coolgardie, across the Nullabor Plain. At every little wayside station groups would gather round the cricketers and ask for autographs. Invariably as the train pulled out, they took up the refrain, 'Look out for Braddy!' and 'Clarrie will bowl you all out!' It became the tune of the wheels as they rolled rhythmically across the desert.

Was is more than coincidence that Grimmett took a wicket with the first ball he bowled against the South Africans a few days later?

Ever since its cricket began, Australia has built up national heroes. One of the memorable experiences of the tour, and there were many, was to meet in the flesh giants of the game who were revered even outside the Antipodes. Many of them were household words from my boyhood. There were Clem Hill and Ernest Jones at Adelaide, and Hugh Trumble at Melbourne where in the stand one day I sat with Van der Merwe and modest Jack Blackham, one of the world's most famous wicket-keepers. He wore a neat goatee beard and the tan of many summers, for he was then one of the only two survivors of the first Australian team that visited England in 1878. He told us how he began to keep wicket – because the regular stumper of his 'fifth-rate' team had missed the train – and with a twinkle in his blue eyes recounted legendary tales of 'WG'.

At Sydney it was as though great characters were walking out of Wisden. In five minutes, at the hotel reception, you could shake hands with MA Noble, Charlie Macartney, Jack Gregory, CB Turner, Herby Collins, Arthur Mailey, Stan McCabe and the little dapper wonder cricketer of the day – Don Bradman.

Something of the same respect has been won by the stars of South African rugby teams as Morkel discovered soon after the team reached the east. He was singled out by a loquacious enthusiast who warmly congratulated him upon making a second visit to Australia – this time with a cricket team. He gave Morkel no chance to deny that he was a member of the 1921 rugby team.

'Don't you remember me?' asked the stranger. 'I played against you in 1921. Why, you don't look a day older. You haven't changed a bit …'

'But I'm not …'

'How do you keep your youth? Do you remember that game … ?'

A little while later, still unable to convince the stranger of his mistake, Morkel politely refused a drink.

'There you are,' he shouted in triumph, 'still a teetotaller! You never would take anything.'

Australia is the home of Christian names. You know that your dance partner is Ethel before you learn that she is Smith. The handshake carries with it the prerogative to use 'Don', 'Bert', 'Jack', and 'Arthur' the next minute.

Sydney – though Melbourne had been my home – seemed to epitomise Australia more than any other town. We read its soul one evening off a single newspaper placard:

SOUTH AFRICA BATS LIVELY
BAN ON KISSING
STATE LOTTERY

Bradman's début, on perhaps the finest ground in the world, was not so devastating as Grimmett's. He fell to an easy 'caught and bowled' by McMillan after scoring 30. Alas, the tomorrows were to tell a very different story.

That night there was a policeman outside the building where the team went to dance. Incidentally I have yet to see prettier or smarter girls than those of Sydney. Like most of the folk in the town, he soon recognised them as South African cricketers.

'Where's the cove who got Bradman?' he asked.

'Why, do you want to arrest him?'

'No, but, by cripes, I'd like to shake his hand.'

By the time the side arrived at Brisbane for the first test match, they had played five games, won one (against South Australia), lost one (against Victoria), and drawn three. They were well below their normal home form.

On the eve of the game Bradman played golf on the pretty Yeerongpilly course, using a club with the same effective swing with which he handled a bat. At the tenth hole he drove off with a low hooked ball that curled beautifully round the dog's leg of the fairway. With a mashie he covered the rest of the 435 yards, dropping his ball dead on the green.

'That's the cove you have to look out for,' observed our caddie. How right he was.

Until the timeless game at Durban came along to take its place as the father of all test match freaks, this match, in the similar humid heat of Queensland, was the most bizarre of all South African international cricket contests. In my time, it was also the unluckiest, for, though the Australians were measurably superior throughout the season, a little less ill fortune in the weather and in taking catches from Bradman would have given the team much needed confidence to fight for the rubber.

Bradman scored 226, to a chorus of 'coo-ees', after being dropped at 10 and 16 by Vincent and Mitchell in the slips. There was a more difficult catch to Morkel at short leg soon afterwards. Bell lost six pounds in weight in a day's bowling. Vincent bowled a ball to Woodfull that passed through the stumps without disturbing the bails, and Mitchell batted for ninety minutes before he scored his first run.

It began pleasantly enough on a fine Friday morning with the team singing 'Sarie Marais' in the dressing-room to Dalton's ukelele. By the end of the day they would have been pleased to be 'terug na die ou Transvaal'.

Because of Bradman, the Australians made 450 – a large but not demoralising total.

All the houses had tin roofs and many spectators climbed on them to see the game. One girl sat perched all day on the top of the toasting iron. Twelve youngsters stood or sat on the boughs of a neighbouring tree.

Enthusiasm and temperature were at their warmest. Towards the wane of the afternoon Taylor could be seen at the end of each over plodding round the edge of the stone-hard wicket. Rather than cross its surface he was walking double the distance.

'What are you doing, 'Erb?' asked McMillan cheerfully.

Without ceasing his measured march, Taylor turned his head. 'I'm keeping to the soft grass,' he replied. At dusk that day he ruminated on cricket – with his feet in a tub of vinegar.

The first unusual incident occurred on Saturday afternoon when 20 000 people packed the Woollongabba ground to capacity. This time the accommodation was literally full. One spectator, exercising his rights as a free Australian citizen, found that the palings of the boundary fence – they call them 'pickets' – were obstructing the view from his seat. So he kicked them off. Other onlookers sitting at fence level adopted the same measures. Then we saw the rare spectacle of a groundsman brandishing a hammer and, accompanied by a policeman, walking round the boundary, nailing up palings. A futile procedure, for no sooner was his back turned than more timber was kicked off into the field. That night they picked up 778 strips of fencing.

All this time the game went on. South Africa had scored 126 for 3 at the close of play on Saturday. As the crowd streamed out of the ground, a lad playfully tossed a cushion into their midst. In a few minutes men, women and children joined wholeheartedly in an old-fashioned pillow fight. So ended the first chapter.

Then the rain began.

It rained incessantly for four days. There was no play on Monday, none again on Tuesday and little on Wednesday. The team went to matinees. They walked about the wet Brisbane pavements. They played cards. They wrote home. And all the time to the sound of dripping rain and the sight of 'Dainty' Ironmonger, the spin bowler, rubbing his hands in gleeful anticipation.

On Wednesday the heavens at last ceased their downpour. The ground looked like a swamp. Grass was inches long on the pitch but, because of the rules, could not be cut. Cameron, from under an umbrella, said it was impossible to play. Woodfull said the conditions looked all right to him. Finally, at four o'clock, the umpires said the game should be resumed. Vincent was roused from a deep sleep at the hotel, and on a wicket that was so slushy that he was afraid to use the roller on it, Cameron continued his side's innings.

There could be only one result on such a pitch, and, after a grim stand, South Africa was beaten by an innings, having scored 170 and 117 to Australia's 450. The game had scarcely restarted when there was a further addition to the side's misfortune. A telegram arrived from the Australian Board of Control at Sydney saying, 'If the game has not restarted, abandon it.'

Late that night, during a dance at which the South Africans were present, one of the dancers (not a cricketer) disagreed with his 'cobber' and hit him over the head with a quart bottle. As he fell, the band discreetly rose and played 'God Save the King'. It was a fitting end to a week of strange events.

Within six weeks the team encountered more rain than it had done throughout the whole of the English tour of 1929.

(From Louis Duffus, Cricketers of the Veld, late 1940s)

Borneo to be wild

Peter Davies

Sobering signs greet arriving passengers at Malaysia's Kuala Lumpur airport. All over the landing hall are posters reminding desperados and fools that 'Drug Trafficking Carries a Mandatory Death Penalty in Malaysia'. This airport is not a good place to loiter with unlocked bags. I spent the day in Kuala Lumpur before connecting to Kuching, the capital of Sarawak. KL, as the locals call the Malaysian capital, resembles nothing so much as a giant building site. Such is the economic flourish in this part of the world that new glass-faced buildings are erected at the speed of a time-lapse nature film. The Malaysian attitude is encapsulated in their 'Vision 2020'. They aim to be a 'fully developed' nation by that year. Huge department stores squat alongside swish hotels, and giant banners remind the world that the Commonwealth Games will be held in KL in 1998.

Some Malaysian traditions haven't succumbed to the march of modernism, however. For instance, dinner. As dusk fell in the bustling Chinatown district of the city, roads were busily cordoned off by police in preparation for dinner and the nightly street market. Vendors fired up portable gas cylinders in their food carts and began bawling their edible wares to passers-by. Much was made of the fruit available, some of which is unique to the region. The most bizarre is the durian – the biggest, worst-smelling fruit in Southeast Asia. This offering is the size and shape of a football clothed in a spiky green shell. Eating a durian is like swallowing crème caramel in a blocked toilet. Its pungent whiff has caused the fruit to be banned on the underground in neighbouring Singapore. Though the stench is awesome, locals munch the sticky yellow flesh with relish, believing the fruit has rejuvenating powers. Far more nasally friendly than the durian is the small, hairy rambutan. Burst open the fruit's red skin and three segments of juicy flesh pop forth, firm like a litchi. I also sampled the mangosteen, which looked like a smooth granadilla, and the watery star fruit.

I met a Canadian girl by the name of Victoria. She was from Victoria, Vancouver. Victoria from Victoria. We nurtured our main-course appetites by roaming through the narrow lanes of market stalls, haggling for the fake R30-Rolexes, imitation Lacoste and Benetton shirts, and pirated videos.

Wandering from stall to colourful stall, tempting aromas wafted from exotic blends of Malay, Chinese and Indian dishes. It was time to eat and we chose the alfresco delights of the Ngan-Kee restaurant. This establishment's most popular item was the 'steamboat', a Chinese-Malaysian variation on a fondue. Skewers of bamboo were brought out on which a myriad of meats had been impaled. These we cooked in a sunken pot of boiling water in the middle of the table and then dipped them in an array of piquant sauces. The bill was calculated by totting up the number of used skewers. I made a note of the delicacies that rapidly disappeared from the table – quails' eggs, abalone, prawn, sea snail, pork and fish balls, cuttlefish, spring rolls, mushrooms, chicken and won ton (a fish and meat combo). Happily, none of the food was still wriggling.

Onward to Kuching in Borneo, a 90-minute flight across the Malaysian peninsula and the South China Sea. Borneo is the world's third largest island, after Greenland and Papua New Guinea. It comprises two Malaysian states – Sarawak, where part of the under-20 World Championships were taking place, and Sabah. Between these is the oil-rich kingdom of Brunei, home to the Sultan, one of the world's richest men. The southern area of the island is Kalimantan, the Indonesian part of Borneo.

Borneo is the island where the ruthless Dayak headhunters plied their trade decades back. The 'Wildmen of Borneo'. So go the romantic notions. Of course, I'd entirely dismissed thoughts of such goings-on persisting in the twilight of the twentieth century. This would have been as silly as small-town Americans thinking lions still stalk the pavements of Gauteng. Then I read an article in *The Malaysia Star* while on the plane. It told of 4 000 people being killed in riots in a remote part of West Kalimantan. The report said many victims had been 'decapitated or had their hearts torn out in an ethnic war of scarcely imaginable savagery, fought according to the ancient principles of black magic'.

As the plane descended, the thick jungle terrain of the island was interrupted only by a wide, cappuccino-coloured river snaking through the emerald foliage. The wilds of Borneo attracted a wad of intrepid British adventurers from the colonial era. One of these doughty Brits, James Brooke, became Rajah of Sarawak in 1841, and a succession of 'white rajahs' reigned for more than a century before Sarawak finally seceded to the British crown after World War II. Independence followed in 1963.

Many tourists travel to Borneo to spend a night or two in a longhouse, a traditional local village under one roof. The longhouse is a collection of individual family dwellings built side by side but sharing a communal veranda. Some of these longhouses can harbour up to 100 families. Though longhouses have been modernised to satisfy the coddled needs of Western tourists, some families still cling to ancient mores. A handful of them keep the head trophies collected by ancestors from headhunting forays.

Unfortunately, most of the longhouses are mere tourist traps these days. So much for the Wildmen. Instead of bones through noses, expect modern Dayak headgear to be a Chicago Bulls cap worn backwards and a pair of bogus Ray-Bans. It was no different down by the river. No ominous wooden canoes disgorging painted warriors in loincloths. The locals seemed to prefer jet skiing in wetsuits along the Kuching waterfront.

The stadium that hosted Group B in the under-20 World Championships was also a monument to modernism, with its hi-tech scoreboard and Citi Golf colour schemes. South Africa's young team had the misfortune to be grouped with powerhouse teams Brazil and France, as well as South Korea. The tone of their tournament was set when they could only manage a goalless draw against the Koreans. With the mighty French and heavily fancied Brazilians to come, they needed a win over the Asians to have any chance of progressing. The second match, against Brazil, saw the United Warriors play their best hour of football in the tournament. They matched, even exceeded, the boys from Brazil, until 15 minutes into the second half. Then two defensive errors were seized upon, and the Brazilians went home 2–0 winners.

The South African No. 9, Benedict McCarthy, was finding the going a little tougher than at the under-20 African Championships. Then again, the Capetonian's life had changed massively in the space of just a few months.

While in Morocco for the African tournament, McCarthy had diligently phoned his agent to tell him that European club scouts were filling his head with stories of fabulous signing-on fees, CEO salaries and fame untold. The Dutch sides Feyenoord and Ajax seemed most interested, but Monaco, AC Milan and Paris St Germain were also sniffing around.

McCarthy's agent is Rob Moore, Cape Town publisher of a batch of sports magazines. Moore had entered the money-soaked world of contemporary soccer back in 1994. He had long dreamed of owning a soccer team and so founded Seven Stars, which played in the national second division. Benedict McCarthy, then 17, had come along for trial matches at the end of 1994. When the goats had finally been shooed from the playing arena, and the trial game got going, it was clear McCarthy was several cuts above the rest. Moore signed the teenager for two sets of playing kit. McCarthy went straight into the first team and ended up joint top scorer in his first season with 28 goals. He also became an under-23 international in his first year with Seven Stars when he played for Mich D'Avray's side against Manchester United's youth team.

In 1996, his second year with the club, a local agent went to the press saying that Inter Milan were after McCarthy. Moore smelt a rat and asked to see documentation. Nothing was received. The rival agent was clearly trying to drive a wedge between the player and his club, to gain control of the player's mind. Once a player starts thinking that his future lies in Milan, and here's his manager and agent telling him to carry on dodging the goats during practice, it can lead to tension. The week after the Milan rumours surfaced, McCarthy was sent off during a game for dissent. His mind was clearly elsewhere.

McCarthy remembered those fake Milanese overtures when he was being seduced by scouts in Morocco. He turned every inquiry over to Moore, who sensed the time was ripe to launch his prodigy on to the global stage. A young player can set himself up for life these days by making a prudent first foray into the moneyed European leagues. Moore was aware that his player was currently on a hot streak. Hot streaks don't last forever. It was time to cash in.

'When he came back from Morocco,' remembers Moore in conversation with me, 'I said we'll go over to Europe and spend one week at a time with a few different clubs. It was a case of not wanting to lose all that momentum he'd built up in Morocco. We had a month or so to get a definite contract. The pressure was on him to perform. The strategy was high risk but with the potential for high rewards.'

When Moore and McCarthy left South Africa, there were four top European clubs keen on the boy from Cape Town – Morocco, AC Milan, Feyenoord and Ajax. The Ajax air tickets came through first. The pair arrived in grey, cloudy Amsterdam one Friday morning in April. That afternoon, McCarthy was plunged into his first training session. The following Tuesday night, Ajax set up a trial match against top amateur club Quick Boys. On the morning of that game Moore told his prodigy that their strategy would be one of pressurising clubs into making a decision. Of not sticking around too long. McCarthy had to shine that night.

The game kicked off. McCarthy's first touch of the ball came with his back to goal. He leapt in the air to meet a knee-high ball, and flecked a back-heeled pass through his legs down to the winger. Moore sat in the stands wondering how someone in such a stressful situation could produce such deft magic with his first touch. Two minutes afterwards, McCarthy hit the bar. Thirteen minutes after that he scored his first goal. In that first half he had three or four certain goals stopped by the keeper. No matter; by the time the ref halted the game, McCarthy had scored twice and laid on two other goals.

Moore and McCarthy sat happily in De Toekomst club bar after the game. Things looked promising. Moore reached down to his bag for his cell phone to call home. His bag wasn't there. The leather holdall containing cash, air tickets, camera and passports had been stolen from the bar of one of Europe's most prestigious clubs. Red-faced officials rushed about. The bag was never found, but the problems were swiftly sorted out. Club directors refunded the money and put a car and a driver at the South African's disposal to sort out their travel documents.

The following afternoon, there was an assessment of the previous night's trial match with Martin Oldenhof, general manager of Ajax. The club's new coach, Morton Olsen, had made a special trip down to see McCarthy play. By half-time he'd told the Ajax scouts that McCarthy had to be signed.

Moore had prepared his demands in typically thorough fashion. Number one was the basic salary. Two, the length of the contract. Three, the bonus structures. Four, the signing-on fee. There were also queries about how much money his parents were going to get, the transfer fee, and air tickets for McCarthy's parents and Moore to visit during the period of the contract. At the end of the meeting the Ajax officials tabled an offer. 'You won't get a better deal in Holland,' they said. But they wanted an answer by Saturday. There would be no chance of going to Feyenoord for a week, or moving on to Milan and Paris.

McCarthy hadn't attended the negotiations. Moore came out of the meeting and the young footballer didn't even ask him what had happened behind those closed doors.

'So I left it. I wanted to see how long he would stay cool for,' recounts Moore. 'I actually had to say, "Don't you want to know what happened in the meeting?" All he asked me was if they wanted to sign him. He wanted to know nothing else. Nothing about money. So I said, "Yes, they want to sign you for five years." His face lit up. I then told him how much money was involved for him personally. I don't think those kind of numbers really sank in.'

After that meeting with Ajax, Moore phoned Feyenoord and told them they needed to talk. On Friday morning Moore sat down with Feyenoord's Hans Hegelstein.

'We sat and negotiated for four hours. They were very keen to get Benni. Hegelstein sent back three times to his computer to run out new copies of the contract, and eventually, when we walked out of there, we had a deal that was 80 per cent better than Ajax's offer. It would really have put Benni among the top earners of Feyenoord. They had to wake up the president of the club in Chicago at 6 a.m. to get approval on certain aspects of the contract they hadn't anticipated. But throughout they were brilliant, and when we walked out of Feyenoord, I said to Benni the deal was unbelievable. He said, "Fine, it's up to you where I play," but later in the day I could sense that he loved Ajax the club, the atmosphere, the facilities. Everything.'

As soon as Moore got back to Amsterdam he phoned Ajax. It was 3 p.m. on the Friday afternoon. He told the club if they wanted an answer by Saturday, they would have to talk as there had been some major developments.

Moore again sat down with Oldenhof. 'You told me you offered the best deal in Holland. You'll think I'm bullshitting you, but here is the written offer from Feyenoord. Now I want to bring it on to a footballing decision. You have to up your offer substantially. I don't want to get into a Chinese auction situation where I go back to Feyenoord, because Benni wants to play for Ajax from a footballing perspective. But we have to reach a situation where he doesn't turn round in a few years' time and say the deal was better at Feyenoord, maybe I should have gone there.'

An hour and a half later, Ajax offered a deal worth double the initial one made 48 hours earlier. The contract was signed. Benedict McCarthy would be transferred to Ajax Amsterdam.

Moore, like most who dabble in the lucrative field of buying and selling footballers, is cagey when it comes to revealing the dollars and cents of the deal.

'All I will tell you is that even if he never makes it at Ajax, never kicks a ball in the first team, he'll never have to work again in his life. I don't want to mention figures, because if people in South Africa know how much he is earning and he goes to an international camp, there might be a bit of animosity, so I shield him. But I tell you one thing, it was interesting to see the Bafana Bafana squad contesting their R7 000 win bonus before the friendly match against England. For players in the Ajax first team, in any league match the win bonus is R45 000. And it doesn't take a genius to know Ajax is going to win about 15 to 20 games a season. This excludes the Dutch Cup and European money. That gives you an indication of the kind of money involved, and that is only the bonuses.'

Ultimately, said Moore, the Ajax legacy for developing talented youth settled the dilemma of which club to join.

'Also, signing for a club like Ajax, with the racial harmony in Amsterdam being probably the most relaxed in the whole of Europe, was, for a young coloured kid from Hanover Park, a major part in our deciding to go with them. But the key thing in the deal was Ajax's record for finding youngsters and turning them into superstars. If you look at the Milans and Paris St Germains of this world, those clubs buy established stars. They're looking for instant success. A young guy trying to learn his trade would probably be on the sidelines for too long. Ajax is very good beyond soccer because they educate you about life, patience, mental requirements. So he couldn't wish for a better club. They look at our overall make-up and work on whatever they need to make sure your feet stay on the ground.'

The celebrations that night were put on hold. They came later. The next morning, McCarthy went shopping in the main street of Amsterdam. He bought himself some jewellery and some presents for his family. He blew R17 000 in an hour.

The next step was to organise suitable digs for Ajax's newest recruit. McCarthy could have bought his own apartment, but Moore warned him against it. 'When it's the seventeenth week in a row that you are playing in the second team, and it's cold and snowing, and you come home to an empty flat with no friends, you are going to be in trouble.'

The club thus set McCarthy up with a local family who would be able to teach a wide-eyed youngster about Amsterdam and provide him with company while he busied himself establishing a network. McCarthy is staying in the suburb of Diemen with a couple in their early thirties who have a young child. They both love football and are knowledgeable about the city. The South African youngster is in good hands.

The final chapter in the Benedict McCarthy fairytale came soon after the Ajax deal had been clinched. National coach Clive Barker called him up to the Bafana Bafana squad for a friendly, ironically against Holland. He thus became the first South African player to represent his country at three different levels in one year – under-20, under-23 and senior international. His debut was rather muted. He came on with 15 minutes to go. South Africa were being given a lesson in possession soccer by the skilful Dutch. McCarthy didn't touch the ball for the first ten minutes, but when he did get some touches in the final five minutes, he didn't give it away. What was important was that he was in the shop window. In South Africa and in Holland.

Contemporary soccer is littered with hot talent that swiftly burns itself out. These days, the challenges are as much mental as physical. Moore, untypically for one with a vested interest, is confident that McCarthy's mental make-up is of the right stuff.

'He's a confident youngster without being arrogant. Very passionate, but very level-headed.' He's also prone to lapses, though, which Moore puts down to the 'exuberance of youth'.

When McCarthy scored the winning goal against Zambia in the under-20 African Championships, he celebrated by running to the corner flag, stripping off his shirt and performing an ecstatic hip-shuffle. As he ran back to the halfway line, the referee asked who had scored the goal. 'Me, ref,' said McCarthy, thinking the official was unsure whom to credit the goal to. Instead the referee took out his yellow card and flashed it at McCarthy in a theatrical fashion. He'd been booked for over-exuberant celebrations. Two bookings in a world tournament mean an automatic one-match suspension. McCarthy would be on thin ice in the semifinal against Ghana. Sure enough, he was booked in the semi. He would thus miss the final of the under-20 African Championships. It was a bitter pill to swallow.

McCarthy had a disappointing under-20 tournament in Malaysia. As did the entire South African side. They scored only two goals in their campaign and were eliminated in the opening round. In the final group game, a 4–2 defeat against France, McCarthy was as subdued as he had been throughout the event. He did make the first goal for his side, however, rising to flick on a cross from the left into the path of Junaid Hartley who buried the half-chance.

In the second half, McCarthy was caught offside more times than he would have liked. He had a great chance midway through the second half, but scuffed a tame shot into the goalkeeper's hands. He was then booked for taking a shot at goal after the whistle had gone. He was substituted soon afterwards, and further admonished by the fussy Jamaican referee for taking his shirt off on the bench. There will be better tournaments in the future for one of South Africa's band of rising soccer stars.

Just as Benedict McCarthy lit up the African under-20 finals, so the rave player in the under-20 World Championships was the Brazilian Adailton. At just 19 years old, he was being called the new Romario or the new Ronaldo. Adailton scored six goals against South Korea and had one disallowed, as his side romped home 10–3. Just as McCarthy was swamped by signature hunters in Morocco (for contracts, not souvenirs), so the full glare of the spotlight bathed Adailton in Malaysia. Telephone number transfer fees and massive salaries were bandied about in the newspapers.

It takes a supremely clear-headed teenager to cope with the demands of the modern game. The harshly critical soccer world will be monitoring every move of the likes of Adailton and McCarthy over the next few yeas. Good luck to them. They'll need it.

(From Peter Davies, Chasing the Game: Sporting Trails from Jo'burg to Jamaica, 1997)

NFO, JEO and the oh so cosy Heroes board that is so far from Springs … and reality

John Perlman

A road sign close to the Nicky Oppenheimer Oval in Randjesfontein, where England opened their tour of South Africa this week, warns motorists: 'Horses have right of way'.

It gave the tourists an early indication of which slice of South African society would be playing host for the day.

It is now an established convention that each cricket tour of South Africa begins with a match between the visitors and the Nicky Oppenheimer XI. The game against England was the sixth.

For the first five games against visiting international teams, the Nicky Oppenheimer XI was captained by Nicky Oppenheimer, taking time off from his job as deputy chairman of Anglo American and De Beers. Against England, NFO, as he's known, took a seat in the pavilion and handed the captaincy over to his son Jonathan. JEO, as he is known, has played in all the tourist games so far and always gets a bowl.

Jonathan Oppenheimer, who bowled four overs of competent seam against Alec Stewart and Mark Ramprakash, played some cricket at Oxford but one of his greatest achievements is celebrated on a handsome wooden board in the main pavilion. In gold and black letters, under the large heading 'HEROES', the board lists the greatest cricketing feats seen at the ground, ever since it was opened in 1991 at a cost of about R5 million.

There are some great names up there, with the deed listed alongside the date of the heroics: 'S Tendulkar for India, 100; S Malik for Pakistan, 135; R Richardson for West Indies, 83; JME Oppenheimer vs Honourable Artillery Company, 5–26'.

The board hangs from one wall of a large terrace below the main pavilion. It is just one part of a shrine to the great game of cricket and the role which the Oppenheimer family has played in it. There are rows of glass-fronted book cabinets with an immense collection of cricketing literature. There are ceramic statues of WG Grace and FR Spofforth ... and of Jonathan and Nicky Oppenheimer.

There is a little lounge area, with couches and armchairs where the family and close friends sit, on cushions embroidered with images of cricket by Nicky's mother Bridget. One shows a young Indian man with flashing bat, a bearded man with determined stare alongside him and a young pace bowler steaming in, wind in hair. The embroidered letters below read: 'NFO, JEO, Tendulker' (*sic*).

The same bearded man, Nicky Oppenheimer, appears alongside Allan Border in a vividly romantic painting done to commemorate the NFO XI's match against the touring Australians. Below the picture of the two skippers – and the artist's impression has NFO matching the intensity of the great Aussie's stare – is the scoreboard from the match, in which NFO's name appears only once – under 'did not bat'.

Not too many of the 2 000 people who turned up to watch the tour opener got to see all this stuff. You needed a special pass to get into the pavilion, unless you happened to be wearing the wide-striped public school-style blazer that is the NFO XI's uniform.

One English journalist discovered this when he tried to get into the players' area to interview Geoffrey Toyana, the young left-hander from Soweto who was top scorer for the home team.

Ironic that, because the fact that the development programme benefits from all this has always been the sugarcoating on a pill that's been difficult to swallow for those concerned to see South African cricket shake off these kinds of upper-class airs.

The Oppenheimer family donate R100 000 a year to the township cricket programme and a further R50 000 from the profits generated by the corporate marquees set up at each game – a small part of the R3,1 million budget for development but enough to make the cricket hierarchy let them make of the day what they will.

Throughout a cloudlessly perfect Highveld day the flags of Britain and South Africa waved in a cooling breeze, alongside a much larger gold and black flag, the colours of the Oppenheimer racing stable – whose horses train in the vast fields nearby – and also the colours of the Nicky Oppenheimer XI.

Gold and black ... entirely appropriate colours, some might say, since the wealth that made all this sporting indulgence possible was generated by decades of determinedly exploiting both.

The family banner was stiffened with a gust of especially hot air when JEO hit England spinner Richard Illingworth for six, and the announcer fairly squealed with delight: 'And a mighty blow by Jonathan Oppenheimer ...'

At least JEO has that much in common with Wayne Radford, the Eastern Transvaal opening batsman whose stirring innings against England the next day set up the home team with a total that almost won them the match. Radford also smashed Illingworth over the ropes, in a wonderful knock of 92 in 118 balls that included 10 fours.

There was more to come as Chad Grainger lashed 58 not out off just 39 balls, hitting seven fours and also getting his Illingsworth with the biggest six of the night.

Easterns are effectively the 10th best provincial team in South Africa – they finished second in the Castle Bowl and the top eight provinces play in the Castle Cup. But some good performances in the domestic series, including a stunning eight wicket win over Transvaal last season, has left them with a strong belief that they are rather good at the slam-bang pyjama pants game.

It was particularly evident in the home team's knock. Batting with the cheery optimism of underdogs, most of the batsmen showed the England attack a half-a-dozen balls worthy of respect, no more.

The PAM Brink stadium doesn't have a HEROES board, but these were real heroics by real cricketers. And they were matched by a man who looked like he'd strayed accidentally on to the pitch from a nearby Billy Bunter lookalike contest.

Whatever else happens to Corrie Jordaan in his cricket career, there is a notch in his belt that represents Atherton and another that stands for Thorpe. Jordaan had Mike Atherton stumped with a most clever bit of bowling, dropping one just a little wider of off-stump after the England skipper had lofted him over mid-off. And soon afterwards he trapped Graham Thorpe leg before.

Jordaan finished with 2–44 on a night when all the bowlers took stick – not quite 5–26 certainly, but then the Honourable Artillery Company aren't exactly England. And Springs, I am happy to say, is not exactly Randjesfontein.

There were less than 500 people in the PAM Brink Stadium when Dominic Cork bowled the first ball of the England tour but around 9 600 applauded warmly at the end.

The game at Randjesfontein might have attracted a better class of car, but I know where I would rather be.

Dust from the mine dumps blew over the ground during the afternoon and braai smoke wafted across at night. The first streaker was so pissed he forgot to take off his blue Y-fronts. And the young man who paraded round the stadium dressed as the Grim Reaper had a broad grin under his cowl as he held aloft his 'Death to England' placard.

Most important of all, the crowd roared lustily for most of a match that was anybody's until the last few overs.

I'm sure that every one of the people there had let imagination run wild and dreamed of playing alongside Hansie Cronje or Hennie le Roux. But I'm equally sure that most of them would agree that there are some things in the world that money can't buy.

In the reality warp that sets in around the Nicky Oppenheimer Oval, you begin to wonder if perhaps that isn't true. Luckily we had Springs the next night and a reminder that real sporting glory is always earned, never bought.

(Sunday Independent, 31 October 1995)

A cricketing tale to rival epic of the Ancient Mariner

Colin Bryden

The pace of cricket is such that there is always time to swap stories. Often they're the same old stories but one tends to listen politely and chuckle or gasp at appropriate moments before droning on oneself.

On Monday, as history was being made at the Wanderers, there was a chance to dust off some tales from the deeper recesses of the memory banks.

Had any of us seen a 300, we asked as Daryll Cullinan moved inexorably, elegantly and unerringly towards the highest score in the history of South African cricket.

I had seen a 299 but it could as easily have been a 280 or a 320. It was scored by Brian Davison, he of the powerful wrists, in the old Rhodesia, playing in an inter-province match in Gwelo, now Gweru. The scorers were from the local army base and worked in shifts. Knowledge of cricket scoring was not a prerequisite and Davison was at his most devastating, scoring at better than a hundred runs an hour.

Not surprisingly, the two scorebooks were irreconcilably at variance when Davison surprised everyone by getting out. The scoreboard said 299. Because 299 was what both he and the public had reason to think he had scored, that was what was entered in the books.

Dougie Ettlinger, the SABC's scorer, wasn't talking about 300. He had seen Eric Rowan score the then-Currie Cup record of 277 not out at Ellis Park 43 years ago and was going on about the slow outfield and the number of threes that were run, when Trevor Chesterfield began a cricketing version of *The Ancient Mariner*.

Chesterfield, of the *Pretoria News*, appears a mild and inoffensive individual. He does, however, have strident views on cricket and is an avid collector of cricket information. If you wanted to know who dismissed

Bradman at Leeds in 1930, for instance, Chesterfield would be a good person to ask.

The tale he told was almost as enthralling as that of the man in Coleridge's epic poem who had 'water, water everywhere, nor any drop to drink'. Chesterfield had watched Gary Sobers set the world Test record of 365 not out against Pakistan at Sabina Park, Kingston, in 1958.

How he had come to do it was the stuff of legend. He had been in Panama, trying to get to New York, when a coup disrupted his plans ... he found a banana boat and worked his passage ... he landed in Kingston with eight days on his hands before the next leg of his odyssey ... he was in a taxi and the driver was listening to the Test commentary ...

All of this had been absorbed with rapt attention as Cullinan moved ever closer to 300. Then he astonished his audience. 'It was sheer good luck,' he said. 'I hadn't known there was a Test match on.' We had believed him about the coup, the banana boat, we could even have accepted it if he had said his boat had been boarded by pirates of the Spanish Main. After all, Henry Morgan had his headquarters at Port Royal, just across the bay from Kingston Town. But a cricket fanatic not knowing the dates of a Test match? Tell us another one.

It was a pleasure to watch Cullinan batting. He has always looked a top-class player. A photographer, not a cricket expert, once confessed that he enjoyed taking pictures of Cullinan simply because of the grace and balance of his strokeplay as viewed close-up through a giant lens.

Eric Rowan, whose record of 306 not out for Transvaal against Natal was set in 1939/40 and survived until his death earlier this year, would have approved. Rowan's record was surpassed by Terence Lazard of Boland in an otherwise meaningless friendly against a substandard Western Province attack just over a month ago. Cullinan's 337 not out against good bowling in a competitive match is an altogether more worthy successor.

(Sunday Times, 31 October 1993)

Gerrie puts hair on patriotic chests

Gavin Evans

There's nothing quite like a big fight, SA style, to bring violence, sex and politics together in an evening's entertainment.

And last Saturday's 'Night of the Heavyweights' at Ellis Park rugby stadium was better than most.

For the local fight fan, it was an altogether satisfying experience. Our boys won and won easily. Better still, Gerrie and Pierre did it against black American opponents.

Male boxing fans, particularly those in the back rows, tend to transfer their own machismo, patriotism and sexual prowess onto the local fistic hero. And heavyweights are best suited for this purpose.

Personally, I prefer the little guys. They're quicker, they avoid more punches and they throw a lot more leather. Generally they rely more on skill and science.

But if you're sitting in the cheap seats and you're not really interested in the finer points of the game, there's nothing like a heavyweight to make you feel proud of the hair on your chest.

You can feel their punches from the back of the stadium, and there's always a lot more blood and snot flying around.

And no doubt about it, Gerrie is a damn good heavyweight – without doubt, the best this country has ever produced. Pound for pound, only Harold Volbrecht has his measure in South Africa. On a good night, he's among the 10 best heavyweights in the world.

So when Gerrie's in good form, you tend to forget his bad nights and bad days. You tend to forget all the terrible things he said about his white South African boxing fans. You tend to forget that he voted a liberal 'no' in the referendum, and publicised it. And most of all, you tend to forget his dismal performances against black Americans John Tate, Mike Weaver and Greg Page.

These days, Gerrie is more valuable than ever for the local white fan, so it's easy to forgive and forget.

For one thing, we don't have any other boxer with a hope in hell of winning a world title – not Brian Mitchell, not even Harold Volbrecht, and certainly not Brian Baronet.

And as the international sporting boycott takes hold, fewer top overseas boxers will be willing to come here. Baronet was in line for a light welterweight title fight against WBA champion Ubaldo Sacco, but pressure from the Argentinian government forced Sacco to withdraw from the Sun City bill, despite a huge purse offer. The overrated Durban golden boy didn't stand a chance, but the cancellation was a portent of things to come.

Gerrie Coetzee, at least, has an outside chance of regaining the WBA title and, though things are becoming more difficult, he is still more or less marketable in America. So he remains the Great White Hope, albeit reluctantly.

That reputation, however, is not entirely advantageous to him. No matter that Gerrie is a genuine non-racist – unlike Kallie Knoetze or his security policeman brother, Bennie. To black boxing fans, he is still a 'boer'.

At a Kaizer Chiefs game, Coetzee's opponent, James Tillis, was introduced to the crowd as 'the guy who's going to beat the white man's hero'. And a few thousand black fans came along to see whether he could do just that.

No matter that from the security of his luxury hotel, Tillis said didn't notice any discrimination in South Africa. He's black and Gerrie's white, and that's what counts. The white fighter, however good-hearted he may be, is always the enemy. By virtue of his position in society, he can't be anything other than the coloniser. There's always the suspicion he'll turn out to be a 'boer'. And if he doesn't, the white fans will still see him that way.

Even if the black boxer is a boycott breaker like Tillis, he's at least more of a known quantity.

It comes out most clearly when *Die Stem* is played and the Ellis Park ladies bring on the orange, white and blue.

When you turn round and face the crowd, you see 30 000 white faces singing earnestly. Gerrie's going to show the blacks and the rest of the world that we can still fight.

The few thousand blacks in the crowd all cheer for Tillis. None sing *Die Stem*. A few even bravely stay seated. But surrounded by drunken patriots, most black fans reluctantly take to their feet.

The racial dimension pops up all over the place in the comments of the spectators.

'Drop your arm, you kaffir' or the more polite 'Hey ref, the African is holding', are mild compared with the unprintable stuff.

But the really choice remarks are reserved for the inter-round ladies. Nowadays black and white women alternate the round change duties. The blondes usually get the biggest cheer, and the black women are virtually ignored.

For the uninitiated, the inter-round ladies are a strange institution. All thighs and calves with matching lips and nails, they bring on the flags and carry the cards indicating the round changes.

But the purpose of the inter-round lady does not end there. No matter how much of a beating the local lad has taken in the previous round, and no matter how much of a cheer he needs to see him through the next one, all is forgotten once she climbs through the ropes.

Three minutes' violence, then a minute's sex, and then back to the violence.

But what of the fights themselves? Well, considering this was Gerrie's first fight in nine months and that he weighed in at eight kgs more than he should have, he put up a splendid performance. Moving smoothly behind his jab, he comprehensively outboxed and outpunched Tillis. I had him winning eight of the 10 rounds.

Tillis fought above himself, but was just not good enough to contain Coetzee. The Texan is a hard puncher who tends to run out of steam after a few rounds. He managed to deck Greg Page, Carl Williams and came close to knocking out Marvis Frazier. But all three picked themselves up to outpoint him easily.

This time he didn't run out of steam, but Gerrie managed to slip most of his Sunday punches and absorbed the rest. All in all, it was an impressive performance and showed that Gerrie still deserves his world ranking.

But to rate him as number one contender, as the WBA have done, is a bit generous.

On his current form, only the fighters out of the top drawer – Holmes, Thomas, Witherspoon, Williams and Page – could be sure of beating him. And he certainly stands an outside chance against WBA champ, Tony Tubbs.

As for the rest, only the slick young hopeful, Johnny du Plooy, impressed. Pierre Coetzer will never make it to the top and Samuel Makhatini remains an unknown quantity.

The luckless Makhatini is yet another victim of the racial dimension to South African boxing. A big fellow with a paralysing left hook, he is said to be the best black heavyweight prospect ever in South Africa.

He turned pro at the same time as the talented Du Plooy and comparisons were inevitable. An eventual showdown seemed on the cards.

But while Du Plooy has had five fights against hand-picked opponents this year, Makhatini has struggled to find anyone to meet him in the ring.

On Saturday night he was put on hold. If the other fights went quickly, he would get his chance. If not, too bad.

As it happened, he was lucky. But as with his previous opponent, Makhatini found himself in with a no-hoper who folded up after two minutes.

And having had to wait seven months for a fight with poor training facilities and a useless trainer (who even forgot to remove the stool from the corner at the beginning of the round), Makhatini looked out of condition.

The problem is that the conflict in the townships has led to most tournaments being cancelled. And white fans are not really interested in watching local black boxers, while the white boxers would rather meet washed-out overseas palookas than hard-hitting prospects like Makhatini.

That's why SA light welterweight champ, Arthur Mayisela, hasn't had a fight in eight months, while Brian Baronet, who has carefully avoided him, is rated number five by the WBA.

So if they ever do meet in the ring, Baronet will probably beat Mayisela and Du Plooy will probably beat Makhatini, and then the white fans and boxing administrators will be able to say, 'We told you so, the blacks just aren't ready'. Or something like that.

(Weekly Mail, 13–19 September 1985)

Vision at Soccer City

Shaun Johnson

Now hold on a minute: is this the same strife-torn, crisis-ridden, race-poisoned South Africa we're all so depressed about? There in the stands, dancing and screeching and hugging each other in paroxysms of patriotism were staidly dressed whites, trendy township teenagers, and a cross-section of just about every other race and class categorisation you can think of.

The occasion was the marvellous final football clash between South Africa and Cameroon, and the climactic moment came when a bubbling Bennet Masinga did the necessary with an inspirational pass from his captain, Neil Tovey. It was 2–2 at the FNB Stadium – appropriately situated midway between Johannesburg and Soweto – and the new South Africa, forced into hiding by the current political crisis, was making a wonderful and welcome reappearance.

For two glorious hours on Saturday, 55 000 South Africans saw a future, and saw it working. 'Isn't it nice to see this multi-racialism,' a fan remarked matter-of-factly in a strong Zulu accent. In the crowd, like islets in a sea of Sowetans, white fathers sat with their pimply, gangly sons, and traded assessments and cold drinks with all in the vicinity. It was for South Africa an extra-ordinary natural, peaceable and – above all – hugely enjoyable affair.

Up went the cry whenever Tovey touched the ball: 'Codesa!' (It was pointed out that the nickname referred to Codesa 1, not Codesa 2, and was therefore highly complimentary.) 'The Doctor!' roared the crowd as Doctor Khumalo stretched an opponent like a rubber band. White fans wearing South Africa's World Cup cricket shirts raised an enormous ANC flag – with a springbok in the middle.

Numbers of people remarked on the tragedy of the fact that the rest of the country was not sharing in, or being touched by, the optimism and happiness of the moment. The television blackout was a sorry reminder that all was not well beyond the stadium fences. But nothing, not missed scoring opportunities or blatant fouls, not irritating announcers or the smog on the horizon, could detract from the experience of those new South Africans lucky enough to be there.

(The Star, 13 July 1992)

You can hear aspiration singing in the trees ...

Luke Alfred

I'M not sure quite what to expect when I arrive at Observatory Golf Course one glorious spring day. But what I find in the car-park, the bump and grind of swampy R'nB as it squeezes out of an open window, the odd personalised number-plate hanging bleakly on a smart car, the undertow of earnest chatter, indicates that I am in the presence of something subtle and – I realise later – something surprisingly big. It is an event about which anecdotes will be told, jokes fashioned, stories cast, but this is all in the future. In the here and now there is only expectation, hope, anxiety.

The occasion is an apparently mundane one: the second round of a qualifying tournament for the Sunshine Tour. But it is a qualifying tournament with a difference. The only golfers here are black ones. Some, but not all, are professionals. All must have a handicap of four or under and be less than 38 years of age. All in all there are 71 of them. Depending on tournament director, Theo Manyama's discretion, there are approximately 10 tour places up for grabs, with those scoring lowest qualifying for the best inducements and those further back in the field qualifying for only some of them.

For now, though, the day is just beginning: there are fat drops of dew on the blades of grass on the edge of the greens, the sacred ibis are threshing in the shadows, quick coffees are being ordered from the club kitchen. On the fairways which fan out from the clubhouse and underneath the trees which line them, a stillness is in the air. Soon the course will be thick with movement, the clink of clubs in golf-bags, the bubble of a ball as it circles the lip and falls into a hole. But for now there is the wide spread of silence and something like a holy calm, a natural bounty that every golfer knows and recognises even if he can't give it a name.

Lucky Shandu and Freddy Shezi have come up from KwaZulu-Natal for the event. Both play at the Maidstone Golf Club near Tongaat, Shandu off a one handicap, Shezi off something slightly higher. Shandu is looking perky in the crisp morning sunshine, the result possibly of scoring a 2-over 74 in cold, windy conditions the day before. Shezi, by contrast, is more demure. He posted an 8-over 80 the previous day and now knows enough to realise that the course, with its wind-pummelled pines and stodgy greens, might just bite him again.

Like Shandu and Shezi, Jeremy Solomons gets in an early start. Solomons and his personalised shadow, Ronald Jansen, are originally from Riversdale in the southern Cape but have been living in Pretoria for 11 and eight years respectively. Solomons, who works as a security guard at the Reserve Bank, hit an 81 on the first day of the tournament. Jansen's handicap isn't quite good enough to allow him a place in the event but what he lacks by way of golfing talent he makes up for in ambition, ambition which takes the form of giving something back to the community from which they came. 'We started to play with the steel pipes you get there by the roof,' says Jansen. 'Then we bend them and play with the ball. Solly [Solomons] and I want to give something back to the club in Riversdale. Start a tournament. I want the trophy to look like that – steel pipes on a wooden base. We'll call it the R&J trophy, for Ronald and Jeremy, because we are the founders of this idea.'

Last to tee off on the second day is a group of three which includes tournament leader, Mawonga Nomwa. Nomwa, from the Soweto Country Club, shot a 71 on day one. Under the difficult conditions, Manyama reckons it was worth 67. On the practice greens beforehand, Mawonga gives the impression he doesn't mind either way. He smiles and is relaxed almost to the point of being casual but you realise first impressions are misleading. After a shot he hurries off after his ball, stalking up the fairway. He starts slowly but in the loop back to the clubhouse his confidence grows. He will win this tournament and so kickstart for the second or third time a career that has stuttered on several occasions.

As Nomwa and his group hurry off for their second nine, so Willie Madiba is reflecting on what might have been. A member of the Pretoria Golf Club in Pretoria West, Madiba is rueing the fact that he was unable to play a practice round on the afternoon prior to the start of the tournament proper. He mutters darkly about going into the two rounds blind, following up his first-round 81 with 81 on day two. He will do better in the future, he vows, play more intelligently, work on that swing. Up above him, on the clubhouse patio, Manyama surveys the scene. He looks at the black talent and can't believe his eyes. 'I look back at what used to happen to us black golfers, not being allowed to go to the Wanderers to practise before the PGA, and think to myself: No, this can't happen,' he says. 'Now I am tournament director of the Sunshine Tour. I keep thinking I'm going to wake up sometime.'

(Sunday Times, August 2002)

What happens when you can't home in on The Road?

Luke Alfred

ALL of us will at one time or another have marvelled over the idea that homing pigeons, released hundreds – even thousands – of kilometres from their home, are able in most instances to fly back safely. The wonder is all the more delicious for not knowing how this happens. Are they somehow attuned to the earth's geomagnetic field, as migrating whales are thought to do? Do they memorise and thus 'read' the landscape across which they have travelled and then follow the route backwards to find home? Nobody quite seems to know and this, surely, is what makes what they do so captivating and so romantic.

I once wrote a story for the newspaper about homing pigeons. I think now that I was not nearly enough attuned to the simple beauty of it all, to the idea that if you release a flock 20 kilometres south of Smithfield, say, they will eventually find their way to their lofts in Judith's Paarl or Reiger Park or Plumstead. They might be tired and thirsty and generally worse for wear but they will arrive home safely. Best of all, I remember now, the 'path' pigeons take to find home is called The Road.

I think my reluctance to embrace the story about the homing pigeons was because they were involved in a race under the aegis of Sun International. The winners of the race didn't earn a crimson rosette and a R100 shopping voucher to the nearest Pick 'n Pay – lots of birdseed here for the winning bird, no doubt – but R1m. Everything was well organised and completely above board but still I couldn't help but feel the tackiness of Sun International, a tackiness that somehow blinded me to the proper story behind the money and advertising and posturing.

Sun International's million-dollar pigeon race aside, there have recently been reports coming out of Britain that more and more pigeons aren't returning to their lofts after having been released far away from home. Nobody quite knows why this should be except to suggest that it probably has to do with the presence of telephone masts for mobile or, as we call them here in South Africa, cell phones. Apparently the electromagnetic radiation generated by the masts is what causes the pigeons to get lost. The masts, generators of powerful microwave radiation, literally scramble the pigeons' homing instincts. They suddenly lose focus, fall off the beam and are lost. They cannot find The Road. I am no expert in these things and I cannot vouch for understanding the cold fear that flickers in a pigeon's eye if they are lost to The Road, but I, like all of you, have seen a lost dog's terror as he or she frantically trots alongside a road or a highway, knowing full well that things are not what they should be and in all probability there is no way back.

What is it then that beats in a pigeon's breast when they fall off their road? Is it fear or terror, or is it closer to what we humans call hysteria? Whatever it is, I think we can assume that it is not pleasant, a feeling best to be avoided and flown around – if at all possible.

As we speak, it seems, there is research being done into the phenomenon in the United Kingdom. The associations and interest groups and lobbyists are out, investigating the problem and thinking about possible solutions. Of several things we can, however, be sure. That the number of lost pigeons in the United Kingdom has grown rapidly; and that when fanciers change their pigeons' routes so as to avoid the masts, the pigeons return home safely. Says Peter Bryant of the British Royal Racing Pigeon Association: 'Their instincts carried them back through hostile fire and they were even parachuted to members of the resistance and made their way back from that during the Second World War,' he said. 'It would be ironic if they were now the victims of an unseen enemy.'

To the best of my exceptionally limited knowledge there have been no such similar reports coming out of South Africa. This is perhaps because this is a large, relatively underpopulated country, not yet stricken with the blight of radio masts. But the time will no doubt come when even pigeons in this large and apparently never-ending land cannot find their road because the signals are blurred.

(SAFm website, 31 January 2004)

Bandages, golf clubs and flash cars are now integral parts of a Springbok training session

John Perlman

IT was 1969 and I had just turned 10. The Springboks are training at the Randburg Club, my friend said, the last practice before they go to Britain and my dad's taking me. Do you want to come with?

Did I want to come with? Does Pinocchio have wooden balls? I mean I had never actually seen a Springbok before.

Nowadays that sounds ridiculous. Even people who have never been to a Test match, who have never seen the Bokke in more than two dimensions, somehow feel that they know them in the flesh. They talk of them in the flesh. They talk of them as friends – Joel, James, Ruben. That's television for you.

Because of TV our memories of Test matches are very precise and somewhat uniform. Everybody saw Joel Stransky's World Cup winning drop-goal from the same camera angle, and relived it again through the same six slow-motion replays. Days, weeks, months afterwards you can settle any arguments about how far out he was when he kicked it, or simply savour the memory, by whipping out the video recording that all of us have kept.

But before then Test match memories, for all but a few, were truly a creation of the mind. We all heard the same radio broadcast – although the crowd always sounded bigger and more excited on a radio with poor reception. But talk about a game, a player, an incident and no two people's memories will be quite the same.

As a kid I had some idea of what the players looked like. I would stare at the team picture they'd put in the Saturday morning papers for hours before kick-off and the general stuff I knew from watching high school games – that locks were large, props had pimples, and centres and wings had tit sidies and kuifs you could flick – helped to fill out the picture a bit.

But these bits of reality only provided the framework. The final picture that unfolded as we gathered round the radio was enhanced, embellished, enlarged by the feverish imaginings of an overheated young mind. And it remained vivid and real for hours and hours afterwards, as I scrummed the family bulldog up and down the lawn, amazing all with my ability to maintain both a furiously exciting commentary and an awesome level of forward dominance.

My dad always recorded each Test on an old reel-to-reel tape and we'd always play them back – sometimes the same evening if the game was thrilling enough. The next day I'd be up at the crack, anxious to get at the newspapers – or the bulldog, if the deliveryman on his scooter happened to be late.

As for Test tickets, my elder brother got a couple by sleeping outside Ellis Park the night before, but by the time I was old enough for that, they'd scrapped the system. But like I said, I did get to watch the Springboks practise.

There were hundreds of us there, that cold drizzly day in Randburg.

We watched them run around the field, wondering how Mof Myburgh, Gawie Carelse and Frik du Preez managed to move at all. We watched them thump into tackling bags hanging on chains from the crossbar and giggled nervously as the posts began to shake.

And when they finally emerged from the showers, bulk beef wrapped in gold and green, we clamoured around them with pens and pages torn from school jotters. Nobody really smiled, but everybody signed. I even managed to shake hands with Carelse, and gulped for an instant as my fingers disappeared. Then they all filed onto the team bus in a silent line and drove away.

The jotter page disappeared in the Bermuda Triangle that was my junk-filled room. But this week I was reminded of that damp day in Randburg 26 years ago. At a wet and muddy Wanderers, another Springbok team had gathered to prepare for another visit to Britain.

So what was different? As I got there, James Small drove up in a red BMW, talking on his cellphone. Then Francois Pienaar arrived, wearing tracksuit pants, rugby boots and carrying a bag of golf clubs.

Somehow the players looked smaller than they did – pure illusion. Kobus Wiese is 11 kg heavier than Carelse was and 5 cm taller. Mark Andrews towers 16 cm over Frik du Preez and weighs three kg more. Ruben Kruger outweighs Jan Ellis, the heaviest of the 69–70 flanks, by 7 kg.

In the dressing room, Rudolf Straeuli took an iron from Pienaar's bag and played a couple of fresh-air shots in the direction of a distinctly uninterested Balie Swart. Kitch Christie was ambling around, chatting quietly to players as they changed – then stepped outside because he was getting bum reception on his cellphone.

Pienaar soon followed, dressed for rugby, but carrying what looked like an eight iron, and proceeded to hit a couple of shots, combining it with a bit of warm-up as he jogged the length of the field in pursuit of the ball he'd just hit. The people sitting in the glass-fronted clubhouse looked relieved that James Dalton hadn't come out with his driver.

Could you imagine Dawie de Villiers taking a couple of swings before training? Or Naas Botha? The grim reverence that surrounds the Springbok team is gone, probably forever.

But business is still business. The three-hour training session began with a sort of touch rugby passing game, refereed by Andre Joubert and punctuated by raucous laughter. Then Christie went to work with the forwards and his assistant Ray Carlson took over the backs.

It started off slow – the forwards going to ground and releasing the ball, the backs slaloming half-pace through a long row of flexible poles – but then built up sharply in intensity. The backs worked quietly and intently, each movement repeated over and over until every pass stuck and every man gasped for breath.

The forwards grumbled and groaned and battered into each other, sometimes with whoops and enormous grins. At one point, Pienaar, Straeuli and Kobus Wiese disappeared into the dressing room to ransack the team's supply of bandages and reappeared looking like extras in a low-budget *Revenge of the Mummies*-type flick. Everybody laughed and carried on chuckling for the next two mauls.

The whole training session seemed to mix serious enjoyment and serious intent. But the last half-hour of the practice passes in grim-faced silence as all the players, forwards and backs, run and jump and stretch carrying arm-aching weights.

Just before that, there was lineout work, and then kick-offs, as Morné du Plessis fired off perfectly flighted balls from a large machine placed on the centre spot and powered down a long extension cord that ran all the way back to the dressing room.

A kick-off machine? I don't think they had those back in '69.

But in '69, at least, a Springbok training session was still a bit of an event. At the Wanderers there were only a couple of blokes there who you could really call fans.

The most serious of them wore olive-green waterproofs and spent a lot of time peering at the players through binoculars. Then again he might have been a scout sent out by Will Carling. Or Princess Di.

Occasionally a car would slow down along Corlett Drive and the driver would pull in for a quick look. But for the rest, all the people there seemed to be there for a purpose, waiting to take players aside for earnest little chats. And the cellphones just kept chirping, a background noise like crickets round a braai fire.

At one point, two little boys came along for a look with their mother. 'How are they going to kick in this mud?' said the younger one. 'Easy man,' said the other. 'They're professionals.'

(Sunday Independent, 5 December 1995)

Great expectations*

Andy Colquhoun

There is no other day quite like in the year. It has a flavour as tangible as a boerewors roll and the virgin promise of a freshly marked rugby field.

It's the first day of the international season and from the moment of waking the clock has only one purpose for me: to countdown to 5 p.m. when the referee's whistle signals the great kick-off and the release of months of stored anticipation.

What makes today so unique is that anything remains possible.

Our hopes and expectations have not been hobbled by dropped passes and missed tackles. The latest gameplan remains unflawed and the pens of the pundits still hover over the freshly charged pots of vitriol.

How I love today.

For those watching the match at home there'll be the morning rush to the bottlestore and the butcher's to stock up on essentials. The family chores are done promptly for the first time this year to barter for a window of peace between 5 p.m. and 7 p.m.

The *Saturday Argus* is picked up even more eagerly for one last poking among the entrails to unpick the secret code of what really is going to happen this afternoon.

And that's the beauty of today, we don't really know and, if we did, where would be the fun anyway?

Will the Springboks be as dazzling as Harry Viljoen hopes to make them? Can the French rise above the daunting odds stacked against them? How will the new boys James, Hall and Fynn go? And the most urgent

*This column appeared on the morning of the opening day of the 2001 season when South Africa played France at Ellis Park.

question of each year: are we at the start of a new Springbok golden age?

If you are fortunate enough to be at Ellis Park, the day has a special and familiar rhythm.

It will dawn cold but squintingly bright and blue-skied. Springbok jerseys will sprout like woodland mushrooms in the shopping malls and you may even sight an impeccably dressed French supporter.

At the stadium the senses are assaulted by the flatulent sound of the plastic horn and the scent of Eau de Rugby – frying onions, naturally.

Down in the changing rooms pristine green and gold jerseys in this year's new design are being unfolded while the French saunter out for their first sniff at the napalm-charged atmosphere of Johannesburg's bullring.

The curtain-raiser provides sporadic interest but the countdown has begun in earnest. The foreplay is the appearance of the tracksuited kickers who go through their drills in the in-goal areas while the stadium announcer cranks up the volume at the appearance of the cheerleaders.

Not long now.

The French appear first, thundering out onto the green as if the fierceness of their entry could earn them a seven-point start.

But no-one in the stands is fooled, for a tumultuous roar greets the arrival of Vossie and Corné and of Breytie and Butch – 15 green-shirted gods sent from heaven to deliver us into the Promised Land.

The forwards look grim; there are a few nervous smiles among the backs, and then it's the anthems as the clock enters its final countdown.

It'll be another year before a page is as blank as this one, our hopes so innocent, our dreams so reckless. I love this moment.

And finally we're ready. The ball is teed up, the referee signals to his touch judges, the players freeze in readiness, and the stadium holds its breath …

(Saturday Argus, 16 June 2001)

Acknowledgements

The editors and publishers of this book would like to thank the following individuals and organisations who have given us permission to include their work in this book.

SA Sports Illustrated for Grant Shimmin, 'From miner to major', 2 September 1996; Telford Vice and Neil Manthorp, 'A dossier of decline', June 2000; Robert Houwing, 'Gibbs could yet be great', March 1999; Peter Davies, '2001: a sports odyssey', October 1994; Mark Keohane, 'Harmony with the hacks', *SASI Fans Guide*; Mark Keohane, 'The great leap backward', January 2004; Andy Capostagno, 'Recipe for success', June 1995; Joel Stransky, 'Sealed with a kick', August 1995.

The *Sunday Times* for Clinton van der Berg, 'Fixed fights, a comeback, Ali: Mike 'The Tank' Schutte talks', 1996; Colin Bryden, 'Death brings outpourings of forgiveness and love to our flawed hero', 9 June 2002; Colin Bryden, 'Glorious last hurrah ends an era', 25 June 1995; Colin Bryden, 'A cricketing tale to rival epic of the Ancient Mariner', 31 October 1993; Luke Alfred, 'You can hear aspiration singing in the trees', August 2002; Dan Retief, 'The final', 25 June 1995; David Isaacson, 'The champion who never was', 13 March 2005.

Witwatersrand University Press for an extract from *Papwa Sewgolum: From Pariah to Legend* by Chris Nicholson (2005), chapter 9.

Random House UK for an extract from *Dancing Shoes is Dead* by Gavin Evans (published by Black Swan, 2002). Reprinted by permission of The Random House Group Ltd.

JM Coetzee for 'Retrospect: the World Cup of Rugby' (*Southern African Review of Books*, July/August 1995) and 'Playing total(itarian) rugby' (*Die Suid-Afrikaan*, August 1988).

Mainstream Publishing for extracts from *Winter Colours: Changing Seasons in World Rugby* by Donald McRae, pp 58–75 and *Dark Trade: Lost in Boxing* by Donald McRae, pp 9–24.

Jeff Zerbst for 'If one nag looks like the rest, must I tip the duds?', *Weekly Mail*, 28 November to 4 December 1986 and 'Nose to nose', *Weekly Mail*, 29 May to 4 June 1987

Charlotte Bauer for 'The cute goodies I found in Equinus' socks drawer', *Weekly Mail*, 5–11 December.

STE Publishers for an extract from *Now Listen Here: The Life and Times of Bill Jardine* by Chris van Wyk, chapter 16.

HarperCollins Publishers for an extract from *White Lightning* by Allan Donald, chapter 20 © Allan Donald 2000. Reprinted by permission of HarperCollins Publishers Ltd.

Andy Capostagno for 'The will to win', *Mail & Guardian*, 27 August 2004.

The *Mail & Guardian* for John Perlman, 'Once upon a short time ago, football was fun', 23–29 August 1985; Gavin Evans, 'Gerrie puts hair on patriotic chests', *Weekly Mail*, 13–19, September 1985, 'The great ring', 8–14 November 1985, 'Fordyce on running', 9–16 October 1986; Fikile-Ntsikelelo Moya, '*Eish*, farewell, Slow Poison', *Mail & Guardian*, 15 August 2003.

Dennis Rubel for 'The death of the running flyhalf', *Weekly Mail*, 21 June 1985 and 'A battle of witlessness twixt brawn and brawn', 27 September 1985.

John Perlman and the *Sunday Independent* for John Perlman, 'NFO, JEO and the oh so cosy Heroes board', *Sunday Independent*, 31 October 1995 and 'Bandages, golf clubs and flash cars are now integral parts of a Springbok training session', 5 December 1995.

Rodney Hartman and the *Sunday Independent* for 'Forget the hype, here was a brave young man', *Sunday Independent*, 11 August 1996.

Penguin Books South Africa for an extract from *Ali: The Life of Ali Bacher* by Rodney Hartman (Penguin Books, 2004) © Ali Bacher.

Gordon Forbes for 'Diary Notes: Paris 1955' and 'Diary Notes: summer 1955' from *A Handful of Summers* (1995)

Andy Colquhoun and the *Saturday Argus* for 'Eats, shouts and leaves', *Saturday Argus*, 18 May 2002 and 'Great expectations', 16 June 2001.

Darrell Bristow-Bovey for 'Tyson 2000', 'Martina Navratilova' and 'Bulls have support from a man wearing a lampshade', originally published in *Business Day* and reprinted in *But I Digress* (Zebra Books, 2003).

Bahapix for 'The life and death of King Kong' by Nat Nakasa (*Drum*, February 1959) and 'Taking the juju out of sport' by Mr Drum (*Drum*, March 1959).

Peter Davies for 'Borneo to be wild' from *Chasing the Game: Sporting Trails from Jo'burg to Jamaica* (1997).

Dan Retief for 'Morné, born to lead the Boks', *Rand Daily Mail*, 17 April 1980 and 'What happens when a Baa-Baa comes home', 15 December 1979.

Shaun Johnson for 'Inside the protected citadel' and 'Vision at Soccer City' from his book *Strange Days Indeed* (1993).

Images24.com/*Drum* for Sibusiso Mseleku, 'Let's play African soccer again', *Drum*, 2 July 1998

Images24.com/*Fair Lady* and Mike Behr for Mike Behr, 'The flip side of Penny', *Fair Lady*, 11 December 1996

Mark Keohane for 'Give our black players more game time, not gym time', *Business Day*, 4 April 2005.

The *Cape Times* for Barney Mthombothi, 'Arabs stand in the way of a successful African bid', *Cape Times*, 13 May 2004.

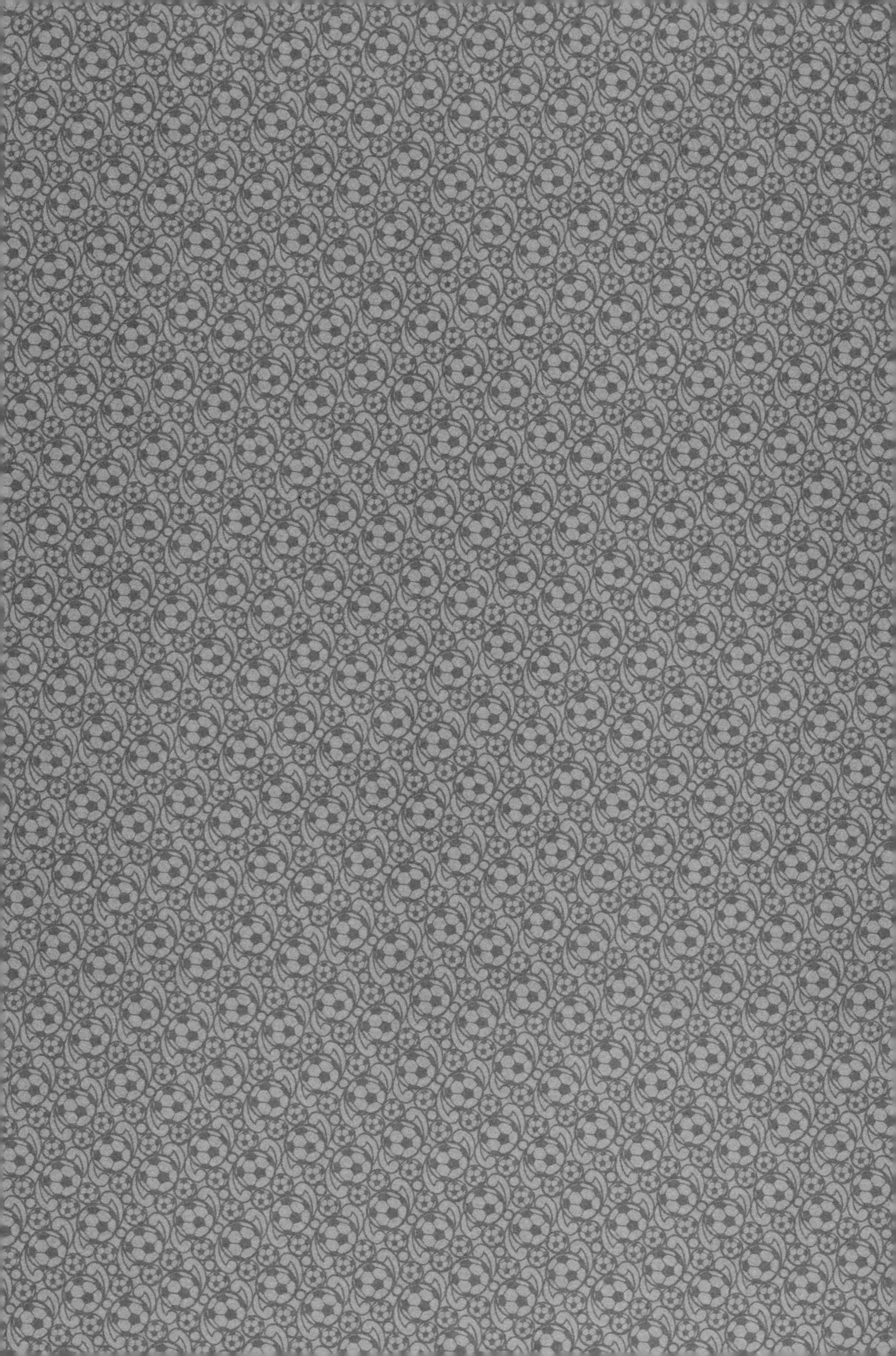